Good Housekeeping

COMPLETE BOOK *of*
HOUSEHOLD
HINTS & TIPS

Good Housekeeping

COMPLETE BOOK of HOUSEHOLD HINTS & TIPS

The Ultimate Home Reference Guide

General Editor: Suzanne Wilkinson
Contributors: Caroline Bloor, Linda Gray,
Patricia Schofield

EBURY PRESS
LONDON

First published 1999

13 5 7 9 10 8 6 4 2

This book has been compiled using material previously published in *Good Housekeeping Complete Book of the Home*, 1994

First published in the United Kingdom in 1999 by Ebury Press
Random House · 20 Vauxhall Bridge Road · London SW1V 2SA

Random House Australia (Pty) Limited
20 Alfred Street · Milsons Point · Sydney, New South Wales · 2061 · Australia

Random House New Zealand Limited
18 Poland Road · Glenfield · Auckland 10 · New Zealand

Random House South Africa (Pty) Limited
Endulini · 5a Jubilee Road · Parktown 2193 · South Africa

The Random House Group Limited Reg. No. 954009

A catalogue record for this book is available from the British Library

ISBN: 0 09 187084 4

Editors: Margot Richardson and Mary Lambert
Illustrations: David Eaton
Design: Lovelock & Co.

Printed and bound in Great Britain by Biddles of Guildford

CONTENTS

EQUIPPING YOUR HOME

EQUIPPING A KITCHEN

The kitchen is one of the most hard-working areas in the house, and therefore its planning needs careful attention.

KITCHEN PLANNING

When planning a new kitchen, even if you are using a professional, it is wise to do a plan yourself. Although a professional kitchen planner is very experienced, only you know how you will use your kitchen. If you are not involved, minor details may be overlooked which will be irritating and make your kitchen less easy to work in.

However, if you decide not to do your own plan you will still need to spend time thinking about your new kitchen because a professional plan will only be as good as your briefing.

Starting points
- Be prepared to take some time to get the kitchen right.
- Think about how you use your current kitchen.
- Make a list of its good and bad features.
- Ask friends for their experiences and any grievances.

AREAS TO CONSIDER
- How much can you afford?
- What activities do you use your kitchen for? For example, cooking only, eating in, socialising, laundry, or supervising children while cooking?
- Will the kitchen be used for any specialised cooking such as stir-frying in a wok, or large-scale preserving?
- How many people will use the kitchen? One person, two adults, or a large family with young children?
- Do you want to eat in the kitchen? Will you include a breakfast bar or table (use a fold-away if space is tight) and do you want to obscure the food preparation area from the dining area?
- What is the maximum number of seats required, and what is the minimum (in a small area) that will be satisfactory?
- Which appliances do you want to include and will you also be keeping any of the existing appliances?
- How much storage space do you need? For example: food that is chilled, frozen, dry, bought in bulk; cleaning products in lockable cupboards away from children; china and glass; rubbish disposal.

DRAWING A SCALE PLAN

The first step is to draw an accurate scale plan of your existing kitchen. Use graph paper and a scale of 1:20, so that 1.2in/30mm represents 2ft/600mm, which is the depth of many kitchen units.

Include all permanent features such as windows and sills, doors (mark the swing areas), chimney breast (external and recess dimensions), mains water supplies and stopcocks, waste outlets and soil pipes, boiler and controls, pipework, radiators and valves, and power points. Note which walls are internal and which are external. Include the ceiling height.

Measuring the kitchen
It is important to measure your kitchen accurately, as even the smallest inaccuracies at this stage will be vital when it comes to installation. You will need two people to do a proper job and it may take a few hours, depending on the size of the room. **It is very**

important to measure everything in metric, as kitchen units and components are always sold in metric sizes. Do not try to convert inches into metric later.

Measuring tips

- Use a metal tape measure.
- Measure walls at floor and ceiling level, and at work-top height.
- Watch out for uneven flooring and corners.
- Double check all measurements.
- Take the overall wall dimensions, then step dimensions, then compare to plus or minus 10mm.

STRUCTURAL CHANGES

If you are short of space you may decide to change the shape of the kitchen. You will need to weigh up the inconvenience of leaving the kitchen as it is with the cost of carrying out the alterations. Relatively easy jobs include raising a window-sill or knocking out a larder.

Moving walls is more costly, but could make all the difference. You may have to apply for approval for alterations under the Building Regulations, depending on the alteration (minor or major). Contact your local authority for advice. For a booklet on the Building Regulations contact the Department of the Environment, Transport and Regions (020 7890 3000). If a professional is carrying out structural work for you, ask if they have obtained the correct permission, because you are ultimately responsible.

Plumbing, wiring and drainage should conform to regulations. If worried about these, contact The Royal Institute of Chartered Surveyors (020 7222 7000) for a building surveyor in your area. They will survey the kitchen and highlight any problems. Surveyors usually charge an hourly fee and a kitchen survey usually takes about two hours.

DESIGNING THE LAYOUT

Once you have the basic shape of your kitchen on paper you can work on the layout. Templates of the standard kitchen units and components on a scale of 1:20 are printed overleaf. Photocopy, and use them to help plan the layout. Alternatively, use card shapes (drawn to scale) of the appliances and furniture you want to include. By moving the shapes around the plan it is possible to assess the pros and cons of different layouts. Aim to create maximum storage space and to position the largest area of work surface between the cooker and sink. Allow for swing areas of doors and windows and the door openings of storage units.

Work triangle

The three main activity areas in a kitchen are food storage (fridge and food cupboards), preparation (sink and work-tops) and cooking (oven or hob, depending on what you use most frequently).

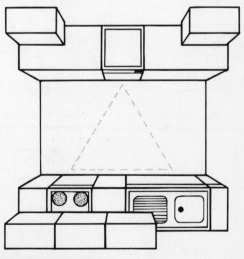

Basic Work Triangle

TEMPLATES FOR KITCHEN UNITS

Wall Units

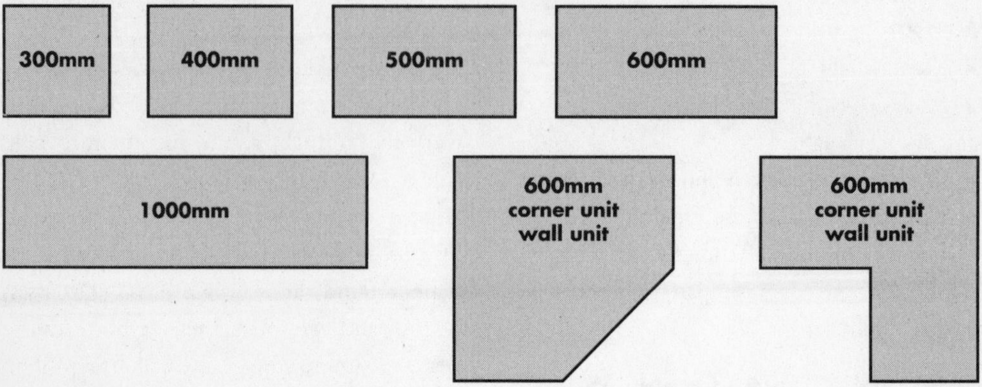

300mm

400mm

500mm

600mm

1000mm

600mm corner unit wall unit

600mm corner unit wall unit

Base Units

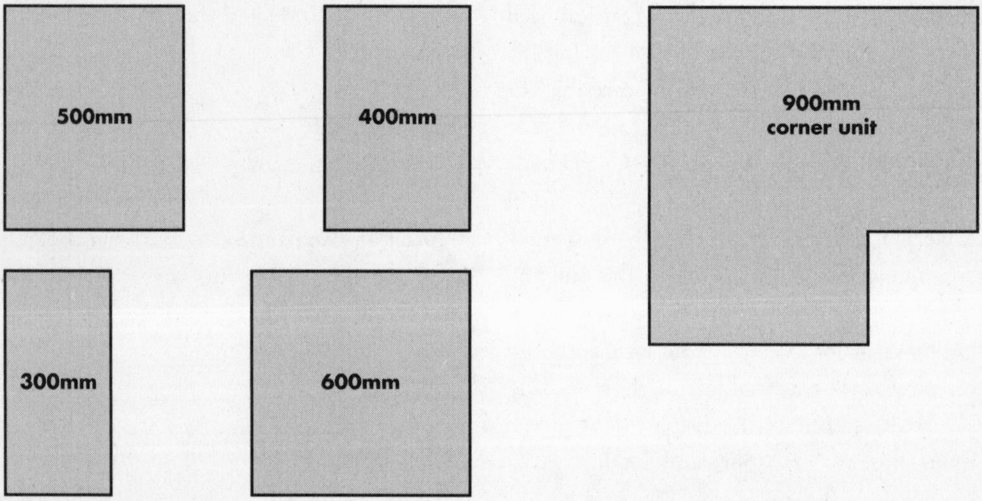

500mm

400mm

900mm corner unit

300mm

600mm

Appliances

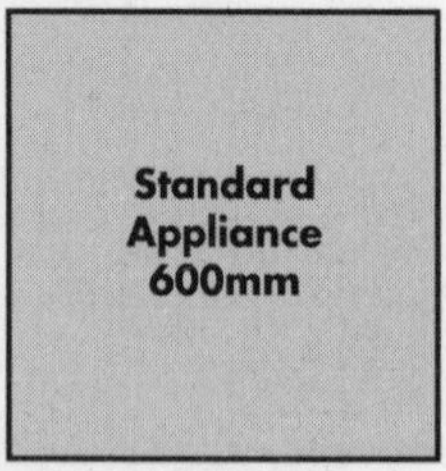

Standard Appliance 600mm

Sink Unit

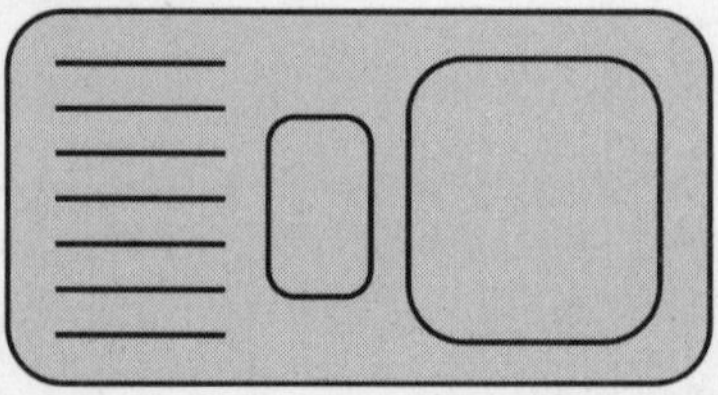

Scale 1:20
(30mm=600mm)

Start your plan by positioning the fridge, sink and oven and draw a line in the shape of a triangle between them. The total sum of the three sides of the triangle should be between 4yd/3.6m and 7¼yd/6.6m. If too long you will find yourself doing tiresome legwork, but if too short it will be cramped. The cooking and sink points should be connected by an unbroken work-top, even if this actually turns a corner.

In a modern kitchen there is often more than one triangle in operation: for example, if you use a microwave as well as your cooker, or if two people use the kitchen at the same time.

BASIC KITCHEN SHAPES

Kitchens are available in many shapes and sizes but there are only five practical layouts which will provide maximum working efficiency. You should be able to match one of these layouts to your own kitchen.

Single galley layout

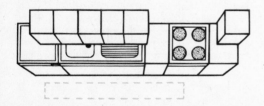

In a single galley kitchen, the units and appliances are lined up against one wall. Most suitable for one or two people, it can be fitted into a very narrow space, but it will need a 3yd/3m run of interrupted wall space. The room should be at least 2yd/1.8m wide to allow enough space for two people to pass each other.

The sink should be placed in the middle with the fridge and cooker at either end with, ideally, the doors of each opening away from the sink for easy access. Allocate as much

work-top space as possible. Choose built-under appliances so you do not lose any of the limited work-top space.

Eating usually has to take place elsewhere, unless a pull-out or flap-down dining table can be included on the wall facing the main run of kitchen units.

Double galley layout

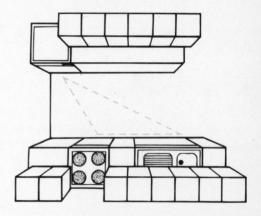

In a double galley kitchen the units and appliances are lined along facing walls. Most layouts will be dictated by the position of existing doors and windows but, ideally, the sink and cooker/hob should be on one side with the fridge and the main storage area on the opposite. This is an easy, straightforward layout for one or two people to work in, although it can cause problems for traffic moving through the kitchen if there are doors situated at both ends.

There needs to be at least 4ft/1.2m between facing units, otherwise it will be difficult for a person to bend down to reach something that is stored in a low-level cupboard. Use 20in/500mm-deep units instead of the standard 24in/600mm.

It's possible to create a feeling of more space by using glass-fronted cabinets instead of those with solid doors.

U-shaped layout

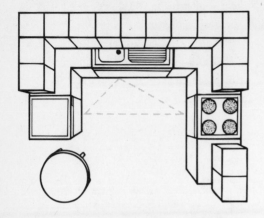

In a U-shaped kitchen, units and appliances are positioned along three walls. It is the most flexible layout and works well in both a small and a large kitchen. There needs to be at least 4ft/1.2m of space between the legs of the U-shape, but in a larger kitchen make sure you keep to the dimensions of the work triangle to prevent unnecessary walking.

This layout can often incorporate a dining area or breakfast bar. This is probably the best layout for both working and safety.

L-shaped layout

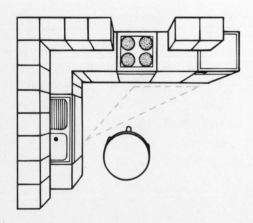

In an L-shaped kitchen the units and appliances are arranged on two adjacent walls. It is suitable for most rooms, except very narrow rooms or rooms with lots of doors. It is a good choice for an awkwardly shaped room because the sides of the L can be adapted to suit most shapes. The work triangle will not be interrupted by through traffic.

It is important to make sure the corner is used effectively, so use a carousel unit or consider a corner sink. Separate the sink, cooker/hob and fridge with stretches of worktop to avoid the three areas of activity becoming congested.

This layout is ideal for incorporating an eating area. It should be able to accommodate two cooks without them constantly getting in each other's way.

Island layout

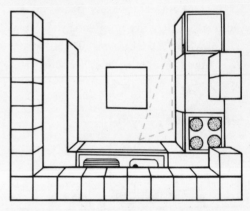

An island layout is usually a U-shaped or L-shaped large kitchen with an island of units in the centre. The island can be used for a hob, but the necessary services (gas or electricity) and cooker-hood ducting will have to be brought to the centre of the room and this is costly. The space between the hob and sink must be a working area only and not a general thoroughfare. It is usually used as another work surface, and is often positioned at a different height.

If the island houses a hob, a cooker hood is ideal, or place a light source or decorative rack for cooking pans or dried flowers above it.

LARGE KITCHEN APPLIANCES

Kitchen appliances such as cookers, dishwashers and fridges are some of the most expensive items bought for the home. As well, they are used with such frequency that an informed choice can make all the difference to the enjoyment of using the kitchen.

COOKERS

Cookers run on gas, electricity or dual fuel.
Their design can be:
- Free-standing.
- Slot-in: fits flush with your work surface and cupboards to give a built-in appearance.
- Built-in: the oven and hob are separate, with the oven built into a special housing usually around waist height, and the hob sited in the work surface. You can mix and match fuels, and you can position them exactly where you want.

HOBS

Hob cooking has become more popular recently. We are steaming and stir-frying more, reflecting healthy eating trends.

ELECTRIC HOBS

These provide a much wider choice than with gas. They are sealed plate, radiant, ceramic or glass-topped.

Built-in hobs

Most models fit into a standard 24in/600mm-deep work-top. If the hole is pre-cut, check measurements before purchasing the hob. A laminated work surface can be cut using a jigsaw, but make a template first. For other work-top material get the hole professionally cut. Electric hobs can be fitted by any qualified electrician.

Radiant

The traditional coiled radiant ring hob is only available on free-standing cookers. Compared with sealed plates, this type is slightly faster to heat up and cool down, but they can be difficult to clean. At high temperatures the rings glow red.

Sealed plate

This type has always been popular in Europe, and is now replacing the traditional radiant ring in the UK. It is inexpensive and relatively easy to install.

As the heat source is a radiant ring covered by a cast-iron plate, the response rate tends to be poor. Compared with other electric hobs it is slow to heat up and it is difficult to maintain a low enough temperature for simmering. When switched off the cooling down period is slow.

To maintain appearance and condition re-blacken the plates with 4 Hob. This will help to prevent rusting.

Some models have red dots in the centre of one or two plates. These have a higher rating relative to the diameter of the sealed plate and therefore a faster boiling time.

A pan sensor is sometimes fitted to one of the plates. This automatically turns the plate down to a simmer once the contents of the pan have come to the boil, and helps prevent liquids boiling over if you are not watching them.

CERAMIC GLASS-TOPPED HOBS

The heating systems are hidden beneath the tough ceramic-glass surface. Patterned zones on the glass surface indicate the size and position of the heat source. All have a safety device which prevents the ceramic-glass from overheating.

There are several types:

Ceramic

Radiant elements are housed under the glass surface. They are coiled like a radiant ring hob, or split and arranged in a series of lines or a star shape. Split elements heat up more quickly than the single coiled ones. Trade names for split elements include Solarglo, Speedglow and Quicklight.

Ceramic hobs are easy to keep clean, provided the manufacturer's instructions are followed properly.

Halogen

Heated by halogen lamps under the glass, which glow when the hob is switched on. This type offers the same benefits as ceramic hobs, plus it is slightly quicker to heat up.

The halogen light glows bright red so put your pan in position first to protect your eyes.

Easy to keep clean provided the manufacturer's instructions are followed.

Due to the cost it is rare to find a hob with four halogen heating zones. Instead this heat source tends to be combined with radiant ceramic zones.

INDUCTION HOBS

These are rare domestically in the UK because of cost, but are used widely in commercial situations. A four-zone hob is about four times the price of halogen.

They are the fastest reacting of the electric hobs, and are comparable with gas.

SAFETY

Ceramic glass-topped hobs retain heat a lot longer than gas, so even when the hob has been turned off it can remain dangerously hot. To avoid any accidents, look for models that have hob-hot warning lights, particularly if you have young children.

Induction cooking differs from normal cooking by heating the pan directly rather than by conducting heat through the hob surface. A spiral copper coil beneath the glass transfers energy directly to the pan by a process known as electromagnetic induction. This process means that no energy is delivered from the coil until a ferrous or iron-based magnetic pan is placed directly over it, and in contact with it, to activate the magnetic field. This makes it much more energy efficient than other electric heat sources, and it is safer because the hob only gets hot where it is in contact with the pan.

GAS HOBS

Any gas appliance, by law, must be installed by a gas fitter registered by CORGI, the Council for Registered Gas Installers.

Gas is a popular choice for hobs, being more responsive than electric ones: quick to heat up and reduce to a simmer. They can take any type of pan, but are often awkward to clean. Look for pan supports that are easily removable.

Look for differently rated burners. This can usually be detected by their size. Large is for fast boiling and the small, less powerful one is for simmering. Some hobs may have identical-sized burners which can be very confusing, so always check the power ratings

COOKWARE CHOICE

To check if your pans are suitable for an induction hob, place a magnet on the base. If it sticks then you can use it. There is a greater variety of pans available than you might at first imagine, such as enamelled pans with an iron base, stainless steel with an appropriate sandwich base and cast-iron pans.

The correct choice of pan is critical when you are using an electric hob. You need good contact with the surface, so avoid using any pans with dents or rough surfaces.

before you buy an appliance.

Ensure the burners are well spaced so all pans fit comfortably, and that the pan supports are well balanced and stable.

For ease of cleaning look for models with easily removable spillage wells.

POINTS TO LOOK FOR ON ALL HOBS

• Hot warning lights on glass-topped hobs.
• Easy-to-use controls with clear markings.
• At least one higher-powered cooking zone for fast boiling on electric hobs.
• Larger cooking zones for big saucepans.
• Drop-down lid on gas hobs to keep kitchen tidy and hob clean, but not intended to be used as a work-top.
• Automatic cut-out systems to cut off gas when the lid is lowered.
• Removable controls for easy cleaning.

OVENS AND GRILLS

Electric is the most popular fuel. Choose from conventional, fan or multi-function ovens.

CONVENTIONAL (STATIC)

This type is found in basic models. Electric elements are in the sides or top and bottom of the oven. These have zoned heating so that the top of the oven is a hotter temperature than the bottom. Some top and bottom elements work independently, which is ideal for base crisping, or for browning the surface of some foods.

Good for traditional cooking: roasts, fruit cakes and bread.

FAN OVENS

Most electric cookers now incorporate a fan that circulates the heat more evenly, so the temperature will stay the same throughout the oven.

In 'fan-assisted' types, the air is heated by electric elements in the oven sides, while in convection ovens the element is wrapped around the fan. The advantages are:
• Cooking is quicker.
• Colour is even, but usually paler and less glossy than on food cooked in a conventional oven.
• Pre-heating is usually unnecessary.
• Repositioning oven shelves is unnecessary, as is swapping trays half-way through the cooking process.
• Good for batch baking (cooking on more than one shelf) because of the even heat distribution.
• Cooking times and temperatures are always reduced from those of traditional ovens but by variable amounts depending on the make of cooker. So always follow the manufacturer's instructions carefully before you start cooking a meal or a recipe.
• One disadvantage of a fan oven is that the food surface may be drier and any topping may be less crisp than in other ovens.

CHANGING OVEN TYPES

Changing from a static to a fan oven takes some adjustment.

Always follow the manufacturer's instructions for cooking times and temperatures, or if you are trying an old favourite recipe reduce the heat by about 50°F/10°C and the time by 10 to 15 minutes. You can always return the dish for further cooking.

Leave space around dishes and at the sides to allow the air currents to circulate.

Check whether the manufacturer recommends grilling with the oven door open or closed.

MULTI-FUNCTION

This type of oven is a combination of a fan and a conventional oven. It therefore provides the user with the maximum versatility. Each option can be used separately or together depending on the type of food you are cooking and the grill can be used with the fan, giving a similar effect to a rotisserie.

A multi-function oven is ideal for batch baking and traditional cooking.

GAS OVENS

Conventional (British) gas ovens

The temperature in the middle of the oven relates to the selected gas mark. The top shelf is slightly hotter, the lower shelf is slightly cooler and the base is cooler still. 'Zoned heat' is ideal for cooking complete meals, where dishes require different temperatures.

Gas is a much moister form of heat than electric, which is particularly noticeable when you bake. It results in cooked food that has a glossy appearance on the outside and a moist texture on the inside.

Brand names for zoned heat are Gyroflo and Cycloheat.

Imported gas ovens

Many built-in gas cookers sold in the UK are of European origin. The burners are concealed under the base of the oven, so that food is crisped from underneath. They are ideal for cooking pizzas and pastries, but you must always avoid using the base plate of the oven as a shelf.

Heat distribution differs from that in a conventional gas oven, so always follow the manufacturer's instructions carefully. Cooking techniques are similar to fan cooking, and heat is more evenly distributed throughout the oven, so you will have to reduce cooking times and temperatures. The amount of reduction does vary depending on the make of cooker, so again, always follow the manufacturer's instructions carefully.

GRILLS

Grilling is done by intense radiant heat at close range. It is quick, and provides even browning over the whole heated area.

Depending on the type of cooker, there is a grill either at the top of the main oven cavity, in the small oven, in both ovens, or in a separate grill cavity.

Electric grills

Most cookers and microwaves with grills use radiant elements which require about 5 minutes of pre-heating. On the more expensive cookers, grills are faster and more efficient and require little or no pre-heating. The more up-to-date models are using a finer heating element wound around a central core. To make cleaning easier this can either be behind a glass sheet or it can be encased in some glass tubing.

Trade names include Quick Grill Ceramic, Ultra Grill, Solar and Quartz Grill.

Gas grills

These are sometimes separate or are situated in the main oven cavity. There are three types to choose from:

Fret burners are situated either at the back or in the middle of the grill cavity. They require no pre-heating, but browning can sometimes be uneven, especially when the grill pan is at full capacity.

Surface combustion burners are concealed behind mesh. This provides a more even heat distribution, resulting in even browning.

Ceramic grill is situated behind a heat-resistant glass panel giving a very even heat distribution. It is easy to clean but it does take longer than a normal gas grill to heat up. Once it is pre-heated, grilling is very fast.

Halogen grills are only found in microwave ovens. (See Microwave Ovens, page 26.)

INSTALLING OVENS AND GRILLS

Built-in/under

These have become increasingly popular as more people opt for fitted kitchens. Compared with free-standing or slot-in models they can be installed at the most convenient height and position.

Fuels can be combined offering maximum versatility.

Before choosing, decide whether you want built-in or built-under. With a built-in, the oven is set into a column-style housing unit, so a cupboard and work-top space is lost.

If space is limited choose a built-under unit which slots under the work-top. Remember you will have to bend down to use the oven and grill.

Built-in ovens come in standard sizes. A single model will fit into a space 24in/600mm wide, deep and high, and a double oven will fit into a space 24in/600mm wide and deep, and 36in/900mm high.

Electric double ovens require a special cooker socket, but single ovens use an ordinary 13-amp socket.

There is a greater choice of electric ovens than gas for built-in positions.

The small oven can be used for cooking, grilling and plate warming.

Free-standing

More traditional in design because they can have an eye-level grill. This is normally available on gas cookers only.

Most electric models have fan or fan-assisted ovens, while only the more expensive models have multi-function ovens. Check the oven is a comfortable height. Some models have a storage drawer which raises the oven above ground level.

The hob is usually the less expensive radiant, sealed plate or gas.

Slot-in

Gives a built-in look. It is streamlined because the cooker is the same height as the adjoining work surface. Unlike a built-in cooker, you can take it with you when you move.

Grills are low level, situated in the main oven cavity or in the second smaller oven. Some manufacturers recommend grilling with the door open, others with the door closed. Consider this if you have children around.

The type of hob depends on the price. Top of the range have either ceramic, halogen or a combination. Some cookers have a gas hob and an electric oven, ie, dual fuel.

COOKER HOODS

These can be installed above built-under or free-standing slot-in cookers to draw grease, odours and steam from the air. There are two types available: recirculating and ducted, and both require some sort of grease filter. Hoods come in two widths, 24in/600mm or 36in/ 900mm. Because hoods rely on moving air in order to operate, they can be noisy when used.

If you are fitting a hood above a gas hob there should be a minimum space of 30in/750mm between the two appliances. There is no specified distance for electric hoods, so follow the manufacturer's recommendations.

RECIRCULATING

The most popular type and the cheapest. It requires no external ducting so it can be sited on an internal wall. It has a grease filter and a charcoal filter for absorbing smells before recirculating clean air back into the room.

DUCTED

If your hob is on an outside wall, choose a ducted hood. They are more expensive than recirculating but performance is superior.

Stale air is ducted through pipes to the outside, so no charcoal filter is necessary. For the most efficient air flow make sure the pipework to the outside wall is as short as possible. A grease filter is necessary.

FILTER TYPES

Whether your cooker hood is of the ducted or recirculating type, it will have a grease filter. There are three types available: metal mesh, foam and paper.

The metal mesh found in expensive models is permanent so only requires cleaning. (See Cooker Hood, page 62.) Foam filters can also be washed in hot soapy water but will need replacing once a year. Paper filters are found on the less expensive cooker hoods, and should be replaced every two to three months as they quickly become saturated with grease.

Charcoal filters are found only in recirculating hoods and can't be washed so will need replacing every six months.

DISHWASHERS

Dishwashers are being regarded more and more as an essential rather than a luxury appliance. Ask any dishwasher owner and they will tell you that they wouldn't be without it, and that they certainly wouldn't revert back to washing-up by hand.

Dishwashers are more hygienic than washing-up by hand. In fact, research on behalf of the Electricity Association has revealed that washing-up by hand increases the presence of germs on dishes by as much as seven times, compared to those washed in a dishwasher. The dishwasher's high wash temperatures – hotter than your hands can bear – and efficiency of the dishwasher detergents play an important role in this result. And when you consider that the average dirty dish cloth can contain up to a million micro-organisms – more than the average kitchen pedal-bin – the contrast in hygiene becomes easier to understand.

CHOOSING A DISHWASHER

Dishwashers are available in a wide range of sizes and capacities, from four to fourteen-place settings. The size of dishwasher that you buy will be determined by:

• space available in your kitchen

- number of people in your household
- how often you entertain.

It makes sense to go for the biggest dishwasher you can fit in if you have a family or entertain regularly. If space is limited, slimline models are a good option, and slot-in models are useful if floor space is at a premium. Generally, you tend to sacrifice wash and dry performance with compact/studio dishwashers compared with full-size models. So go for the largest you can accommodate.

SIZES

Full-size

- Width 24in/600mm.
- Majority will wash up to 12 place settings, although a few models will wash up to 14.
- Free standing; fits under a work-top.
- For easy plumbing, put it adjacent to the sink.

Slimline

- Width 18in/450mm.
- Will wash up to eight place settings.
- Free standing; fits under a work-top.
- For easy plumbing, put it adjacent to the sink.

Slot-in

- Width 20in/500mm.
- Will wash up to eight place settings.
- Designed to fit in a kitchen cupboard without having to pull the kitchen fitments apart.
- Height and depth is reduced so all the pipework fits behind the machine and the cupboard plinth is kept in place.
- For easy plumbing, put under the sink.

Compact/Studio

- Sits on the work-top, or some can be built-in. Some models are designed to fit inside a

kitchen cupboard.
- Will wash up to four place settings.
- Models that sit on the work-top are about the size of a combination microwave.
- Wash and dry performance generally inferior to full-size models.

WASH PROGRAMMES

Most dishwashers take in cold water only (cold fill) and offer a range of wash programmes to allow you to select the one suitable to the degree of soiling and type of load.

Some dishwashers offer an array of programmes.

Main programmes

Normal: usually at 150°F/65°C. For general use, suitable for most loads, including normal to heavily soiled china and saucepans.

Intensive: a longer wash, usually at 150°F/65°C with pre-wash and extra rinses. For heavily soiled china, saucepans and bakeware.

Economy: the temperature is usually between 120–130°F/50–55°C. For light soiling and delicate items, eg, glasses and plastic ware.

Other programmes

Gentle and quick washes: useful for washing lightly soiled crockery and delicate items. Some quick washes are for half-loads only.

Rinse-and-hold cycle or pre-wash: loosens food to prevent it drying on to items if you are waiting to wash a full load.

Plate-warming cycle: utilises the drying cycle to heat items in the dishwasher, but is uneconomical.

Half-load washes: you load only one basket. Tend to be uneconomical as they use more than half the water and electricity needed for a full load.

Freshen up: rinses loads that have been stored for some time.

Drying cycle

Full-sized dishwashers usually have a drying cycle. There are two different methods used:

Hot air drying (element): most effective drying method but uses slightly more electricity. An element heats the air to dry items in the dishwasher.

Residual heat (hot rinse): uses the residual heat from the final rinse to dry the load.

POINTS TO CONSIDER WHEN CHOOSING

In general you get what you pay for in terms of performance and quality. So it is worth trying to spend as much as you can afford as you should get a machine that will last longer.

• As a general rule, the more expensive the machine the better the insulation and the quieter it will be during the wash cycle.

• Good range of economy programmes.

• If you have an economy-7 meter a delay timer will allow you to make use of cheap-rate electricity.

• Anti-flood device.

• Hot air drying (element) rather than by residual heat (hot rinse).

• If you have plenty of excess hot water (for example, if your water is heated by a Rayburn) look for a hot-fill model.

• Stage of wash indicator.

• Door that will stay open at a right angle to make loading easier.

• Sturdy, smooth running baskets that pull out fully.

• Easy-to-clean filters. Blocked filters will impair the washing process.

• Refill indicators for rinse aid and salt. You need rinse aid to avoid streaking and improve

SAVE WATER AND ENERGY

Dishwashers are wrongly labelled as water guzzlers. Increasingly, they use less water. The latest machines use as little as 4 gallons/18 litres of water (equal to two washing-up bowls) to wash 12 place settings on a normal wash programme. Washing by hand uses more than two washing-up bowlfuls, and most water of all is wasted by rinsing off one or two items under a running tap.

With the introduction of concentrated dishwasher powders, dishwashers are becoming more energy efficient. This is because the enzymes in these detergents work at their maximum efficiency at 100–120°F/40–50°C, allowing dishwashers to use lower wash temperatures without sacrificing performance, and to therefore reduce energy consumption. Dishwashers are beginning to offer 'Bio-phase programming' designed to maximise the benefits of these enzyme-based detergents by extending the period the wash water is held above 100°F/40°C and below 120°F/50°C. Bio-phase programming claims to give washing performance as good as using a 150°F/65°C programme, but obviously using less energy.

Heat-exchange systems are another development in dishwasher technology. These work by a heat exchanger, within the dishwasher, taking heat from the main wash water and using it in the subsequent rinses. This feature claims to reduce energy consumption by 13 per cent, water usage by 5 per cent and programme time by 7 per cent, compared with a normally heated standard wash.

drying, and salt works with the water softener in the machine to help prevent the build-up of any limescale.

• Good supports in the top basket for glasses and small items.

• Adjustable upper basket heights so you can fit in large dishes and tall glasses. With some dishwashers this can be done when the basket is fully loaded. Compact machines don't have adjustable baskets.

REFRIGERATORS

Refrigerators are available in a range of sizes to fit on table tops (2.9cu ft/82 litres), under work-tops and full kitchen height (13.6cu ft/384.5 litres).

To fit flush with work units they tend to be 24in/600mm deep and between 20–24in/500–600mm wide.

The majority of fridges and freezers work on a condensation mechanism. The coolant draws heat from the cabinet as it is circulated by a condenser motor.

There are a few small fridge units (maximum capacity of 2cu ft/57 litres) which operate by an absorption mechanism. Because the unit is so small there is no compressor motor. These fridges have a very small ice box and are ideal for locations such as dining rooms because they are virtually silent and vibration free.

There are two main types of fridge construction: larder, and those with an ice box.

LARDER FRIDGES

These don't have an ice box so all the space can be used for storing food. They are also the cheapest to run.

The cabinet is coldest at the bottom, just above the salad box, because cold air sinks.

FRIDGES WITH AN ICE BOX

As well as the fridge compartment there is a compartment at the top for storing commercially frozen food and making ice cubes. The ice box will have a star rating to indicate how long food can be safely kept in it (see box, overleaf).

The fridge is coldest at the top, adjacent to the ice box.

POINTS TO CONSIDER WHEN CHOOSING

Size
Factors will be the size of your kitchen and the storage space required. If you have a separate freezer you won't need a fridge with an ice box unless you need a lot of ice cubes.

Shelves and Storage
• Fridges with adjustable and folding shelves are more convenient for storing bottles and large containers. Removable door shelves give flexibility for fitting items and are easier to clean than moulded fittings.

• Shelves are usually plastic-coated metal or glass. A variety of shelf positions gives flexibility of storage.

• A solid surface like glass prevents items tipping and can easily be wiped clean.

• Some salad compartments have humidity control to retain the moisture around salad vegetables. Two separate salad compartments are useful for allowing separation of different types of food.

Controls
• May be inside the fridge or along the top edge. Higher external controls will be more child proof but inconvenient if you are small.

• Built-in thermometers and temperature displays are useful for at-a-glance assurance that everything is working properly, but for accurate measurements a separate thermometer inside is advisable.

Door hanging

• Most fridges have reversible doors so that the hinge can be moved from one side to the other to make it hang on the right or left. Check before buying.

Other features

• A grille that encloses the condenser (the wires across the back of the fridge) reduces the operating noise and is also cleaner as it can't trap dust.

• Inside will also be easier to clean if the

fridge has an enclosed evaporator plate behind the back wall, rather than protruding into the storage space.

• Both types of fridge are available with an auto-defrost system (see page 25).

FREEZERS

There are two main types, upright and chest freezers. Choosing the type depends upon where the freezer is to be situated and the space available.

UPRIGHT FREEZERS

Upright freezers vary in size between small table-top models (1.7cu ft/49 litres) holding 35lb/16kg of food; to full kitchen-unit height (about 5ft 9in/1,750mm) holding 197lb/89kg of food (11.1cu ft/317 litres).

They generally measure 18in/450mm to 24in/600mm wide and are about 24in/600mm deep.

Food is stacked on shelves and in pull-out drawers giving convenient and accessible storage. This type of arrangement suits storage of regular-shaped packets rather than large bulky items.

Upright freezers are usually designed to complement fridges. They have reversible doors to match.

POINTS TO CONSIDER
WHEN CHOOSING

Storage

• The drawers are either plastic-coated wire mesh or solid plastic with solid fronts. Look for easy-to-grip recess handles with easy-glide drawers, especially considering that they will be heavy with food. Stops on the drawers prevent them tipping out when opened.

• The drawers are much easier to sort through than shelves.

STAR RATINGS AND STORAGE TIMES

Commercially frozen foods can be stored in an ice box or freezer compartment depending upon its rating, as follows:

1 week Compartment at 20°F/–6°C

1 month Compartment at 10°F/–12°C

3 months Compartment at 0°F/–18°C

Compartments with the above star rating cannot be used for freezing down fresh food.

6 months (depending upon food type; refer to manufacturer's instruction book) Compartment at 0°F/–18°C

- Extra features may include a twist-and-serve ice maker. Once the cubes are made they can be tipped out into a small drawer. They take up valuable storage space.

Controls

- Like fridges, some models have thermometers and temperature read-outs.
- Audible alarms and indicator lights are a good idea to ensure a rise in temperature (from power failure or door left open) doesn't go unnoticed.
- Indicator lights for the fast-freeze operation are also a useful reminder.

Defrosting

A flip-out defrost spout is useful to drain the melted water from the freezer.

CHEST FREEZERS

These are available in a range of capacities from 4cu ft/114 litres) to 17.2cu ft (492 litres).

Food is stacked in to the chest and hanging, removable baskets. Chest freezers cater for more awkwardly shaped items that may jam in the drawers of an upright freezer. They are usually about the same height (34in/855mm) and slightly deeper (26in/665mm) than a work-top and can be from 21in/540mm up to 52in/1,325mm wide.

POINTS TO CONSIDER WHEN CHOOSING

- The design of the chest freezer means that the cold air is kept around the food, as opposed to an upright freezer where the cold air can flow out of the bottom when the door is opened. They therefore retain the temperature well when opened and as a result use less electricity and so can be a cheaper option in the long term.
- The food is not as accessible as in an upright freezer. Some packets of food may need to be moved to get to food underneath. People who are not very tall may also have difficulty bending over to reach food stored at the bottom of the cabinet.
- A self-supporting lid helps access.
- If a chest freezer is to be kept in a garage or out-house, look for one with a built-in skin condenser to prevent condensation which otherwise encourages rust formation.

Defrosting

- Chest freezers normally need defrosting once a year unless they are low-frost (see Chest freezers: low frost, page 25).
- A drainage spout is recommended to help clean out the bottom of the freezer.

FAST-FREEZE FUNCTIONS

Most freezers have an area for fast freezing. In uprights it is usually the top shelf; for chests a partitioned area at one end.

Manufacturers recommend that the fast-freeze setting is switched on 24 hours before fresh food is added to the freezer and left on for another 24 hours. This increases the operation of the condenser and takes the freezer temperature down to –14°F/–26°C. Before buying, check the maximum recommended quantity of food that can be frozen down at once. This may be important if you tend to freeze a lot of fresh-picked fruit or bulk-bought meat.

Some freezers don't include a fast-freeze option. This may be because they have integral frost-free systems or the manufacturer suggests just turning up the control to the maximum cold temperature for a period of 24 hours.

Fast-freeze trays can be useful accessories to have for the open-freezing of soft fruits or vegetables.

FRIDGE FREEZERS

These are upright units which combine fridge and freezer cabinets. These are put usually one above the other. As a general rule, the freezer is at the bottom unless it is less than about 3cu ft (86 litres) in size.

American-style units may have the fridge and freezer side by side with separate doors, or stacked with double doors for each compartment. They are therefore wider than conventional, upright fridge freezers. Extra features are incorporated, such as drinks dispensers, accessible from the outside.

Under work-top fridge freezers are also available but the freezer space is limited.

Some three-door models are also made. The smaller, middle compartment can be set to operate as a fridge, as a zero-degree compartment, or as a freezer giving additional storage depending upon demands. The zero-degree setting is designed for safe storage of ready-cooked meals, meat and fish.

Fridge freezers are available with equal capacities, or one larger than the other.

Controls

The two compartments may be controlled by a single compressor or two separate compressors. Separate compressors give greater flexibility to maintain the separate compartments at their best temperatures. It also means that the freezer can be switched off independently for defrosting on manual defrost models, or the fridge only switched off if you go away for a period of time, such as a holiday.

TIP If there is only one compressor, check the fast-freeze operation. If the manufacturer suggests just turning up the control this may also over-chill the fridge compartment.

RECOMMENDED OPERATING TEMPERATURES

Fridge:	32–41°F/0°C–5°C
Zero/Chiller Compartment:	32–37°F/0°C–3°C
Freezer:	0°F/–18°C

To check the fridge temperature, immerse a thermometer in a bowl of water. Leave in position for several hours and read without withdrawing the thermometer. It is not satisfactory to place a thermometer on the shelves. This will measure air temperature, not the temperature of the food.

ELECTRICITY CONSUMPTION

Fridges and freezers carry a label stating the energy consumption figures (as from January 1995). The appliances are given a rating between A and G (A being the most economical) for energy use and state how much electricity will be used over a year (this is stated in kWh: 1 kWh = 1 unit of electricity).

INSTALLATION

Free standing

For efficient and safe operation, fridges and freezers should have a gap of at least 1¼in/3cm around the sides and top of the unit. (Check with the manufacturer for the exact measurement details.)

The position of the fridge or freezer can affect the efficiency during use. In a hot room it will obviously have to work harder. Never position one right next to a cooker or heater.

Built-in

Built-in fridges and freezers are fitted into the kitchen units, often with a matching door.

The fitting is usually secure at the top with height adjustments made at the base.

TYPES OF DEFROST SYSTEMS

Fridges: auto-defrost

In traditional fridges, ice and frost build up on the evaporator plate on the back inside wall and must be defrosted manually every few months, by switching off the fridge. This is not very common nowadays.

Auto-defrost fridges will do this automatically. The temperature rises slightly to melt the frost. The water automatically drains to the rear of the appliance, where it evaporates naturally. However, if there is an ice-box this must be defrosted manually.

Upright freezers: frost free

Frost-free freezers need no defrosting as there is no build-up of frost.

A fan circulates cool, dry air throughout the cabinet. There is no water vapour to form frost around the walls or on the food. Because there is no frost the freezer is always running at maximum efficiency and returns to temperature quickly after the door has been opened. Although they are more expensive to buy they are more convenient to use. As well as needing no defrosting, the drawers run smoothly, the food packages do not frost up so they do not stick together and labels are clear.

Some storage space is lost due to the fan housing, and running costs are higher (from 20 per cent more) because the fan is constantly running, but the freezer itself is always running at optimum efficiency.

The frost-free feature is only found on freezers or fridge freezers with a larger capacity.

Fridge freezers: auto-defrost/frost-free

Combined fridge freezers may have one of the following three defrosting systems:

Auto-defrost fridge only: the fridge automatically clears any frost build-up but the freezer compartment will need manual defrosting.

Auto-defrost fridge and frost-free freezer: both compartments need no defrosting. The fridge automatically defrosts and the freezer, being frost-free, has no frost build-up.

Frost-free fridge and freezer: the air that circulates in the freezer to keep it frost free also circulates into the fridge. Manufacturers claim the drier atmosphere in the fridge, as well as the freezer, extends the storage of food as the conditions are even less favourable to bacteria and moulds.

Chest freezers: low frost

Chest freezers need defrosting once a year. A low-frost chest freezer reduces the frost build-up by about 80 per cent, so defrosting can be left for five years. Running costs should be reduced because the freezer is running more efficiently than conventional models.

Once conventional freezers have reached the correct temperature the compressor switches off. The air in the freezer then gradually warms and, as it does, expands slightly. The excess volume of air is pushed out between the door seal. The compressor then cuts back in, to prevent the freezer from warming. It cools the air, which shrinks it again, and moist air is sucked back into the compartment. This is a continuous process and moist air is always being introduced, which builds up as frost.

The low-frost freezers have a separate compartment which acts as a 'lung'. The expanded warming air is pushed into this space and drawn back in as the air shrinks. No new moist air is introduced except when the freezer is opened.

MICROWAVE OVENS

HOW THEY WORK

A microwave cooker works by generating electromagnetic waves. They are produced by a device within the oven called a magnetron.

Microwaves are attracted by water and will enter the food on all its exposed surfaces to a depth of 1¼in/3cm, causing the molecules to vibrate. In foods which are thicker than this, cooking takes place by conductivity: heat produced by the vibrating molecules gradually moves through the food. Unlike conventional cooking there is no external heat, which is why food does not brown.

Microwave energy travels through the air but no heat is generated until it is absorbed by the food. That is why it works so fast, because no energy is wasted. Microwaves can pass through certain substances without harming them, such as plastic and china. They will not pass through metal, but are reflected by it.

Microwave ovens work more quickly than conventional cookers and use one-quarter of the energy of a conventional cooker depending on what you are cooking.

TYPES OF MICROWAVE

There are three main types, depending on the type of cooking you want to do.
Microwave only: the most basic option. It will cook, re-heat and defrost.
Microwave and grill: will also brown food.
Combination oven: combines microwaves, grill and convection cooking (like a normal electric oven) and is the most versatile.

MICROWAVE ONLY

A microwave will re-heat, cook and defrost food. It is a boon to the cook in a hurry and a useful back-up to a conventional oven. It is most useful for re-heating foods which do not need to be browned such as pre-cooked meals and liquids. If you have a freezer, it is ideal for defrosting food quickly.

TIP In an 800-watt microwave it takes 10 to 12 minutes to defrost four pork chops and 4 to 5 minutes to re-heat a plated adult-size meal.

Most useful for
- Re-heating pre-cooked ready meals.
- Re-heating plated meals.
- Re-heating liquids such as soups or beverages.
- Cooking vegetables.
- Cooking fish.
- Defrosting bread, meat and poultry.
- Making jam.

MICROWAVE AND GRILL

These have a grill sited in the ceiling and are slightly more expensive than a microwave only. They are the most popular option because they will also brown the surface of foods. You can use the microwave only, the grill only and usually both together.

However, the grills are not suitable for cooking thicker cuts of meat all the way through because they are not as powerful as a conventional grill: ratings are about 1.3kW compared to 3kW. Even so, these machines have an advantage in that they can be plugged into an ordinary 13-amp socket. Instead, use grill and microwave together or microwave followed by grill.

Most useful for
- Grilling breaded products.
- Grilling meat products such as sausages and chops.

- Re-heating and browning ready meals.
- Re-heating foods with a cheese or potato topping.

Grill types

There are three types of grill used in a microwave and grill. They vary in performance, ease of cleaning and cost. Grilling is generally carried out with the door shut. Check the kW rating, which determines how powerful it is. They are usually around 1.3kW.

Radiant Similar to a conventional cooker grill element but smaller. It is the cheapest option but takes the longest time to brown because you need to pre-heat the elements for eight to ten minutes. Because grilling takes longer food can dry out more than when conventional grilling. After cooking fatty foods the element can be difficult to clean. Some ovens allow you to grill with the door open, which is useful, if you want to cook high-fat foods, to prevent excessive splashing.

Quartz Consists of a ceramic tube encasing fine elements, sited at the top of the oven behind a mesh. Heat is instant so there is no need to pre-heat. This grill is the quickest and tends to give the most even results. It is sited behind the ceiling panel so is easy to clean. Some quartz grills have variable power settings, but these have limited use because, for the majority of foods, high power is needed.

Halogen Has halogen bulbs set at the top of the oven, behind a mesh. The heat is instant, but a halogen grill browns only slightly quicker than a radiant element grill. It is sited behind the ceiling panel so is easy to clean. These tend to be the most expensive.

COMBINATION MICROWAVES

These are more expensive than microwave and grills. They combine a microwave, grill and convection oven, and allow you to cook by microwave only, grill only and convection only (roast and bake); microwave and convection together (combination cooking); and usually microwave and grill together. Some models allow you to use convection and grill together, which is useful for more rapid browning.

With all these options, combination microwaves are very versatile and can be used in place of a standard cooker. They are ideal for one or two people because they are smaller to heat, saving energy, take up less space, and can be positioned at a convenient height for the user.

In an 800W combination microwave it takes about 36 minutes to cook a 4lb/1.8kg chicken compared to 1 hour 40 minutes in a conventional oven. Four baked apples will take about 7 minutes, compared to an hour in a conventional oven.

Most suitable for

- Roasting meat and vegetables.
- Baking pastry and bread.
- Baking cakes.
- Baking jacket potatoes.

Grill types

The types available are the same as in microwave and grills.

Additionally, some models have a hot-air grill. Air from the convection fan is used, but this type of grill does not tend to brown very quickly or evenly.

POINTS TO CONSIDER WHEN CHOOSING

Type of controls

Choose between dial or key-pad.

- Models with dial control usually have fewer programmes and are cheaper. It is not very easy to set times accurately using dial control so check that the calibrations for the first five minutes (most frequently used) are clearly marked.

• Models with key-pad control use a digital display and enable you to set a more accurate cooking time. With microwave cooking this is important because seconds are critical. They tend to have a range of programmes. A key-pad is easier to clean.

Power levels

• When cooking by microwave the most frequently used power settings are high, medium and low, and it is unnecessary to have nine or ten power levels.

• Whatever the wattage of your microwave, the High/Full setting will always be 100 per cent of the power output.

• Some combination ovens only have pre-set programmes for combination cooking. This means the microwave power level and convection temperature is pre-set, eg medium microwave and 350°F/180°C. These can limit your choice if you want to use recipes other than just those in the instruction manual. A model which allows you to select your own settings is the most versatile.

• Make sure the oven has a full range of temperatures available for convection cooking.

WATTAGES

The wattage of a microwave indicates the maximum power output of the oven and relates to how fast it will work. The higher the wattage the quicker the microwave will re-heat. It is important to know the wattage of your microwave so you can calculate cooking and re-heating times.

The optimum wattage is about 750 watts. Lower wattages, such as 600 watts, are not as fast, whereas higher wattages, such as 1,000 watts, may heat food too rapidly and result in

drying and undesirable, uneven cooking.

MICROWAVE SAFETY

Microwave ovens are safe appliances. They will only work if the door is firmly shut. A microwave door has at least two switches, which will cut off the power if the door is not shut properly. Keep the oven door and hinges clean and inspect regularly for corrosion.

If you are worried about microwave leakage, contact the manufacturer, who will send a service engineer to check the oven with accurate equipment.

Microwave leakage detectors are available from electrical stores, but they are not always completely accurate.

WASHING MACHINES

The most common type of washing machine has a porthole door at the front. This type can wash a maximum cotton load of 11lb/5kg, or 5½lb/2.5kg of synthetics (one set of double bed linen).

Standard dimensions to fit under a kitchen work-top measure 33½in/850mm high, 24in/600mm wide and 24in/600mm deep.

Slimline models are the same height but not as deep:18in/450mm or 13in/320mm.

WASH PROGRAMMES

The main programme dial selects the wash cycle, which is set to correspond to the wash care labels that are on all clothes. Some machines automatically set the temperature while others are fitted with a separate temperature control. This gives greater flexibility to use lower temperatures with different wash cycles.

Spin speeds are automatically set, depending upon the programme selected. Full agitation cotton washes have a maximum spin (between 900 and 1,400 rpm), while the easy-care and wool programmes with less agitation use a lower spin (500 to 900 rpm). Spin speeds can often be lowered using an option button.

A lower spin speed (eg 900 rpm) does not necessarily mean that the spin is not as thorough as a high speed spin (eg 1,100 rpm); the machine may just spin for longer to compensate.

A rinse-and-hold option (also called delay spin or Creaseguard) stops the machine during the final rinse when the easy-care programmes are used. This holds the clothes in the water and the machine will not spin until it is reset. This reduces creasing, as clothes can be removed from the drum immediately after spinning rather than left sitting wet in the drum at the end of a wash.

On some models this happens automatically while on others the rinse hold will only come into play if the option button has been used.

SOAK OR SPRAY?

Automatic washing machines work in one of two ways. Most manufacturers sell both types.

Traditionally, automatic machines take in a predetermined amount of water and the clothes are rolled around in the drum with the water and detergent solution.

More recent machines use a sensor-spray system, which is more economical on water. There are two stages in this system.

First, the drum is filled with an amount of water that depends upon the amount of clothes, using a minimum requirement of water. This saves on the amount of electricity used to heat the water.

Second, the water is circulated and sprayed back on to the clothes by being either scooped up by paddles on the drum or re-pumped

from the bottom and showered in at the top of the drum. The latter has the advantage of using all the detergent that may otherwise be trapped in the washing machine's pipework.

Different manufacturers adopt different names for the shower system: Hotpoint, Aquarius; Candy, Aquamix; Zanussi, Jetsystem; and they tend to be more expensive than the traditional machines.

There are a few models that also have the sensor system on the rinses for even greater water savings.

OTHER FEATURES

• Ball Valve (also described with trade names such as Eco-lock) is positioned in the bottom of the drum and prevents detergent falling straight into the pipework and being wasted.

• Imbalance spin protector regulates the speed and length of the spin. If clothes are unevenly distributed in the drum this will prevent the bearings being unnecessarily strained. Some machines operate short spins to try to even out the load before spinning.

• Bio-enzyme phase (or bio-phase). To take full advantage of the enzymes in biological detergents the water temperature is held at around 100–120°F/40–50°C so that stains can be broken down.

PROGRAMME OPTIONS

Half load cuts down (but does not halve) the amount of water used in the main wash on traditional (soaking) machines. Reduces the rinse water used in sensor-spray machines.

Delay timer allows you to set the machine to wash when you want. The wash can be set to finish when you will be able to sort it, or you can take advantage of Economy 7 electricity. (If you intend to make use of this facility, a smoke alarm fitted in the kitchen is recommended.)

Quick wash is designed to freshen up lightly

soiled items, this option may be a separate, cooler wash programme selected on the dial (takes about 30 minutes). Some machines have a limited maximum load for this programme and may also reduce the number of rinses.

Economy option may be similar to a quick-wash option by reducing the wash temperature or the length of the programme. Alternatively, it may reduce the temperature and extend the programme time to compensate. Check that you get a machine with the type of programme you want, and don't confuse a quick and an economy wash.

USEFUL FEATURES

- An extra rinse button allows you to increase the number of rinses. Useful for those with sensitive skin.
- Stage of wash indicators allow you to see how far the wash has progressed, at a glance.
- Rinse and spin programmes are useful for finishing off hand washing.
- If you frequently use different programmes, separate wash temperature and programme controls will help to give you some greater versatility.
- Accessible filters at the front of the machine (a small, square door which hinges open) save items like buttons from collecting in the pump, so reducing the necessity to call out a service engineer. Some machines don't have this access to the filter but claim to have a self-cleaning filter.

TUMBLE-DRIERS

There are two types, vented or condenser. Vented driers are more common.

The basic operation of tumble-driers is simple: you set the drying time according to the amount of clothes. Suggested drying times are usually given on the machine. All programmes have a cool-down period just before the end of the drying cycle.

VENTED

As the name suggests, the damp air from the drier is vented outside via a hose. The vent hose is connected to the front, back, or side of the tumble-drier and can be connected permanently through a window or wall. You will need special fixtures and will probably require a builder to install them. If a permanent fixture is not possible a flexible hose can be put out of a window, but you will need to keep the window fully open throughout the drying session.

CONDENSER

These do not need venting or plumbing. The damp air is cooled and the condensed water collected in a reservoir. The water is emptied from the drawer or can be piped away. (It is suitable for using in steam irons.) This makes the positioning of the drier less restrictive.

Look for condenser driers that have a warning light to remind you to empty the water drawer.

Condenser driers are more expensive than vented driers.

SIZES

Standard

Both models are available in standard size: height 33½in/850mm, width 24in/600mm and depth 24in/600mm. They are the same size as full-size automatic washing machines and can be stacked on top to save space. Permanent stacking kits are available but you must have the same brand of washing machine and tumble-drier.

Standard driers will dry a 9–11lb/4–5kg load of cotton items (a normal maximum wash load).

Compact

Only vented models are available as a compact size (height 26in/670mm, width 19in/490mm). They are a convenient size to sit on a work-top or hang on the wall, and will dry about 6½lb/3kg of cottons at one time.

POINTS TO CONSIDER WHEN CHOOSING

- Basic machines have two heat settings, for cotton and synthetics. Some models may also have a cool setting for airing dried clothes.
- Reverse tumbling action changes the direction of the drum during drying to reduce tangling and assist drying.
- An intermittent tumble after the drying cycle has finished helps to minimise the creasing until you have the time to put the clothes away.
- More sophisticated models have sensors: some lower the heat as the load dries to reduce creasing and prevent over-drying.
- Moisture-sensitive models are programmable and switch off when the clothes are dry. A convenient feature is that they can be set to switch off when the clothes are 'iron dry' or 'cupboard dry'.

Filters

- All tumble-driers have filters that need clearing of fluff on a regular basis. Some models have indicator lights to remind you. Check to see that the filter is easily accessible: one at the front of the drum is more convenient to clean than one at the back.

WASHER-DRIERS

These look just like automatic washing machines but are also able to tumble-dry in the same drum.

They are convenient, carrying out both operations where space is limited. The machine has to be plumbed in where a washing machine would normally fit. The washing capacities are similar to full-sized washing machines but you can only dry half the maximum load, 5½lb/2.5kg cotton, so you must remove half the load after washing.

For drying, the water is condensed using cold water and is pumped away down the washing-machine piping. As the drum is the same size as a washing machine rather than a tumble-drier, there is less room for the clothes to tumble and the result is not as good.

POINTS TO CONSIDER WHEN CHOOSING

- Washing programmes and features are generally the same as for washing machines, but because a drier is also incorporated there are generally fewer extra options.
- The drying cycles have two temperatures to correspond to fabric types.
- All washer-driers can carry out a continuous operation, washing followed by drying, provided you are washing only half the machine's load capacity.
- They can also be used as a washing machine only, or as a drier only.

BATHROOM FIXTURES & FITTINGS

A new bathroom adds an extra personal touch to your home. Consider the choice of colours, materials, fittings and positions in the room.

The main limiting factors are permanent fittings such as windows, doors and plumbing connections. Some piping can be fairly easily moved or extended, but probably the greatest influence is the position of the toilet soil pipe.

PLANNING A BATHROOM

First, consider the space available and the fittings required. Measure the room and mark the plan out on graph paper. **NB: work in metric, as this is how bathroom fittings are always sold.**

Remember to allow for manoeuvring, or the 'activity space', around the fitting (see illustration below). Space is needed for bending over fittings such as a basin, and climbing in

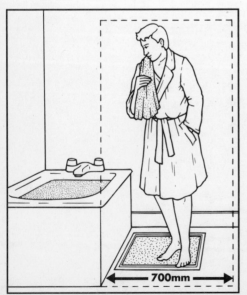

700mm

and out of baths. Access for cleaning should also be considered. Some activity spaces can overlap (see right), as fittings are unlikely to be used at the same time.

Siting the toilet, bidet, basin and bath in line is an efficient way to run water pipes.

The final decision to make is the actual style and colour for the fittings. Light, pale shades and co-ordinates will give an illusion of space in small rooms. Dark colours give the impression of intimacy and warmth but show dirt easily.

Lighting should also be considered at this stage as artificial or natural light will affect the look of a bathroom.

Built-in units can be used to fill spaces. They provide useful storage space and help to tidy up corners that may be difficult to clean.

BATHS

Acrylic

Lightweight, and the most common type of bath. They are warm to the touch, less slippery than metal and stain resistant, but will scratch easily. Light scratches can be removed using metal polish. Deep scratches may be removed by the manufacturer. The moulded acrylic is reinforced with fibreglass and mounted on a galvanised steel frame to give strength. A variety of shapes are available.

Enamelled

Pressed steel baths are coated with vitreous enamel and fired to give the hard finish. Cast-iron baths have a porcelain enamel. Both types of enamel can be damaged by abrasive cleaners and some limescale removers.

RECOMMENDED ACTIVITY SPACES

Bath: 28in/700mm-wide standing area along the side.

Basin: 40in/1,000mm-wide area extending 28in/700mm from the front of the basin. Remember to allow space above for bending down over it. Don't fit a shelf or cupboard above a basin unit so that people using it will bang their head, or drop things into the sink.

Toilet and Bidet: allow a total width of 32in/800mm each, extending 24in/600mm back from the front edge of each. Less space is needed at the sides if they are placed next to each other. Bidets are designed to be used facing the taps, so knee room at the sides must be allowed.

Shower: 28in/700mm standing space in front of the opening.

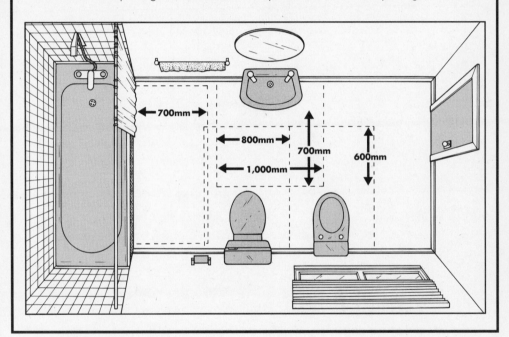

SIZES AND SHAPES

The standard size for a bath is 5ft 6in/1,700mm long x 28in/700mm wide. The average height is 20–24in/500–550mm. Alternative sizes available are smaller baths, starting at about 47in/1,200mm long, and unusually shaped styles, such as corner units. Contoured baths, usually made from acrylic, are shaped to trace the outline of the body, and are slightly more economical on the water that is needed.

All these baths have a rectangular outer frame which usually has panels down the sides and ends. An embossed surface improves the grip and is safer, especially if the bath is to be used with a shower attachment.

Traditional Victorian-shaped baths are freestanding with feet and can still be obtained in cast iron.

A bath usually has the taps positioned at the end of the bath, but some designs have them fitted on the side or they are placed in the corner.

WASH BASINS

Made from vitreous china, kiln fired and glazed. Like normal china, the finish is smooth with a high gloss and hard wearing but will crack or chip if treated roughly.

SIZES AND SHAPES

Pedestal

As well as supporting the bowl the pedestal hides the pipes. The bowl is still usually fixed to the wall, so it is at a height of about 32in/800mm.

Available in a variety of styles and shapes.

Wall mounted

Vary from large to small hand basins which will fit into small cloakrooms. Because they are fixed to the wall the pipes may be exposed, although half pedestals may be fitted.

Counter top

The bowl is sunk to sit level with a wash stand or vanity unit. Cupboards underneath hide the pipework and provide tidy storage.

TOILETS

Like basins, these are made from vitreous china. They consist of two main parts, the pan and the cistern.

TYPES OF FLUSHING SYSTEM

Wash-down: the most common type of mechanism where water washes down from the cistern through the pan.

Syphonic: a quiet and efficient method where the water from the pan is drawn out by a syphoning action.

Shredding and pumping unit: this enables the toilet to be installed almost anywhere in the house. The discharge is shredded so that it can be pumped through a narrower pipe. Being smaller, the discharge pipe can be run behind the wall. An electrical connection is needed to operate the pump.

They are an option for an additional toilet in the house. Permission must be obtained from the local authority before installation.

SIZES AND SHAPES

Close-couple

The cistern sits on the pan to give the look of a single unit. The pan sits on a pedestal (floor standing), but this can leave a space behind the toilet that is difficult to clean.

Low-level

The cistern is mounted a small way (about 37in/935mm) above the pan, connected with a small flush pipe.

High-level

The cistern is fixed on the wall high above the pan with a joining pipe. The cistern has a pull chain to flush the toilet.

Back-to-the-wall

Floor standing, but completely encloses the pipe work so that it is flush with the wall behind. It has a neat appearance and a smooth finish for cleaning.

Wall-hung

The pan and piping are enclosed and supported against the wall. The floor below is clear and easier to clean.

Concealed cistern

The cistern is positioned with a unit or behind the wall with only the flush handle protruding. It may be fitted with a back-to-the-wall or wall-hung toilet pan.

TOILET SEATS

Some manufacturers offer seats with different heights, particularly suitable for the disabled. They fit on to standard toilet-seat fittings.

BIDETS

A low-level wash basin made of vitreous china, like toilets and basins. Originally designed for personal hygiene, they are also used as a foot bath in Britain.

There are two main types, and they both need good, balanced water pressures in order to work effectively.

Over-the-rim

A mixer tap fills the bidet with hot and cold water, like a basin. The tap may have a swivel head to give directional water sprays.

The over-the-rim is the most common type made by UK manufacturers.

Below-the-rim/Box rim

More expensive, and looks more like a toilet. It is filled from under the rim.

Either type of bidet may also have an ascending spray or douche supply. The inlet nozzle is set in the base of the bowl giving an upward spray. High water pressure is needed for this type of bidet to be effective.

Before buying a bidet, check that it conforms to your local water regulations. It may need special installation to meet backflow prevention requirements specified by the water company. Consulting a qualified plumber is recommended.

Like toilets bidets may be wall hung or floor standing. They are usually the same height as a toilet, and should be positioned as close to the toilet as possible.

TAPS

A variety of materials are used for taps and bathroom fittings. The most common are chrome or a gold-effect coating. Brass taps are also available and are sometimes coated with a coloured plastic finish.

The size, position and type of taps for baths, basins and bidets are restricted by the size and number of fitting holes.

Look for taps that comply to BS 5412/3 or EN 200, as this ensures that the tap allows water to pass through at an acceptable and practical rate. Taps to this standard should also satisfy water by-laws against wastage and contamination.

Pillar

These come as pairs for hot and cold water. The water enters the tap vertically, so they must be mounted on a level surface. They are generally small and neat with a twist top. Traditional styles have a cross-shaped handle.

Mixer

Water is supplied via a central tap. A dual mixer supplies the hot and cold together but keeps the two separate within the tap. A true mixer combines the water through the tap and needs equal water pressures for accuracy.

Mixer taps may consist of a single unit with the taps connected to the spout.

A three-piece unit has the controls and taps mounted on to the basin or bath separately.

A bath/shower mixer has a diverter to send water to the attached shower head.

Single lever

As the name suggests, the tap is a single unit with a rotating control and lever. The flow of water is controlled by raising or lowering the lever, while the temperature is varied by rotating the control.

This tap style requires only one fitting hole.

PLUGS

Modern mixer taps often incorporate the plug control. Pop up plugs are operated by a lever. There is no plug chain connected to the bath overflow.

Alternatively, a twisting plug control may be mounted on the side of a bath.

SHOWERS

The main factor affecting a choice of shower will be the type of water system in your house. If you're not sure which type of system you have, ask a plumber to investigate for you: see Fitting a Shower, below.

If your hot and cold water are both supplied from a hot-water cylinder (in the airing cupboard) or a cold-water tank (in the loft) you can choose between a mixer shower (preferably thermostatic) or a power shower (a mixer shower with an extra pressure boost).

If your house does not have a hot-water cylinder or constant hot water, you need an instantaneous electric shower. The cold water supply, direct from the mains, is heated by the shower as it is needed.

An exception is for combination gas boilers (with gas-heated mains-pressure water), when you need a mixer shower. However, check first with your local gas company.

FITTING A SHOWER

The base of the cold-water tank needs to be at least 39in/1m above the shower head for a mixer shower. This is described as a 'head of pressure' and the greater the distance, the greater the shower flow. If there isn't sufficient head of pressure – perhaps if you live in a flat

– you will have to install a booster pump. With an electric shower (supplied direct from the mains), the only way to increase the pressure is to buy one with a higher wattage, or a power shower.

Check that your water supply can cope with the type of shower you are considering. Showers with a high flow rate must not drain the water-storage system too quickly.

Always check foreign imported brands as they may not fit British plumbing systems or comply with UK water regulations.

Professional advice

Advice on your water system and appropriate installations can be obtained from a qualified plumber. Suitable local contacts can be obtained from the Institute of Plumbing.

For advice on electrical work and a local electrician contact the National Inspection Council for Electrical Installation Contracting (NICEIC) on 020 7582 7746.

All gas appliances and connection must be carried out by a plumber who is CORGI-registered (Council for Registered Gas Installers).

Sealing

Make sure that the area around a bath where a shower is to be installed is suitably sealed. Traditional grout is not durable enough against constant sprays of water. Use a silicon sealer; colours to match fittings are available.

TYPES OF SHOWERS

All types of showers can be installed over the bath, or in a separate shower cubicle, except bath/shower mixers.

Bath/shower mixer

The cheapest and easiest to install. Water is diverted from the hot and cold bath taps using a shower mixer which fits over existing taps. Alternatively, a new tap which mixes the water and includes a shower head can be used to replace the individual taps.

Adaptors that fit over the taps come as two types. The simplest only takes water from the taps, and has to be removed to fill the bath. A slightly more complex system clips permanently over the taps but has a diverter which switches the water from the shower through a tap into the bath. Some of this type may also have a temperature control for the shower that is separate from and independent of the two taps.

No plumbing is needed (except if fitting a new mixer tap), but you still need an adequate head of water (see Fitting a Shower, left) and preferably equal pressure from the hot and cold water supply.

This type of system is likely to suffer from draw-off. Water drawn elsewhere in the house, such as flushing a toilet or filling a basin, will cause the shower to run hot.

Look for an automatic diverter which sends water back into the bath if the supply pressure drops too low.

Mixer shower

A wall-mounted shower which draws water from the hot water cylinder and cold water tank. Some have separate temperature and flow controls. There are three types.

• Manual: as with taps, you mix hot and cold water. The shower is gravity fed and needs at least 39in/1m head of pressure. These can also suffer from draw-off (see above) so are best fitted with separate hot and cold supply pipes.

• Thermostatic: the temperature control has a build-in stabiliser so that water stays at the same temperature. It can't run too hot, and shouldn't be affected when water is drawn off elsewhere. Some can even be locked within a

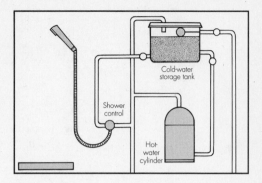

certain temperature range for safety.

• Pressure balance: balances the water supply pressures.

Instantaneous shower

The shower draws water from the rising cold-water mains only and heats it using electricity or gas. The shower is instantly hot and can be taken any time because the supply is not dependent on the stored hot water that may run out. They are a good choice if you don't have a lot of stored hot water.

Electric showers must be fitted with a separate power switch for safety. It can be a cord-pull switch in the bathroom or a switch outside to isolate the power. If in doubt, check with a qualified electrician. For a local electrician contact the National Inspection Council for Electrical Contracting (020 7582 7746).

Usually, the water temperature is manually controlled, but some have a temperature stabiliser so they aren't affected by draw-off

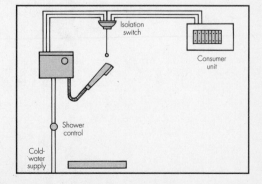

from other taps. The flow rate depends upon the shower's ability to raise the cold-water temperature, particularly in winter. Look for a shower with a power rating of at least 8kW.

The rate of flow may be reduced as the temperature is adjusted: more water can go through if it doesn't need heating, whereas colder water requires more heating, so the flow is slower.

Power shower

To achieve a power shower you can fit:
• A mixer shower with an integral pump to increase the water flow. The temperature is manually controlled, like a normal mixer shower taking water from the cold water tank and hot water cylinder.

They can be fitted where there would otherwise be an insufficient head of water, requiring only 3in/7.6cm head of pressure.
• An additional electric booster pump on an existing mixer shower system. This allows thermostatic control and can be fitted somewhere out of the way, such as in the airing cupboard next to the water cylinder.

A power shower is ideal if you suffer from low water pressure or water flow. A power pump can achieve as much pressure as 30–90ft/ 9–27m head of pressure. The pressure and type of flow from the shower head can be varied to give effects such as a needle jet or soft foam-effect spray.

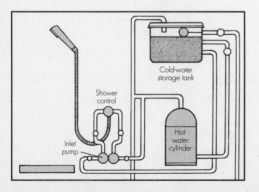

The higher the wattage the greater the flow of water.

POINTS TO CONSIDER WHEN CHOOSING

• A separate on/off switch, independent from the temperature control so that the temperature stays set where you prefer it.
• Some kind of marking, such as LED lights, to help you select your chosen temperature.
• Maximum temperature cut-out to prevent scalding.
• BS 3456 and BEAB approval for electric showers.

SHOWER HEADS

Fixed wall mounted

• The hose to the shower head is concealed behind the wall. Only the actual head is fixed to the wall, but it can be pivoted to change the direction of the spray. Traditional fixed heads have a large circular head connected by rigid exposed pipes. You are not able to adjust the height of the shower.
• The support for the shower head is fixed in one position on the wall. The wall bracket cannot be adjusted in height but the shower head can be unclipped from the bracket for use. The water hose hangs freely from the shower head.

Slide rail

The shower support is fitted on a wall-mounted slide rail, so that the height can be varied and the head can also be unclipped.

Spray variations

The actual head will also affect the power and effect from the shower. They can give a variety of spray types. The greatest variation is on power showers, where a jet, a soft spray or a normal shower effect can be achieved.

Self-cleaning

• Look for a shower head that is self-draining, so that no limescale is formed.

• Self-cleaning heads have internal plastic pins which will protrude through the spray holes when not in use and keep them free from scale.

Individual shower heads offering the designs above can often be bought as replacements compatible with current fittings.

SHOWER ENCLOSURES

Surfaces need to be cleaned easily to prevent the build-up of limescale or mould. Whichever type you choose, the area around the shower needs to be protected from the water spray.

Shower cubicles

• These may be built into a corner or alcove in the bathroom or other room, using two or three walls as part of the shower enclosure.

• Free-standing cubicles don't rely on any interior walls as frames but will need a wall to support the plumbing. The unit has its own four side panels and sometimes a top to contain water vapour.

• Usually they can be purchased as complete kits, including the shower tray.

Shapes and sizes

• Square shower trays are between 28in/700mm and 36in/900mm square.

• Rectangular trays are usually 47in/1,200mm long by 24in/600mm wide.

Different shaped trays, such as curved or triangular, can be purchased to fit into corners.

For a neat edge with a tiled wall, look for a tray with a special tiling lip.

Look for slip-resistant trays, but bear in mind that if the base is too rough it may be difficult to keep a clean appearance.

Construction

Shower trays are usually available in colours to match existing bathroom furniture.

• Ceramic shower trays are the most durable and most expensive. They are made from fireclay, which is stronger than the ceramics used for basins and toilets.

• Acrylic trays are made from the same material as acrylic baths, are warmer to touch than ceramic and are the cheapest option.

• Resin trays are stronger than acrylic, but lighter and cheaper than ceramic.

SHOWER CURTAINS

The cheapest and simplest screening to put along a bath/shower, and can easily be pulled out of the way when the bath itself is needed.

For a simple rail between two walls look for a spring-loaded telescopic rail. A curtain rail fitted with brackets can be fitted between two walls, or in an L-shape or U-shape around a bath. The rail normally comes with the rings or fittings for the curtain.

Mildew and a build-up of soapy deposits in the folds are the main problems associated with shower curtains. Look for PVC, which can be wiped clean, or washable nylon, polyester or cotton.

BATH SCREENS

Usually made from toughened plastic or rigid glass, these are more permanent than curtains.

• A single-panel fixed screen can fit to reach halfway along the side of the bath and may be fixed or hinged for easy access.

• Screens made of several hinged panels will fold flat to be kept out of the way.

Check that the screen will make a good seal with the bath before purchasing.

LIGHTING

Lighting is a necessity in the home, and used creatively it can enhance your decor considerably. Good lighting gives a feeling of space, enhances decor and highlights areas of interest such as paintings and alcoves; and is essential for many practical activities.

The most effective artificial lighting combines three forms called general, accent and task.

General

Good background lighting is necessary for efficiency and safety, and can be supplemented by directional lighting, used as required.

Accent

This provides highlights and shadows which make the room more interesting. It is also sometimes called 'mood' lighting.

Low-voltage fittings are suitable and unobtrusive, especially if recessed.

Task

Task lighting needs to be bright enough for the job in hand, such as work at a desk, needlework or chopping food, but it must not provide any glare.

Working with inadequate light may lead to eye strain, and the older we get the more light we need. Visually-demanding tasks can be carried out by a window during the day, but an additional light source is often necessary in the evening and at night.

Daylight-simulation bulbs

Daylight-simulation bulbs are useful for task lighting. These blue bulbs give out less of the yellow light given out by ordinary tungsten bulbs. They show colours more correctly, and are therefore good for hobbies such as needlecraft and art. The bulbs are available as tungsten, (bayonet and screw fittings) fluorescent and spotlights. They can be obtained from needlecraft and art shops, or from specialist lighting suppliers.

QUALIFIED ELECTRICIANS

In the UK electrical contractors do not have to comply with any of the official regulations. This means that anyone can carry out electrical work, so it is important to choose someone who will work properly and safely. The trade association for electrical contractors is the Electrical Contractors' Association; they will provide details of members (020 7229 1266). The National Inspection Council for Electrical Installation Contracting is a consumer safety organisation. It carries out detailed inspections of electrical contractors and specifies compliance with national regulations. Contact for details of local approved contractors (020 7582 7746).

TYPE OF LIGHT FITTINGS

Select fittings for their light quality, and then their appearance.

CEILING LIGHTS

Give all-round lighting but need accent and task lighting to enhance them. The shape and size of the shade determines the direction and spread of light (A).

PENDANTS

A variation of ceiling lighting with a rise-and-fall facility. Especially useful for people who can't climb to change a light bulb.

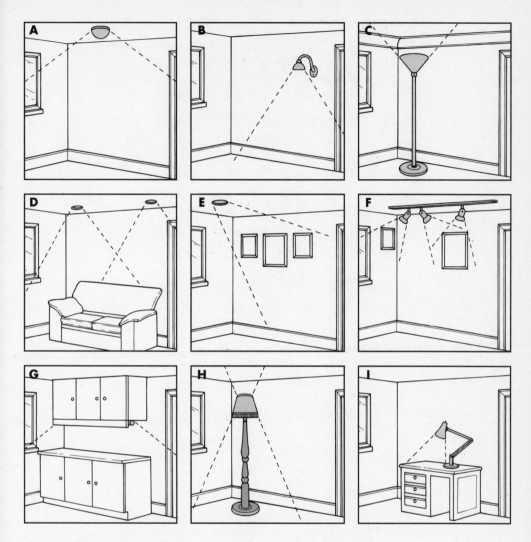

The amount of light depends on the height at which the pendant is hung, the type of bulb and the shade. A pendant should relate to the room size.

WALL LIGHTS

Give a decorative effect. They contribute to general lighting but also help illuminate particular objects (B).

UPLIGHTERS

Light the ceiling, and this light is then reflected back to provide soft gentle illumination. They are really a way to achieve accent lighting (C).

Uplighters are only suitable to use if the ceiling is in good condition, is of a reasonable height and a pale colour. Don't use them if the ceiling is low or dark, as it will absorb the light, rather than reflect it, or if the ceiling has an uneven surface. The ideal ceilings to use for uplighters are period ceilings, with wonderful, original mouldings or cornices.

Uplighters may be wall mounted, free standing, or suspended on a stem from the ceiling. They can be placed on the floor for a dramatic effect, behind large, bushy plants or in corners that would otherwise be dark.

DOWNLIGHTS

Illuminate the carpet and furniture, and are usually recessed or semi-recessed into the ceilings. They achieve a clean, unfussy look and are useful for emphasising particular areas of a room (D).

Give thought to the reflector you choose: a gold reflector is a good choice for earthy tones and wood but not for pastel shades.

Make sure the beams of the downlights merge into each other so that you don't get pools of light. This will be dictated by the bulb and housing. For example, a halogen bulb in a recessed fitting will be more concentrated than a tungsten bulb in a surface fitting.

WALL WASHERS

Provide light like a downlight, but directional, to accent a wall or picture (E).

SPOTLIGHTS

Provide adjustable, directional lighting, with a dramatic effect (F).

Not all spotlights require a track mounting; they can be fixed directly on to the wall and ceiling or clipped on to shelves to accent areas or objects.

While most fittings obscure the bulb, some don't, so choose them carefully.

STRIP LIGHTING

Used a lot in kitchens. It contributes to general, accent and task lighting. The source of light is usually concealed (G).

STANDARD LAMP

A free-standing floor lamp that provides general or directional light depending on the shape of the shade. Provides a flexible source of light as it can be moved around. Standard lamps tend to be used in traditional settings, but there are modern equivalents (H).

TABLE LAMPS

Provide accent lighting and contribute to general lighting in a small area. Their light tends to be multi-directional.

DESK LAMPS

The ultimate task lamps. They provide concentrated light in a particular area. An adjustable head, such as Anglepoise, allows you to alter the angle (I).

TIP If table or standard lamps provide general lighting, have them wired on the same electrical circuit. They can then be switched on together or dimmed simultaneously.

PLANNING LIGHTING

Consider the following:

1 Practicalities: eg, can fittings be recessed into the ceiling?
2 Space and mood: how is the area used, what is its ambience; or is it multi-functional, so the lighting needs to be flexible?
3 Design and colour schemes: textures, walls, ceilings and curtains.
4 Any special features: eg, fireplaces, paintings and alcoves.
5 Would the installation of dual switches and

SAFETY TIPS

- Never work in your own shadow.
- Make sure all work surfaces are well lit.
- Avoid positioning lights where they may dazzle.
- Don't trail flexes over work-tops or near water.

BATHROOM SAFETY TIPS

- It should not be possible to touch any piece of electrical equipment while using the bath or shower.
- In Britain, only pull-cord switches are allowed inside the bathroom, and if a dimmer switch is used it has to be wired outside the door.
- All bathroom light fittings should be either double insulated with no metal parts that can be touched, or properly earthed.

dimmers be useful and improve the lighting?

6 Quality of light required in a specific area, the type of fixture which will provide this, and whether it will look aesthetically pleasing.

7 Location of sockets and switches: traditionally, sockets are 18in/46cm and switches are 51in/1.3m above the floor.

BATHROOM

As well as general lighting, task lighting is needed for shaving and applying make-up.

The mirror is often sited above the washbasin. Ideally, it should be lit on three sides with long incandescent tubes or lots of small low-wattage pearl bulbs, or for a strong clear light install a fluorescent fitting with a diffuser, behind a valance or pelmet.

TYPES OF SWITCHES

STANDARD SWITCHES

These vary according to design and application. Standard, plate switches are available in white with various sizes of rocker control, or in decorative brass or metal. Architrave plate switches can be mounted on narrow door architraves.

Ceiling-mounted switches operated by a pull cord are usually used in bathrooms for safety, because wet hands could cause an electric shock.

DIMMER SWITCHES

These work by reducing the voltage passing through a bulb. This will not only cut down on the amount of electricity used, but also prolong the bulb's life. They are inexpensive to buy and provide an easy means of changing the mood of the room at the turn of a dial.

They are easy to install. It is possible to wire them to all kinds of fittings from floor and table lights to ceiling and wall lights, but do not use dimmers with fluorescent fittings.

ONE- AND TWO-WAY SWITCHING

A one-way switch means that the lights linked to the switch are controlled only from one switch position. A two-way switch is linked to a second switch to control the light. In most homes the commonest use of this is on the staircase, so lights can be switched on or off from either the bottom or top of the staircase, and on bedside wall lights.

GARDEN LIGHTING

With the advent of outdoor entertaining and summer barbecues this form of lighting has become more in demand. Installing just a few lights will have a dramatic effect outside as a little light goes a long way. Look for appropriate IEC standards.

Illumination

Use indoor mains-wired floodlights to cast a bright, even light over drives and lawns and to deter any predatory burglars. The higher you make the position of the light the wider the beam becomes.

Effect

Outline shrubs and trees by using spotlights at ground level. For best effect, the light should be placed the same distance from the feature as the feature is high.

Entertaining

Strings of lights with weatherproof cable provide a party atmosphere. Available from hire shops. For instant light, use flares and candles that are protected against breezes.

Safety

Guide the way down steps with post-mounted lights along the way.

Security

Use an infra-red detector light which switches on when it detects body heat within its range.

TYPES OF EXTERIOR LIGHTING

Low-voltage lights

These are clipped to waterproof cable which is attached to a transformer. This converts mains voltage (240 volts) to 12 or 24 volts so that if you accidentally cut through the cable with a mower, you will come to no harm. The advantages of this type are that the cable need not be buried and it can be installed by a competent DIYer.

Mains lighting

Permanent garden lighting should have a separate circuit. It should have waterproof sockets, a PVC cable encased in a plastic

---

LIGHTING AND THE ENVIRONMENT

If every household in the UK bought just one energy-saving light bulb (for use where light is needed for long periods each day), this country would save power equal to the output of one large power station. This would help cut down on carbon dioxide emissions, and so the use of these bulbs helps to reduce the threat of global warming.

---

conduit buried at least 20in/50cm deep, a current breaker (RCD) and a fuse. It should be installed either by a qualified electrician or an expert DIYer.

The advantage of mains lighting systems is that you can have much more lighting than on a low-voltage system, for practical rather than decorative use.

Solar lighting

Solar panels absorb sunshine during daylight hours and then convert it into electricity, which is stored in a battery.

The advantage is that you have no installation or running costs, but solar lighting will only give a decorative glow and efficiency depends upon the amount of sunshine absorbed.

Security lighting

See Security Lighting, page 196.

FLOORING

Flooring is the most hard-working area in the home so it must be functional to withstand abrasion, weight and spills, yet still be decorative. As well, the colour, texture and finish must blend in with the rest of the decor.

Who doesn't admire the cool stone slabs or rich terracotta tiles of Mediterranean villas? But, when it comes to the crunch, most of us opt for foot-friendly carpets or inexpensive, easy-to-clean vinyl. However, there may be other alternatives worth considering.

HARD FLOORING

BRICK TERRACOTTA PAVING

Suitable for kitchens and dining areas, outhouses and conservatories.

This is warm and rustic, and available in many shades. Different patterns can be laid by positioning the bricks at different angles, eg herringbone style.

The York Handmade Brick Company (01347 838881) has a good selection and will advise on installation and sealing.

Pros
- Can be laid directly on to the damp-proof course.
- Non-slip.
- Stain and grease resistant.
- Can be sealed.

Cons
- Hard.

CERAMIC TILES

Suitable for kitchens, bathrooms, hallways, and conservatories. Should be floor strength and laid on to a solid floor which should be perfectly flat. The International Abrasion Resistance Grades include four ratings. Class III is suitable for kitchens and Class IV for bathrooms. Whether matt, glazed or unglazed, there's a huge range of colours, styles and patterns available.

Sizes vary from tiny mosaic tiles to 1ft/30cm square, and hexagonal, rectangular and interlocking shapes.

Pros
- Impervious to water and chemicals.
- Cool.
- Low maintenance.
- Chips and scratches are less noticeable in unglazed tiles because the colour is distributed throughout the tile.

Cons
- Dishes will crack if dropped on to them.
- Noisy.
- Can be tiring on the feet.
- Slippery when wet.
- Hygienic, but attract dust in a bathroom when damp, due to condensation.

QUARRY AND TERRACOTTA TILES

Suitable for kitchens, halls, conservatories and porches.

Various different colours are achieved by the use of clays from different areas of the UK and the world, as well as the materials used to fire the kiln which bakes them. Gas-fired kilns make a plain, uniform-coloured tile, while the irregular-coloured Spanish or Mexican tiles vary from cream to deep russet from a fuel of almond or coconut shells.

Tile shapes vary: squares (4in/10cm or 16in/40cm), rectangles, hexagons, octagons and shapes, with clipstones or insets and borders.

Encaustic tiles are made from different-coloured clays. The overall effect can be similar to a geometric patterned or oriental rug with border, set into the floor.

Acrylic seals will maintain the natural colour of the tiles, while linseed oil will darken and change the colour during its life. Quarry tiles have a more regular appearance and are generally not sealed.

Pros
- Can improve in appearance with age.
- Hard wearing.
- Impervious to water.
- A little softer underfoot than ceramic tiles.

Cons
- Cold and noisy.
- Break if a hard object is dropped on them.

TIP If using glazed ceramic insets, sink these in ⅛in/3mm to minimise the wear of the glazed surface.

SLATE

Suitable for halls, porches, conservatories.

British slate is quarried in Wales and Cornwall; African and Chinese slate is richly coloured, but expensive. A good range of colours and finishes include diamond sawn with a smooth matt finish; riven, where the slate is naturally split with a textured surface; and fine rubbed with a light sheen. Treat with a mix of linseed oil and turps for extra lustre.

Pros
- Hard wearing.
- Easy to maintain.
- Impervious to water.

Cons
- Brittle and heavy, so needs a strong sub-floor.

- Some types have an uneven surface.
- Will stain, but this will fade over time.
- Cold and noisy.

STONE

Suitable for kitchens, halls and utility areas.

Includes granite, sandstone, limestone, and York stone, which have a variable texture and colour. It is usually cut into simple shapes: square or oblong.

Pros and Cons
As slate.

TERRAZZO

Suitable for halls, porches, kitchens and bathrooms.

Made from marble chippings and dust set into cement, and is mottled rather than veined like real marble. Takes its colour from whatever type of marble has been used; a large range of colours is available. It looks smooth and elegant but is very expensive.

Pros
- Hard wearing and impervious to water and staining.
- Built-in lustre, but can be polished.
- Improves with age.

Cons
- Heavy so the sub-floor must be sound and strong.
- Cold to the touch.
- Noisy.
- The polished surface can be slippery, especially when wet.

WOOD

Suitable for throughout the house, with the exception of wet areas such as bathrooms.

There is a wide choice of woods and

finishes available. Use clear grades of ash, beech and maple for cool modern interiors, and the more subtle tones of rustic grades to bring warmth to traditional rooms. Oak is available in a wide range of grades from rustic knotty to the clear straight-grained qualities found in the classic parquet floors of France and Italy. Ash, oak, beech and maple are all well-established hard-wearing woods suitable for a wide variety of areas, while cherry is quite new to flooring, bringing a feeling of softness and warmth.

Surfaces can be lacquered, oiled or waxed. Popular branded ranges include mainly lacquered finishes, but more oiled products are becoming available for heavy traffic areas. Oil is less shiny than lacquer, and brings out the grain and texture of the wood. Strips and boards provide a good background to rugs and furniture.

Blocks, battens and tiles can be used to create herringbone and other parquet patterns. If laying over floorboards, install a layer of plywood first.

Recent developments in adhesive and mechanical fixing systems allow easy installation over existing floorboards, concrete or any level base such as plywood, chipboard, etc. The thickness of the flooring is important. When nailing to joists or battens, do not use products under ¼in/19mm in thickness. Overlay flooring, which comes in thickness from ⅜in/8mm upwards, can be used where it is totally supported, for example over floorboards or concrete.

Solid and laminated branded ranges include Junckers, Kahrs, Tarkett, Vigers and Wicanders. Wicanders Wood-O-Cork has a cork core sandwiched beneath the wood, which is protected by a vinyl-wear layer on the surface. If buying non-branded products, check they have been properly kiln-dried and beware of reclaimed timber from derelict buildings where changes in humidity may well have affected the dimensional stability of the wood itself.

Pros
- Durable and can improve with age.
- Warm and stylish.
- Easy-to-clean surface.

Cons
- Not waterproof, so avoid over-wetting.
- Can be dented by heels and castors.

RENOVATING OLD FLOORBOARDS

Renovating old wooden floors is only worth the effort if they are in good condition. Hammer down protruding nails, fill in nail holes or gaps, and remove sharp edges or splinters. These can then be sanded, stained darker or bleached a lighter colour, and sealed or varnished.

When sanding down, use the sander along the length of the board, never across. Remove all traces of dust, and then wipe over with white spirit. Bleach, stain or paint.

LIGHTENING WOOD

Scrub with domestic bleach and leave to dry. Repeat until the correct colour is achieved. Thoroughly wash the floor with water. Allow to dry. The wood grain may have expanded slightly due to the water: if so, sand it down before sealing.

STAINING

A good range of colours is available, and they can be combined with a varnish.

Choose either oil, water or spirit-based stains. Oil-based tend to give a more even colour but are slower to dry. Apply with a clean dry cloth, along the grain. It's easier to concentrate on one floorboard at a time. Repeat until the required depth of colour is achieved. Dry, and then seal.

SEALING

Use either wax or a polyurethane varnish.

Polyurethane varnish

Varnishes can darken and yellow the wood, but they are tough, water resistant and easy to maintain. Choose from gloss, satin and matt finishes. Gloss is the toughest, but shows up dust and marks easily.

Apply across the grain, finishing with long brush strokes down the grain. Apply three coats in areas of heavy wear. Sand in between coats to give the next one something to grip to.

Wax

Not as tough or as water resistant. Needs frequent re-treating. Seal the floor with a floor sealer to prevent dirt penetrating the wood. Apply wax thinly with a soft cloth, leave, and then buff up the surface with a floor polisher. Polish with a soft cloth.

SEMI-HARD FLOORING

LINOLEUM

Suitable for kitchens, bathrooms, conservatories.

Linoleum is processed from wood flour, cork, linseed oil and various resins baked together, rolled under pressure and then pressed on to a strong jute backing.

Available in sheet or tile form. Sheet form should be professionally laid, but tiles are not difficult to lay.

Pros
- Hard wearing.
- Quiet and warm.
- Springy underfoot.
- Designs with borders, motifs and patterns can be tailor-made, but it is best to have them professionally done.
- Does not indent as readily as vinyl – but protective cups should be used under castors.
- Improves with age as the linseed oil oxidises and destroys surface bacteria.
- Resistant to minor burns and fading.

Cons
- Over-wetting can damage the finish and cause rotting.

VINYL

Suitable for kitchens, bathrooms, playrooms, halls, porches.

Manufacturers have at last come up with stunning new ranges with more than a hint of

TIPS FOR FITTING VINYL

- If you are fitting it round a lot of awkward shapes in the bathroom for example, it's easier to lay tiles, but if it's a rectangular-shaped room, sheet vinyl will give a better result.
- Cut a little larger than the actual size because it does shrink slightly when laid. Trim to fit after several weeks.
- If you've chosen a geometric pattern, try and square it up with the line of the doorway so that it runs either at right angles or parallel.
- Leave the vinyl in the room in which it is to be laid for at least 24 hours beforehand, either opened up flat, or loosely rolled.

the Continent about them: rustic reds, deep blues and grey flecks, symmetrical designs and bold borders and insets.

It's a flexible plastic surface available in sheets (generally 2, 3 or 4yd/m widths) or tile form. It can be cushioned with expanded PVC foam sandwiched under the wear layer. A thickness of at least 0.06in/1.4mm is the best choice. Price varies according to thickness of wear layer (0.2 to 0.4mm) and the cushioning.

Sophisticated hard vinyls such as Amtico look realistically like wood, quarry tiles and marble. They should be professionally fitted.

Special safety flooring is available; good for bathrooms.

Pros

• Very versatile.
• Cushioned vinyl is very comfortable and warm.
• Tiles are very easy to fit because they are flexible. Some have self-adhesive backing.
• Waterproof and resistant to oil and most domestic cleaning agents.
• Easy to clean because of its smooth impervious surface.

Cons

• Cheap flooring can scuff so choose the thickest you can.
• Will burn and mark if something hot is placed on it.
• Dents, and can be damaged by dragging heavy appliances and furniture across the surface. Stand heavy equipment on hardboard or special discs.

CARPET

Thanks to advances in fibre technology, today's carpets are better value than ever before – a far cry from the 1950s when the choice available was restricted to either wool or nylon. In the UK, synthetic carpets now account for 80 per cent of all sold.

CHOOSING A CARPET

There are several factors to consider when choosing a new carpet:
• Cost: the maximum you can realistically afford.
• Durability: how much wear and tear the carpet is likely to get.
• The purpose of the room it will go in (eg bedroom, living room or hallway).
• How long you want it to last.
This will give you some indication of the quality required, the type of fibre, the depth and the density of the pile.

DURABILITY

This is determined by looking at the denseness of the pile and also its resilience. You can check this by pressing your hand on the pile and monitoring how long it takes to spring back into shape; the faster it does the better. Short, dense piles are more durable than long shag piles.

Carpets are made in a variety of weights: light, medium and heavy. A combination of 80 per cent wool to 20 per cent nylon is probably one of the most durable blends, if the construction is good.

Synthetic carpets now look more like wool than they used to, and they have fewer problems with static electricity as the fibres are now treated to reduce it.

WHICH FIBRE?

Acrylic

Often blended with other fibres, it's particularly suitable for bedrooms and other low-duty areas. Not very common.

Pros

- Lightweight carpet with a wool-type texture.
- Does not absorb dirt and stains easily.

Cons

Not as durable as other fibres.

Polyester

A suitable choice for bedrooms.

Pros

- Reasonable resistance to abrasion.
- Does not fade easily.
- Warm feel.

Cons

- Cheap versions which haven't been treated are prone to soiling.
- Once the pile has been flattened it's difficult to restore.

Polypropylene

Suitable for kitchens and bathrooms. About a quarter of British tufted carpets have a polypropylene pile or one that is blended with other fibres. Blends of 50 per cent wool and polypropylene are very popular, and if they have a good proportion of wool it helps to prevent the pile from flattening permanently.

Pros

- Good value.
- Non-absorbent and easy to clean.
- Withstands abrasion well.
- Colourfast.
- Low in static.

Cons

- Traditionally harsh textured, but new ranges are softer.
- Will flatten more easily than wool so polypropylene is often used in low loop pile constructions (so the pile does not crush as easily).

Wool

Generally blended with 20 per cent nylon for greater resilience and durability.

Suitable for heavy-duty areas. For maximum durability always look for a short, dense pile.

Pros

- Inherently good resistance to soiling and wear.
- Soft and comfortable.
- Good insulation properties.
- Does not burn readily.
- The pile does not easily flatten so retains its appearance well.

Cons

- Can rot if left wet.
- All wool is expensive, but you get what you pay for. A better option is to go for an 80/20 wool/nylon mix.

NATURAL-FIBRE FLOOR COVERINGS

Suitable for all dry areas.

These traditional coverings have been around since the days of the Ancient Egyptians but have become more popular in recent years as they provide a warm, muted background for many styles of room, contemporary or period. They provide a good range of rich colours and interesting weaves; are hard wearing; and do not suffer from static.

Choose natural-fibre flooring with a latex backing for a total fitted look. The backing helps it to stay flat and keep its shape. Extra underlay will increase the comfort and insulation of a natural-fibre floor covering, which can be fitted or loose.

COIR

Thick, rough fibre which protects the inner section of the coconut from the casing. Coir matting has become more sophisticated in recent years, and can be combined with sisal or other natural materials which can be dyed exciting shades. Often backed with latex or vinyl, to prevent the dust from penetrating through and improve its durability.

Pros
• Relatively cheap and hard-wearing (although not as durable as sisal or seagrass).

Cons
• Uncomfortable on bare feet.
• Needs to be tightly fitted or it waves, looking untidy and becoming a hazard.
• Lengths need to be stitched together.

SEAGRASS AND RUSH

Woven into plaits and herringbones which look great in old rooms, especially with stone.

Pros
• Much tougher fibre and a smoother surface than coir.
• Warm underfoot.
• Inexpensive.
• Good stain-resistance.

Cons
• Can be slippery, so if using on stairs lay the grain parallel to the stair tread.

SISAL

A fibre produced from the leaves of the plant, *Agave sisalana* by a special spinning process. Types of weave include herringbone, plaid, bouclé and panama.

Pros
• Soft and hard wearing.
• Inexpensive.
• Dyes well, so is available in a good range of colours.

Cons
• Very porous fibre, so stains can be hard to remove.

CLEANING IN THE HOME

A–Z CLEANERS

There is almost always a ready solution for any household cleaning problem, but before starting it is helpful to be aware of common cleaning materials and substances.

ABRASIVES

Any material used to rub or abrade surface. Available in differing degrees of fineness from metal polish cleaners to cream cleaners. You can feel how abrasive a material is between your thumb and forefinger. When using an abrasive cleaner, follow the grain of whatever you are rubbing.

SCOURERS

Metal

For the toughest jobs on hard surfaces. May be formed of a ball of metal coils, or look like wire wool.
(Include Vileda Heavy Duty Scouring Pad, Spontex Tough Scourer [stainless steel] Goldilocks [brass].)

Nylon

Traditionally made of green nylon. Gentler than metal, but will still scratch delicate surfaces. May be in thick squares, or bonded on to sponge cleaners.
(Include Vileda Super Scourers, Vileda Washmaids, Spontex Washups, Spontex 'Brisk', Minky Sponge Scourer.)

Non-stick nylon

Similar to above, but a softer nylon, traditionally white, and bonded on to sponge cloths. Good for rougher cleaning on delicate surfaces such as baths.
(Include Spontex 'Nonstick Brisk', Vileda Non-Scratch Washmaids.)

SPECIAL CLEANERS

Non-stick: rough but not sharp surface

Vileda Scrunge looks like melted plastic on one side of a synthetic sponge, and is recommended for all household surfaces, including stainless steel, ceramics, enamel, glass and non-stick cookware.

Brillo Lite is similar to traditional Brillo, with soap pellets inside. The outer material is woven plastic over foam and must be wetted to make use of the soap. Recommended for all surfaces, including ceramics, microwaves, glass and non-stick surfaces.

Brillo metal scourers must be wetted to get the benefit of the soap pellets inside. Designed for tough cleaning, but will rust if kept for more than one job.

ACETIC ACID

This is a common acid; a dilute form is household vinegar.

ALCOHOL

Dissolves grease and evaporates quickly, although not as effective as dry-cleaning fluids. As a solvent it is excellent for cleaning glass because it removes oils and waxes. Most commonly used is methylated spirits and vodka (but not gin, which contains juniper berry stain, and not surgical spirit, which is composed of alcohol and castor oil).

ALKALIS

Household alkalis include ammonia and some soda compounds. They will harm certain materials, including wool, silk and aluminium.

Ammonia is an alkaline gas dissolved in water. For household use, its strength varies from 5 to 15 per cent. It is great at cutting through grease and removing dirt from floors and walls. Can be used for stain removal as it is a mild bleach. Be careful, however: ammonia is poisonous.

DRY-CLEANING FLUIDS

These are particularly effective for stains caused by grease, oil and adhesive tape. Most proprietary dry-cleaning stain removers contain a grease solvent and are sold under a variety of trade names, for example Dabitoff, K2r; and both as a liquid or a spray.

Dry cleaning solvents dissolve the grease which holds the stain on. Don't flood the fabric with cleaning fluid. Several applications are best. The spray variety contains the solvent to dissolve the grease and an absorption powder to take the grease away and control ring marks. Carefully follow the directions about the suggested distance for using the spray, and wait for the powder to dry completely before brushing it off.

HOUSEHOLD BLEACH

This is a strong chlorine bleach, with a strong swimming-pool smell, and is usually made from sodium hypochlorite. It can range in concentration from about 5 per cent and has detergents and perfumes added. It is sold under trade names such as Domestos, Parozone and Vortex.

Bleach should be used with great care because it can weaken fabrics and fade colours.

Milton is sodium hypochlorite, about 2 per cent concentration. For cleaning, it is used diluted 1 part to 4 parts water, and there is no need to rinse afterwards.

HYDROGEN PEROXIDE

A mild, slow-acting bleach safer for all fabrics. It has a different chemical composition to the hypochlorites. Its percentage strength varies. It is one of the slowest-acting bleaches and therefore the easiest to control. It is available from chemists.

SILICONES

Used in furniture and floor polishes. They act by lubricating the polish, making it easier to spread, so that an even film reflects light and appears glossy.

Silicone textile finishes give resistance to wear, water, weathering and stains because they form a film that acts as a barrier to make the surface more durable.

SODIUM BICARBONATE

Baking soda or bicarbonate of soda. It removes stains from china, cleans your teeth, deodorises drains, cleans your fridge, eliminates stomach aches which are caused by gas, and acts as a rising agent in biscuits and cakes. It also brings a sparkle to jewellery, neutralises bee stings (because it is an alkali), cleans glass, tiles and porcelain, and helps to kills odours.

SODIUM CARBONATE

See Washing Soda, page 55

SOLVENTS

A substance used to dissolve another substance, such as grease, which attracts and holds dirt on to a surface.

Water is the safest and best solvent. Try it first on all washable materials.

Alternatively, to dissolve and remove grease-based substances you need to choose a grease-based solvent (such as dry-cleaning fluids).

TURPENTINE

An oil-based solvent that is obtained from pine and fir trees.

It is used in certain paints, varnishes and waxes, and as an ingredient of furniture polishes and waxes. It will remove paint stains and grease.

Turpentine is flammable and poisonous.

VINEGAR

About 5 per cent acetic acid. If using vinegar for stain removal, it is always best to use white vinegar because it is colourless (malt vinegar and wine vinegar may stain).

WASHING SODA

Sodium carbonate. It is a cheap and effective cleaner, is inexpensive and is sold in most supermarkets; and is sometimes referred to as washing or soda crystals. Useful for cleaning drains, greasy pots and pans, and can also be used as a water softener.

CLEANING SURFACES A–Z

BAMBOO

See Basketware, page 56

BARBECUES

Refer to the manufacturer's instructions if you have retained them.

ASH PAN

Line with aluminium foil to hold the coals and ash, and also reflect the heat towards the food. The foil and ashes can simply be lifted out when cold.

Don't line gas barbecues with foil; it will obscure the burners.

GRILLS

There are two main types: chrome-plated, like ordinary oven shelves, and porcelain-coated (which look black). Both types are easier to clean while still warm.

Use a solution of washing-up liquid in warm water. Abrasive cleaners or oven cleaners should be avoided as they will damage the coating. A brass-bristled brush will help remove food (brass is softer than steel and won't damage coatings). Avoid the bristles clogging with grease by first rubbing food remains off the grill with crumpled aluminium foil. Porcelain-coated grills can be washed in the dishwasher. (At GHI we find the chrome can be washed in a dishwasher too, but this may be at the user's discretion.)

CASING

Usually made from aluminium, coated with a black paint or enamelled steel. Wipe clean with washing-up liquid to remove grease marks. Don't use abrasive cleaners. If the paintwork is looking shabby, touch up with a heat-resistant metal spray paint on the aluminium or enamel (eg Plasti-Kote Bar-B-Q Paint). Paint after priming the area.

VIEWING WINDOWS

Some gas and kettle barbecues have glass windows which should be wiped over with a detergent solution. Use a ceramic hob scraper to remove burnt-on splashes.

FRAME

Check the legs and frame, as steel frames may be susceptible to rust. Use a rust-preventing metal paint to touch up if required.

Don't neglect any wood on the frame. About once a year, treat with preserving wood varnish after rubbing down the old finish with sandpaper.

GAS BARBECUES

Volcanic rocks

Fats and oils will be absorbed by the rocks and then vaporised as the rocks are heated. To clean thoroughly at the end of cooking, close the lid and heat on high for five to ten minutes. Turn the rocks to expose the clean side before each use. Replace the rocks about every five years.

Gas burners

Disassemble and clean every two to three months, as insects may find the burner tubes cosy homes and cause flash backs. Check the manufacturer's details for disassembling the unit for cleaning.

Barbecue-cleaning kits are available that include a de-greaser, a wire brush and touch-up paint. (For example, B&Q Barbecue Cleaning Set or Thermos Clean-up Kit.)

STORAGE

Before storing for the winter, wipe clean metal parts with vegetable oil to prevent damp corroding them.

Cover permanently built barbecues with plastic sheeting to protect from severe weather.

Gas barbecues should not be stored indoors with the cylinder attached. Disconnect, using a plug or cap to seal off the valve outlet. Store the barbecue indoors and the cylinder outdoors only, in a well-ventilated area.

BASKETWARE

Basketware may be made from one of many materials: bamboo, rattan, wicker or willow. It is used for furniture, ornamental baskets and hampers. Large items may come with care instructions, so follow these where possible.

CANE

Generally, imported baskets are made with split cane. They may have a light seal or varnish. For general cleaning wipe down with water. For heavier dirt you may need to use a solution of washing-up liquid, but anything harsher may break through the seal and damage the cane underneath.

WILLOW

Mainly used for hampers and similar baskets. Usually unsealed, so clean as above. Don't over-wet or leave basketware to soak.

If staining occurs and cannot be removed with normal washing it may respond to gentle bleaching. This is likely to whiten the cane. Varnish if you wish to re-colour.

TIP If a stain does not respond to bleaching, varnish the basket with a coloured polyurethane wood varnish to cover the stain.

BAMBOO

A hollow cane, often split for weaving. Wipe clean with a solution of washing-up liquid, then dry with a cloth.

BATHROOM SURFACES

If you know the manufacturer of your bathroom suite, contact them for cleaning advice. Follow all the cleaning-product recommendations carefully.

BATHS

Acrylic

Daily care: Rinsing and drying the bath after every use – if you have the time – will prevent water staining. Clean daily with an all-purpose bathroom cleaner endorsed by the British Bathroom Council to prevent build-up of dirt and scum. A product with a spray applicator is quick and easy to use, and just needs wiping with a damp cloth.

For real convenience a bathroom cleaner mousse is simply sprayed on, left and then rinsed off. However, it will not remove heavy build-up of scum, and is expensive compared to conventional cleaning products.

Thorough care: Once a week, give the bath a thorough clean, paying particular attention to scum build-up. For stubborn marks, use a nylon bristle brush but not an abrasive cleaner. Look for the British Bathroom Council's logo on literature that comes with recommended products. In a hard-water area use a limescale cleaner. Pay particular attention to the area around the taps where limescale can gather, and to the taps themselves.

Maintenance: To remove fine scratches, rub gently with metal polish, and then clean the bath afterwards.

Vitreous enamel-coated cast iron or steel

Daily care: See Baths, Acrylic

Thorough care: Clean as for acrylic baths, but look for a product recommended by the Vitreous Enamel Association.

Cleaning products with anti-limescale ingredients may cause enamel to dull, so are not recommended. To remove limescale try using a plastic scourer and neat concentrated washing-up liquid – this job requires lots of elbow grease. With enamelled surfaces avoiding limescale is down to prevention rather than cure.

Maintenance: For re-enamelling ask for advice from the Vitreous Enamel Association (07071 226 716). This is only worthwhile if your bath is of some value, perhaps because it is a Victorian cast-iron bath that would be hard to replace.

Whirlpool and spa baths

Although most are self-draining, it's important to clean out the scum left in the pipework.

About once a week fill the bath with warm water and add a cleaning agent: the manufacturer's proprietary product or a cupful of Milton. Allow to circulate for five minutes. Empty the bath, re-fill with clean water, and circulate for a further five minutes to rinse. Some whirlpool and spa baths will dose the pipework automatically with disinfectant.

BASINS

Clean daily with an all-purpose bathroom cleaner. Wipe with a damp cloth. Once a week, wipe over the outside and the pedestal.

TIP After cleaning, make sure the plug hole is thoroughly rinsed as bathroom cleaners can damage the coating. Brass or gold-plated plug holes should be buffed dry after use to prevent them from discolouring.

SEALANT

The sealant between baths or basins is difficult to clean effectively. Use a fungicidal spray to remove mould, and spray regularly to prevent re-growth. Once the sealant is discoloured the only solution is to replace it.

TOILETS

Daily care: Clean every day to keep germs at bay. Wipe the rim of the bowl and the seat with a solution of washing-up liquid. Seats range from polyester to solid oak, but can all be cleaned in this way.

To clean the bowl, either use a bathroom cleaner with added disinfectant, or fit an in-cistern cleaner or a bowl cleaner, both of which will release cleaner or bleach into the bowl after every flush.

Thorough care: At least once a week, wipe the outside of the toilet bowl and the cistern with a solution of washing-up liquid or a bathroom cleaner.

To clean the bowl thoroughly, use a liquid or powder cleaner and a toilet brush, paying particular attention to under the rim. Keep the brush clean by rinsing in a flush of bleach after every use.

If you live in a hard-water area, regularly use a toilet cleaner with a built-in limescale remover. To remove limescale in the bowl use a limescale remover with a thick gel consistency so it can stick to the vertical bowl surface. For heavy deposits empty the water from the bowl first. Bail out the water by hand or, if the cistern is accessible, tie up the float-operated inlet valve (otherwise known as the ballcock) and flush the toilet. (This lowers the water and stops the cistern from filling it again.)

TIP Do not use two different toilet cleaners at the same time, even if one is bleach. When they mix, toxic gases can be released into the bathroom.

TIP Do not leave toilet cleaner in contact with the surface longer than recommended, or the cleaner will penetrate through worn areas or cracks in the glaze and cause the surface to discolour. Remember this if going on holiday.

SHOWERS

Daily care: Clean the shower tray with an all-purpose bathroom cleaner.

Thorough care: If you are in a hard-water area use a limescale cleaner once a week.

Clean shower screens with a solution of washing-up liquid. On folding shower screens pay particular attention to the hinging mechanism, which can get grubby.

Damp areas will be susceptible to mould, which appears as black spores. To remove it, spray with a fungicide. Regularly re-spray any susceptible areas to prevent further growth. Make sure you spray when everyone has finished in the bathroom so it is not immediately washed off.

To remove mould from shower curtains see Mildew, page 131.

Descale shower heads using a liquid descaler, available in conveniently measured sachets or in a bottle. An old toothbrush is useful to dislodge any particularly stubborn scaly deposits.

If grout between tiles is dirty and discoloured, apply a whitening product which also contains a fungicide. Tile Guard has a foam applicator that makes it easy to apply. Alternatively, you can use a solution of diluted household bleach (one part bleach to four parts water) and an old toothbrush, although this doesn't contain mould inhibitors.

TAPS

Includes chrome, plastic, gold and brass finishes.

Daily care: Many products used in the bathroom, such as denture creams, toothpaste and strong detergents, can damage the protective coating on taps, particularly those with a gold or brass finish. Ideally, after every use, wipe the taps free from such products and then buff dry. Clean regularly with a solution of washing-up liquid, rinse and dry. Do not use an abrasive cleaner.

Thorough care: To remove heavy limescale deposits soak a cloth in a proprietary descaler and wrap it around the tap. Do not leave for longer than the recommended time. Rinse thoroughly and dry.

WALLS

See Kitchen Surfaces, page 78

FLOORS

See Flooring, page 65

BOOKS

Valuable books should be stored correctly to avoid damage. Don't let them slump on partly filled shelves. Invest in some book ends. Large and heavy books such as atlases or the Bible should be kept flat.

Keep them in a cool room (about 60°F/15°C). Too much heat can damage leather bindings and make the adhesive brittle. Sunlight fades covers, and dampness will cause mildew and other moulds.

Dust books at least once a year. Do them one at a time using a fine paint or unused blusher brush. Holding the book closed, gently brush along the edges. Never bang the book as it will damage the bindings.

TIP Once a year, fan the pages of those books which are left undisturbed on your book shelf. This will help remove dust.

Valuable books may need professional treatment for bookworm, rust or mildew, in which case contact your local specialist bookseller, museum or The Institute of Paper Conservation (01886 832323).

BRASS

See Metals, page 79

BRUSHES

See Paint Brushes, page 84

BROOMS AND CLEANING BRUSHES

These pick up a lot of dirt which should be removed regularly. Wear household gloves and pick out the larger particles by hand.

Nylon brushes are easier to wash than bristle brushes. They won't rot or go mouldy, and they are softer. Wash them in a warm, mild detergent solution with a final rinse in cold water to stiffen the bristles. Then hang them up to dry.

TIP Do not store brushes and brooms so that they rest on their bristles as this flattens them and destroys their effectiveness. Use the hanging hook or lean the brush head end upwards.

CANE

See Basketware, page 56

CARPETS

See Carpets, page 106

CERAMIC FLOOR TILES

See Flooring, page 65

CERAMIC WALL TILES

See Kitchen Surfaces, page 76

CHANDELIERS

Turn off the electricity before starting to clean. For thorough cleaning, remove as much of the chandelier as possible. It is easier with two people to keep the chandelier intact, if possible. Use a warm solution of washing-up liquid and pat dry with a lint free cloth.

For occasional cleaning use Antiquax Crystal & Chandelier Cleaner. Clean *in situ* by spraying on and allowing the cleaner to run off along with the dirt. Remember to protect the floor underneath with a polythene sheet covered by an old towel and newspaper.

CHOPPING BOARDS

PLASTIC

There are two types: polythylene (HDPE) and polypropylene (PP). Polypropylene can withstand higher temperatures and therefore can be washed in the dishwasher, which is the most hygienic method. They are also more resistant to staining and less likely to stress crack. However, if not labelled, the two types of materials are difficult to distinguish. If in doubt, follow the manufacturer's instructions. Otherwise, clean in hot soapy water, dry thoroughly and wipe over with an anti-bacterial solution such as Dettox cleanser or Milton (one part to four parts water). There is no need to rinse.

If stained, soak overnight in a mild solution of bleach. Then wash in hot soapy water.

LAMINATED MELAMINE

This type often has a picture on one side. It is not dishwasher proof and should never be soaked. Wipe over with a solution of washing-up liquid and dry immediately.

WOOD

Hold the board under very hot water and occasionally wipe over with an anti-bacterial solution. Never soak as this will swell the wood, which cracks upon drying. Leave to dry naturally, resting on one long edge. Drying flat can cause warping and with all chopping boards the warm, moist conditions under the board speed up the multiplication of bacteria.

COFFEE MAKERS

TIP Coffee beans are oily and any residue turns rancid and impairs the flavour of the next batch of coffee made.

PLUNGER POTS/CAFETIERES

Remove the plunger and unscrew the rod from the filter assembly. Wash the filter and the glass beaker in hot soapy water or the dishwasher if appropriate. Bicarbonate of soda will remove any stains on a bone china beaker. Buff brass or chrome frames with a soft cloth.

ELECTRIC FILTERS

Always unplug. Allow the machine to cool down before cleaning.

The filter holder and nylon filters should be washed by hand in warm soapy water. Glass jugs can be washed by hand or in the dishwasher. Wipe the body of the machine with a damp cloth.

Descale every eight to ten weeks in a hard-water area or every six months in areas of moderately hard water. Only use proprietary descalers that specifically state they are suitable for plastic kettles and/or coffee makers.

TIP If your coffee starts taking longer to filter through then the filter needs descaling.

ELECTRIC ESPRESSO/ CAPPUCCINO MACHINES

Descale in the same way as a filter machine but never try to force open the lid of the water tank. Immediately after use wait until the pressure has subsided and the lid comes off easily. Wash the filter very carefully as espresso grains are extremely fine.

Make sure you wash the steam/cappuccino nozzle thoroughly. Most are removable and should be washed by hand. If you haven't used the machine for a while it is a good idea to check the nozzle before you switch it on. If necessary, use a pin to unblock it.

COMBINATION OVENS

See Microwaves/Combination Ovens, page 83

COMPACT DISCS

See Stereo Equipment, page 87

COMPUTER EQUIPMENT

Wipe the screen and keyboard with a soft cloth. To remove any dirt or fingerprints always use a special computer cleaner.

For ingrained grease, dust or dirt on the exterior of equipment and keyboards, use Foamclene, an antistatic foam cleaner which neutralises the static charge. Spray on to the cloth, not directly on to the equipment. For cleaning the screen use Screenclens antistatic wipes. Your instruction manual should recommend the best cleaners that you can use for your machine.

TIP Never place a computer in direct sunlight as this will cause discoloration. If it is not going to be used for a while, place a cover over it to avoid dust.

COOKERS

Prevent it from getting too dirty in the first place. Wipe up spills and splashes on the hob or in the oven as soon as it is practical, preferably while still warm so that the spill has not solidified. For major cleaning, switch the cooker off at the mains if the switch is accessible.

OVENS

Most modern cookers have stay-clean oven linings, otherwise called easy clean or catalytic. (The oven sides are rough to the touch.) Never attempt to clean these as it will damage the finish and render them useless. They work by vaporising the splashes from cooking at high temperatures during cooking.

TIP Self-cleaning ovens work at an optimum temperature of 390°F/200°C, but if you are a low-temperature cook, turn the oven to 425°F/220°C for 30 minutes each week to stop the linings clogging up and to keep them working efficiently.

If you have a cooker with pyrolytic cleaning you will have a special high-temperature dial. This reaches about 930°F/500°C, which carbonises any deposits in the cooker and leaves the inside really clean. Any remaining ash can be wiped away using a damp cloth.

To clean ordinary enamel linings and oven floor, use a proprietary liquid, paste, impregnated pad or aerosol oven cleaner approved by the Vitreous Enamel Development Council. Make sure the oven cleaner doesn't come in contact with any stay-clean liners and always wear rubber gloves. Most oven cleaners contain corrosive chemicals that can damage the skin. You should also open a window and make sure the room is well ventilated.

TIP To make cleaning easier: before you begin, place a bowl of water in the oven and heat the oven on a high temperature for 20 minutes. The steam produced will help loosen the dirt and grease and make it easier to clean. To avoid diluting the oven cleaner wipe away condensation with cloth or a paper towel.

TIP After cleaning, use a cloth to smear a thin paste of bicarbonate of soda and water on enamel linings. It dries to leave a protective coating that absorbs greasy soiling and makes it easier to clean next time you clean the oven. It looks messy, but it is effective.

COMBINATION OVENS

See Microwaves/Combination Ovens, page 83

OVEN SHELVES

The easiest way to clean the oven shelves is to put them in the dishwasher. You may have to remove the top basket, and make sure the spray arms can rotate freely.

TIP You may find it easier to remove the racks before the drying cycle. Stubborn residue will chip off easily with the back of a knife.

If you do not have a dishwasher, soak off the soiling in a hot biological washing powder solution. Any remaining deposits can be removed with a mild, abrasive cream cleaner or impregnated pad. If you have to resort to an oven-cleaner, check it is suitable on chrome.

OVEN DOOR

Remove cooked-on deposits with a ceramic hob scraper. If the glass in the door is removable, soak in a solution of biological washing powder. If the door can't be removed, use an oven spray cleaner.

COOKER HOOD

Whether you have a ducted or recirculating cooker hood, it is important to clean and/or replace the filters regularly. New filters are available from cooker manufacturers, kitchen specialist shops or department stores.

Charcoal filters Only found in recirculating hoods, and remove odours. They are not washable so will need replacing about every six months.

Grease filters are made from foam, metal or paper. Paper filters are not washable and need replacing every two months. Metal and foam can be cleaned in a hot solution of washing-up liquid, and should be soaked for a few hours if they are really greasy. Alternatively, metal filters can be washed in the dishwasher, but always check the manufacturer's instructions first. Although washable, foam filters will need replacing about every six to 12 months.

Filters are removed by unclipping the hood and sliding them out. The replacement is then simply clipped back into place. If you buy filters directly from the manufacturer then they will be cut to size. 'Universal' ones bought from a department store may need trimming.

COOL BOXES

Food and drink marks that have stained the inside of a box can be removed with a proprietary stain remover.

TIP   To remove odours, use a solution of bicarbonate of soda. Before you store the box, wipe out with an anti-bacterial solution and leave the lid off, to allow air to circulate.

COPPER

See Metals, page 79

CROCKERY

Most china can be put in the dishwasher with the exception of hand-painted and antique pieces. Check it is labelled as dishwasher safe. Use a detergent recommended by the china manufacturer. Load the dishwasher so that pieces do not touch each other, to avoid risk of any chipping.

HAND WASHING

Use a hot solution of washing-up liquid, and a soft brush, cloth or mop. Avoid scouring pads, harsh abrasives, bleach or soda which can damage the surface or dull patterns, especially gold and silver decoration. Use a plastic washing-up bowl to prevent knocking china on the sink itself. After washing, rinse each piece in clear, warm water, drain, then dry and

polish with a soft tea towel. Do not stack wet pieces on top of each other because the footing is often unglazed and may scratch the piece that is underneath.

TIP   If cups are stained use a proprietary stain remover. Alternatively, try soaking the china in a solution of biological washing powder.

TIP   Bar Keepers Friend will help to remove pencil-type marks caused by minute deposits of metal from cutlery.

Use a soft brush to clean china with a raised pattern. China which is kept on display should also be wiped occasionally, first with a damp cloth and then with a dry one.

Earthenware and stoneware are much tougher than china so they are oven proof, dishwasher proof and can withstand boiling temperatures.

CUPBOARDS

See Kitchen Surfaces, page 76

CURTAINS

See Curtains, page 108

CUTLERY

See Silver, page 80

TIP   Don't mix silver and stainless steel cutlery in a dishwasher as it will cause the silver to turn black. Don't allow dry dishwasher detergent to come into contact with silver items as it will make black spots to appear. Remove and dry (if necessary) silver cutlery immediately at the end of the dishwasher cycle, as any salt residue which is not removed will cause staining and pitting.

STAINLESS STEEL

Check if it can be washed in the dishwasher. Occasionally polish with a proprietary stainless-steel cleaner to maintain the mirror finish. Wash thoroughly after cleaning.

Dishwasher tip

Always remove stainless-steel cutlery immediately at the end of the dishwasher cycle. The humid atmosphere inside the machine may cause 'rust' marks to appear, particularly on poorer-quality stainless steel. (The rust marks are corrosion pits, although the pits are barely visible.)

For the same reason, never use the rinse and hold cycle. If the dishwasher is not to be switched on for a while, rinse food deposits off by hand.

After refilling the salt container, make sure to run the dishwasher through the rinse programme before washing stainless-steel cutlery in the machine.

Staining

Although tough and relatively stain free, stainless steel still needs a certain amount of care. Permanent staining or etching on stainless steel is caused by contact with a dip-type silver cleaner.

Hot grease may leave a stubborn rainbow-coloured mark. Mineral salts in tap water can cause a white film if not dried off thoroughly and prolonged contact with acidic foods, such as vinegar, also causes staining. A proprietary stainless-steel cleaner will remove most marks. Wash the cutlery thoroughly after cleaning.

To remove tea stains from teaspoons use a proprietary stain remover and then soak overnight. Always rinse and wash them thoroughly. For stubborn marks use Bar Keepers Friend.

Dishwasher safe?

Wooden handles are not dishwasher safe since wood tends to swell and crack. Plain-coloured plastic-handled cutlery can be washed in the dishwasher, but patterned ones are not suitable since the pattern can lift off.

DECANTERS AND CARAFES

To remove port and sherry stains in the base of a decanter, fill it with a warm solution of biological washing powder and leave to soak. If the stain is stubborn, try adding two tablespoons of rice to the liquid and gently swirling it round. This will act as an abrasive and help loosen the dirt. After cleaning you should rinse the decanter thoroughly in warm (not hot) water.

If unsuccessful, use a stain remover.

To dry, stand upside down in a wide-necked jug to drain and become thoroughly dry before it is stored. If draining is not appropriate, the Manor House Decanter Drier, a gauze tube filled with moisture-absorbing crystals, can be hung inside.

If the stopper is stuck, wrap a cotton cloth soaked in very hot water around the neck to expand the glass. Also dribble some warm oil around the edge of the stopper.

DEEP-FAT FRYERS

Modern electric deep-fat fryers incorporate filters to reduce airborne grease from escaping in the steam. To reduce odour, some models also have charcoal and paper filters. These need to be replaced. Apply to the manufacturer.

To make washing up easier, the lids of most

fryers are detachable and some can even be put in the dishwasher, but always check the manufacturer's instructions first.

The inside of the fryer needs to be thoroughly cleaned every time the oil is changed – every six uses. Once the oil has been emptied clean the tank with a plastic scouring pad and washing-up liquid, taking care not to damage any non-stick coating. Wipe over the outside with a damp cloth and a non-abrasive cleaner. Always store the fryer with the lid slightly ajar to allow air to circulate, and wipe out before use.

DISHWASHERS

Switch off electricity supply. Clean the filters after each use. If they are blocked it will really impair the machine's performance.

The spray arms should be cleaned in a solution of washing-up liquid. Direct running water through the inlet of the spray arm to check that the water can escape through the holes and no grains of rice or food debris are blocking them.

Wipe the exterior of the machine with a damp cloth and a solution of washing-up liquid. If the machine is not going to be used for a long time, leave the door ajar to allow air to circulate inside.

TIP If the dishwasher is not performing well check that:
- the baskets are not overloaded
- the spray arms are not blocked
- the correct detergent and programme has been chosen
- the filter is clean.

There are some specialist cleaners on the market which will de-scale and freshen. Use them occasionally and always follow the manufacturer's instructions.

EXTRACTOR FANS

Unplug at the mains. Remove the outer cover and wash it in a warm solution of washing-up liquid; rinse and dry. Wipe the fan blades with a damp cloth wrung out in a solution of washing-up liquid. Avoid getting them wet and ensure that everything is dry before replacing the fan's cover.

FIREPLACES

Wherever possible, keep the fireplace manufacturer's cleaning instructions.

Made of either cast or wrought iron, both are the same material but shaped in a different way. Cast iron is produced in a mould and tends to be more brittle, whereas wrought iron is hammered into shape.

Before any cleaning, remove all rust using a wire brush or wire wool. Wear goggles to protect yourself from flaking particles. Severe cases may need treating with a chemical rust remover; always closely follow the manufacturer's instructions.

Re-blacken iron using a black grate polish (such as Liberon Iron Paste, Zebo Black Grate Polish) or a heat-resistant paint such as a barbecue paint (Plasti-Kote Bar-B-Q Paint).

FLOORING

Always use doormats to catch grit and mud trodden in from outside. Vacuum or sweep hard floors regularly to avoid surface scratching by grit.

Follow manufacturers' recommendations for sealants and polishes. Apply polish in thin coats. Use wax in liquid or solid form for wood or acrylic emulsion.

To remove build-up of polish, use a cloth

moistened with white spirit. Remove stains with repeated gentle action, rather than a severe single treatment. Re-apply polish.

VINYL

A popular choice, and easy to maintain. Most vinyls have a clear wear layer on the top which consists of various forms of polyurethane. Simply sweep with a soft brush or vacuum, and wipe over with a damp cloth or sponge using a solution of detergent or floor cleaner. Follow by rinsing.

TIP It is advisable to rinse the floor, otherwise a build-up of detergent occurs which can become smeary and feels sticky every time you walk on it.

Remove any noticeable scuff marks on the floor with a cloth that has been dipped in neat washing-up liquid or white spirit. Then rinse off thoroughly.

TIP If you have pets as well as children in the kitchen, you may want to use a disinfectant cleaner such as Dettox on the floor. Use diluted and then rinse off. These products are cleaners as well as disinfectants.

LINOLEUM

Sweep or vacuum the surface to remove grit and dust. Clean with a mop or cloth dampened with a solution of detergent or floor cleaner. Use water sparingly. Rinse after washing.

For stubborn marks rub lightly with a fine nylon pad, and neat detergent. Cigarette burns can be removed; they won't melt lino whereas they will vinyl.

Polishing isn't strictly necessary. Without it, the lino will have more of a satin, matt finish. Polishes give a glossier finish. Use an emulsion water-based polish, especially in kitchens and bathrooms, such as Johnson's Klear. Apply only a thin coat at a time and allow to dry completely before applying

---

FLOOR POLISHES

There are three different types. You cannot mix them, ie solvent and water based. If you start with one you have to stay with it.

Solid wax polish Old-fashioned type, sold in a flat tin like shoe polish. Generally a wax, it is solvent based and suitable for unvarnished wooden floors and cork. Hard work to apply and has to be done by hand and buffed up to shine. The shine lasts a long time.

Liquid wax polish A solvent-based liquid, sold in a tin with a screw top opening. It can be applied with an electric floor polisher. Suitable for the same floors as the solid wax, and is easier to apply but may

need more applications. Has to be polished well to give a good shine.

With both these polishes a good shine is not achieved by lots of polish but by hard buffing. The more buffing, the harder the finish, since the friction builds up heat which drives off the solvent leaving the wax gleaming.

Water-based emulsion polishes Generally silicone polishes. They are easy to apply because they are often self-shining. Simply apply them and leave to dry. They are reasonably long lasting and claim to make the floor easier to keep clean because the gloss repels dirt.

another one, otherwise you may get a milky appearance. Apply twice a year to give a natural shine and help protect the surface. Do not wax polish.

CERAMIC TILES

Scratching is less noticeable on unglazed tiles, which need minimal maintenance. Sweep them, then wash with a mild detergent solution. Rinse with clear water, then buff with a soft cloth tied round a mop or broom head. Don't polish as they will become slippery and more difficult to clean. Remove stubborn stains on unglazed tiles with an abrasive cleaner such as Jif.

Terracotta tiles

These are porous and therefore need to be sealed. Use either a traditional linseed oil and beeswax-based seal, suitable for all terracotta tiles, or a synthetic water-based acrylic seal.

Check with your supplier that the acrylic seal you are intending to use is suitable for your tiles. Acrylic seals keep the natural colour of tiles; oils darken it initially, but the colour will fade again in time.

After sealing, build up a hard finish. Wax immediately with two or three coats of oil sealant, followed by more sealant once a week for four to six weeks; then only when worn patches start to appear. Wax acrylic-sealed floors once a week for four to six weeks; then as necessary.

For the first year after installation terracotta tiles mature in character. Most suppliers have their own special cleaner, sealant and polish so it is worth making enquiries at the point of sale and using recommended products.

WOOD

Wood flooring will be sealed with either a polyurethane or acrylic varnish, or left unsealed and waxed.

If you don't know what's on your floor, put two or three drops of water on the surface. If the surface turns white this indicates that the floor has a wax finish. (Don't worry, the white marks will disappear as it dries.) If the water beads on the surface, the flooring has been sealed with polyurethane or varnish.

Sealed wood

This is the most usual treatment for wooden floors. Sealed floors only need to be swept and damp mopped. Don't use too much water as wood swells.

It's not strictly necessary, but you can apply an emulsion polish, such as Johnson's Klear, on top of the varnish. This gives the surface shine and an extra wear layer which takes care of a lot of minor scratches. But after several applications, this will have to be removed using a proprietary wax remover or a floor cleaner with a little ammonia added.

TIP Don't be tempted to apply a wax, even if it is non-slip, on top of a sealed wooden floor. You will make it very slippery.

Unsealed and waxed

This type of finish is less common because it's harder work to maintain.

Sweep regularly and polish occasionally with wax polish. A new floor will take a long time to build up a traditional-looking finish. Be careful about too much wax as it will leave a tacky surface and attract the dirt. Apply sparingly, infrequently and then buff well afterwards. Polish occasionally when worn patches appear in the surface with a non-slip floor polish. Remove any fruit, milk and coffee stains with a dilute solution of washing-up liquid.

TIP Don't be tempted to apply a varnish on top of a waxed floor. You will end up with a gooey mess as the varnish won't dry.

Removing wax

On waxed floors, polish and dirt builds up over time. The only way to clean them is to remove the wax and start again. To do this use a cloth moistened with white spirit. Let it soak in, and as the wax and dirt begin to dissolve wipe them off with crumpled newspaper. Scrub obstinate parts by hand or with abrasive pads on a floor polisher. When the polish is removed from the floor, finish by damp mopping with clean water. Allow the floor to dry completely before applying new polish. Work over small sections at a time.

CORK

Cork has the advantage of disguising dirt with its mottled appearance. It is an absorbent material so is normally sold sealed.

Factory-sealed cork tiles with a vinyl wear layer are simply wiped clean with a damp mop using a solution of washing-up liquid. If you wish to give an extra protective layer, especially in the kitchen or bathroom, apply an emulsion polish. Never over-wet, and take care not to damage the seal or wear layer by dragging appliances or furniture over it.

CERAMIC TILES

Wipe over with a solution of washing-up liquid. Rinse and wipe dry. Never polish ceramic tiles as they will be too slippery. Dirty grout can be tackled with a soft brush dipped in a mild solution of bleach. Rinse well.

QUARRY TILES

Quarry tiles are available in glazed or unglazed types. Glazed quarry tiles only need mopping with a solution of household cleaner. Unglazed can be treated with a liquid or solid wax polish, preferably the slip-resistant type, buffing well. Unglazed tiles are reasonably stain resistant due to a low surface porosity, but they are not stain proof.

Tackle stubborn marks with very fine steel wool dipped in white spirit. Then wash, rinse, dry and reapply polish, buffing well.

Quarry tiles are the same colour all the way through so wear patches are not apparent, although the surface can dull with excessive wear. Pigmented wax dressing or polish may help to enhance a very dull surface.

To restore faded colour, remove the polish with steel wool and white spirit, then wash and rinse them. When the tiles are dry, sparingly apply a pigmented wax polish, eg Cardinal Red Tile Polish, and buff well.

When quarry tiles are first laid, white patches may appear on the surface. This is due to the lime content of the concrete sub-floor. Until the patchiness has faded, do not polish the tiles.

TERRAZZO

This is a mixture of cement and marble chips. It just needs damp mopping with a mild detergent solution.

STONE FLOORS

Include slate, flagstones, granite and marble. Damp mop with a mild detergent solution.

FLOWERS

Use a hair dryer on the cool setting or a feather duster to get rid of any surface dust that has accumulated.

SILK AND POLYESTER

Don't immerse the flowers in water, since the stems may have a wire base which will then rust. Wipe the leaves gently with a damp cloth, supporting them at the same time with the other hand.

DRIED

Look for a proprietary petal spray such as Petal Fresh which precipitates the dust, brings up the colours, and prevents the dried flower arrangement from shedding its leaves. This is readily available from garden centres, some florists and gift shops.

FOOD MIXERS/ PROCESSORS

Disconnect from the electrical supply before cleaning. Pushers, lids and bowls are usually dishwasher proof, but always check manufacturer's instructions first. The blades should be cleaned in a hot solution of washing-up liquid using a kitchen brush, not a cloth; they may cut through this. Any food stains can be wiped away using a damp cloth and a very mild solution of bleach.

FREEZERS

DEFROSTING

Freezers need defrosting when the frost is about 1¼–1½in/3–4cm thick. Load the contents of your freezer in a basket or other suitable container, wrap the food in newspaper, cover with a duvet and put it in a cold place.

To speed up defrosting, place containers of hot but not boiling water in the cabinet. Ice can be scraped off using a wooden spoon or plastic scraper, but never use a knife or anything with a sharp edge as this could damage the cabinet interior. When all the ice has melted, wipe the freezer dry, replace the food and switch on again.

CLEANING

To clean and freshen the freezer, wash with a solution of warm water and bicarbonate of soda (1tbsp/15ml to 1.7 pints/1 litre). A solution of washing-up liquid might taint the plastic. On stains, use neat bicarbonate of soda on a damp cloth.

Clean the outside with a solution of washing-up liquid, rinse and wipe dry.

Lingering odours

If the freezer smells strongly, wash out as above then wipe the interior with a sterilising fluid or branded fridge-freezer cleaner. Dry with a soft cloth and leave the door open to allow air to circulate.

FURNITURE

There are many different types of wood finishes, but they can be roughly divided into three main areas:

French-polished The finish has been achieved by the repeated application of shellac (varnish) dissolved in spirit to give a satiny finish.

Lacquered This accounts for the majority of the furniture we buy. A hard-wearing finish that may be applied to solid wood, or on top of a veneer (either wood, paper foil or plastic). A veneer is usually applied on top of chipboard or medium-density fibreboard (MDF), and then lacquered to seal the whole piece, and for protection against any knocks and scratches.

Waxed Wax polish is built up by repeated rubbing with wax and turpentine to give a rich deep shine.

FRENCH-POLISHED FURNITURE

Treat as for waxed furniture.

Serious damage on valuable, French-polished pieces should be repaired professionally. Contact either the Association of Master Upholsterers (01633 215454) or the British Antique Furniture Restorers' Association (01305 854822) for companies that carry out furniture restoration.

LACQUERED FURNITURE

It's not necessary to polish lacquered furniture. The hard-wearing lacquer is designed to protect the wood against heat and moisture and so doesn't need additional protection. The polish won't be able to penetrate the lacquer – it just gives the surface a shine.

Wipe over the furniture with a damp duster. Use a fine, water-mist spray directly on to the duster to avoid over-wetting the wood. The water will help the dust stick to the duster, preventing it from becoming airborne.

WARNING ON WAXED FURNITURE

Don't be tempted to use furniture polishes with added silicones, or aerosol polishes. These give an instant shine and make the polish easier to buff, but the film does not fill scratches or other surface blemishes as a wax does. More importantly, the solvents can soften the underlying layers of wax. If used too frequently, the surface acquires a slight milky look for which there is no cure, short of stripping down and resurfacing the furniture.

Furniture cream waxes present a similar problem. They contain a high percentage of solvents (used to make the wax easier to apply) that can also soften the lower layers of wax, to the extent that you can remove as much old wax as the new wax being applied.

POLISH: WHAT IT DOES

The basic purpose of a polish is to assist in the removal of surface dirt and to help encourage the dust to stick to the duster. Polishes also provide surface protection and revive the shine, leaving a finish which is easier to dust than a dull one. For wooden furniture, polish also helps enhance the colour and grain.

Wipe dry and buff with a soft, dry duster.

To remove grease and fingermarks, use a damp cloth and a mild solution of soap flakes. Take care not to over-wet. Dry thoroughly with a soft cloth. Use an occasional application of a good furniture polish to revive the shine when it starts to disappear.

WAXED FURNITURE

Unsealed furniture doesn't have a protective lacquer, so it needs to be waxed from time to time to give it protection against damaging elements such as heat and moisture.

Dust waxed furniture regularly with a soft cloth to remove dust and to revive the shine. Remove sticky marks with a cloth wrung out in a warm, mild solution of soap flakes, taking care not to over-wet. Dry thoroughly with a soft cloth.

Occasionally, apply a wax polish – only once, or at most twice, a year. Solid wax, as opposed to creams, produces the best results but it requires lots of elbow grease.

REMOVING MARKS

Where furniture is antique or valuable it is best to have marks and dents removed professionally. Contact either the Association of Master Upholsterers (01633 215454) or the British Antique Furniture Restorers'

Association (01305 854822) for companies who carry out furniture restoration work.

TIP   To minimise marks, stand flower vases, glasses or hot cups on mats, so that the heat or liquid doesn't damage the surface. Place self-adhesive felt pads underneath ornaments to prevent them from scratching the surface.

Heat marks

White marks caused by heat often indicate that the finish has been damaged. Before calling in a professional refinisher, try the following methods.

If the surface is not roughened you may be able to burnish out the mark with a cream metal polish rubbed briskly in the direction of the grain. Then polish lightly with a wax polish. Alternatively, you can use a proprietary product such as Mr Sheen Classic Topps Ringaway or Liberon Ring Remover. Work in small sections at a time, wiping away the paste at frequent intervals to assess the progress made that you have made.

Where the surface has roughened, use some very fine steel wool that has been dipped in liquid wax polish. This method, however, should be used with extreme care on veneered finishes.

Water marks

To remove ring marks caused by wet glasses, vases or plant pots follow the suggestions for heat marks.

TREATING MARKS

The golden rule when treating marks on furniture is to go carefully. Start with the mildest method first. Repeated milder methods are far more effective than one, very harsh treatment.

Try home remedies before spending money on proprietary cleaners you may not use again. Read all the instructions carefully, work in a well-ventilated place and keep children out of the way.

Test proprietary ring removers on a hidden area first.

WAX TIPS

- Don't apply wax over a build-up of dirty wax or on a dusty surface. You'll seal in the dirt. Dust and clean first.
- Apply wax polishes sparingly. If you put it on too thickly it will dry before you have finished polishing, leaving the surface smeary and difficult to buff. If wax is applied too frequently or thickly, it will build up, making the surface sticky and will attract dirt. Run your finger across the surface. If it smears, then you have used too much polish.

If the dye in the wax polish is darker than the wood, it will darken it. If you use a lighter coloured polish on dark wood, take care that no residue is left in the crevices because it will show up as the wax dries out.

Allow the wax to dry before buffing to achieve a better shine with less effort.

To remove a build-up of wax, soak a cloth in white spirit and wipe the wood, following the direction of the grain, until all the dirt has been removed. Allow to dry and then wipe over with a clean, dry cloth. Alternatively, use a proprietary product such as Rustin's Surface Cleaner. The surface can then be repolished with a wax paste.

Scratch marks

Light scratches can often be masked using a similar-coloured wax crayon or shoe polish. Apply, and leave for a while before buffing the area briskly.

Alternatively, use proprietary products such as Mr Sheen Classic Topps Scratch Cover, Rustins Scratch Cover or Liberon Retouch Crayon. All are available for light, medium and dark wood, but test colour match in a hidden area first.

GLASSES

Avoid putting lead-crystal glasses in the dishwasher as the detergent will etch and dull the surface. Always wash in warm water, using washing-up liquid. Rinse in water of the same temperature, drain and dry with a soft cloth. Cotton tea-towels tend to leave fluff, so linen is preferable.

Do not store glasses stacked one inside the other as they may stick. Store the right way up as the top rim is the most delicate part and prone to chipping. Take care when drying wine glasses as the stems can easily snap.

HOBS

GLASS-TOPPED

Includes all ceramic, halogen and induction kitchen hobs.

Turn the hob off and make sure the surface is cool before cleaning. The only exception is sugar-based spills. With these, turn off the heat immediately, remove the pan and, with extreme care, wipe the glass before continuing cooking. If you leave the sugar, it will crystallise on to the glass surface during cooling, causing pitting.

WHY DOES ETCHING OCCUR IN THE DISHWASHER?

With time, glassware can start to etch due to the general wear and tear from everyday use. Different qualities of glass will etch at different rates. The etching attacks the glaze and causes the glass to develop very fine cracks and scratches on the surface.

These areas can attract calcium deposits from the dishwasher water. This then gives the glassware an unattractive milky appearance. If this happens to your glassware, top up your rinse aid, salt and detergent levels.

It is more likely that the cloudiness will be permanently etched on to the glass surface. Oversoftened hard water, high drying temperature, alkaline detergent solution and the components of the glass all contribute to the problem.

However, you can try washing the glasses in the dishwasher with citric acid crystals. Fill the detergent dispenser with the citric acid and run the glasses through a normal wash (don't add any detergent). The citric acid acts as a limescale remover and will descale the dishwasher at the same time, but follow the dishwasher detergent manufacturer's recommended dosage.

It is also important to make sure that the salt regeneration unit is always topped up and is correctly adjusted to suit your local water supply.

Lead crystal is the most susceptible to damage and should not be washed in a dishwasher as it is too soft.

Light soiling can be easily removed with a paper towel or a clean damp cloth. It is important to use a specialist hob cleaner recommended by the hob manufacturer such as Easy-Do Cleaner Conditioner for ceramic hobs. These are less abrasive than general-purpose cream cleaners, so they won't damage the glass.

Really stubborn stains and cooked-on food deposits should be removed using a ceramic hob scraper. Don't use any other type of blade, as it may not be sharp or flexible enough and could damage the glass.

Conditioning

Once the hob is clean, use a conditioner to protect the glass. This may already be incorporated in the cleaner, come as a separate product, or alternatively you could wipe over with a conditioning cloth.

Remember to reseal the cloth after use to stop it from drying out.

To avoid scratches, always lift pans, never drag them when moving them around the hob. Check the base of the pan is clean, dry and dirt free.

SEALED PLATES

Sealed plates have now replaced radiant rings. Make sure they are turned off. To clean, use a scourer and cream cleaner, rubbing in a circular pattern following the grooves on the hob plates.

Conditioning

Involves polishing and blackening to avoid rusting and to maintain colour. There are proprietary products such as 4 Hobs and Minky Cloths to do this. Most contain oils and graphite, so wear rubber gloves when applying because they can be messy. Use a strong cloth as the steel plates have quite a rough texture.

Once the conditioner has been applied, the plates should be pre-heated, during which period a slight amount of smoke and smell will develop. This is quite normal.

TIP Don't lay saucepan lids face down on adjacent unused hobs while you are checking the cooking. The condensation in the lid will encourage rusting.

GAS

Pan supports and spillage wells make gas hobs more fiddly to clean. If you have a dishwasher, check to see if the parts are dishwasher safe. Otherwise use a cream cleaner, recommended by the Vitreous Enamel Development Council, and a damp cloth.

Also remove the controls as dirt can build up behind them. Some just pull off.

Clean metal surround on hobs with a proprietary metal cleaner.

HOUSE-PLANTS

Like other household items, plants get dusty. Dust spoils the appearance of the foliage, blocks the leaf pores so that the plant can no longer breathe properly, and forms a light-blocking screen.

To remove it, you need to wash the leaves during the day so that they will be dry before nightfall. When the foliage is very dirty it should be dusted with a soft cloth before washing, otherwise when you do wash it a strongly adhesive mud forms upon drying.

Foliage tends to become tired and dull looking as it ages. Many plant-polishing products are available, as wipe-on liquids and aerosol sprays. Aerosols are quick to apply, but are often not suitable for repeat treatments.

TIP When cleaning and polishing the leaf

support it in your hand and never press down on the surface. Wipe the top surface only of the leaves (not the under surface where the cell openings are). Do not wash or polish very young leaves.

Use ordinary milk, which produces a shine. Alternatively, use a Minky Leaf Cleaning Cloth.

Cacti, succulents and plants with hairy leaves should not be sprayed or washed. Use a soft brush to remove the dust.

ICE-CREAM MAKERS

Many ice-cream recipes use raw eggs so hygiene is essential to reduce the risk of salmonella. Models with a removable bowl are much easier to clean than those with a fixed one. In both cases, however, you should use a hot solution of washing-up liquid. Always dry thoroughly before use.

IRONS

The soleplates of modern irons vary. Most have an aluminium or chrome-plated base or a ceramic-coated aluminium soleplate. Check the manufacturer's instructions before cleaning.

To remove burnt-on deposits on the soleplate, whether spray starch or melted deposit of synthetic fibre, try the gentlest treatment first.

Use a proprietary soleplate cleaner or an impregnated cloth from Minky.

Alternatively, heat the iron on a warm setting and rub at the edge of the board across a damp, loosely woven cloth which is held taut over the edge of the ironing board.

Use a moistened plastic scouring pad gently to avoid scratching. Make sure the iron is plate down, as this will stop dirt falling into the steam holes and clogging them up.

Descaling

Limescale reduces efficiency, so regular descaling is necessary. Most irons take tap water, but if you live in a particularly hard area try using demineralised water. You can buy a bottle to demineralise tap water at home.

To descale an iron use a proprietary scale remover and always follow the manufacturer's instructions. Some models come with a built-in anti-scale device, either in the form of a valve or a removable section on the soleplate. These attract limescale and therefore require cleaning or replacing every few weeks.

JEWELLERY

Needs care if it is to remain in perfect condition and, if real, keep its value. A jeweller will ensure that the piece is not likely to break, has loose stones or damaged claws.

TIP Have jewellery revalued while it is being cleaned. The value of jewellery continues to grow and inadequate insurance might mean you are unable to replace a treasured piece.

TURQUOISE AND OPALS

These are porous stones so should never be immersed in water. Simply polish with a soft dry chamois leather and use a soft bristle brush to clean the claws.

PEARLS

Never wash in water. Oils from the skin help to maintain their gleam, so wear them as much as possible (but not while applying make-up, scent or hair spray). Rub them with a chamois leather from time to time.

MARCASITE

Never wash. Polish with a soft brush, then rub with a chamois leather.

AMETHYSTS, DIAMONDS, RUBIES AND SAPPHIRES

These are all hard stones so they can be cleaned in a solution of washing-up liquid, scrubbing gently with a soft toothbrush or an eyebrow brush. Rinse in lukewarm water and then dip quickly into surgical spirit to remove any remaining detergent film before draining on absorbent paper and buffing with a chamois leather.

These particular stones can also be cleaned by immersion in a proprietary jewellery care kit such as Goddard's Gold and Platinum Cleaning Liquid.

Although diamonds are extremely hard they have a grain, similar to that of wood, and a hard knock could split them. Diamonds may also scratch other diamonds if they are stored close together.

EMERALDS

Are softer than other precious stones and can chip easily. They can be cleaned, with care, in a warm solution of washing-up liquid.

TIP Always wash jewellery in a plastic bowl with an old towel or cloth in the base. This will prevent pieces getting damaged, or disappearing down the plug hole. Put the plug in just in case of an accident.

JUICERS

Juicers have many parts to clean. It should be done immediately after use to avoid the fruit and vegetable pulp sticking and staining.

Most juicer attachments are not dishwasher safe so check the manufacturer's instructions.

Using a kitchen brush or a specially provided cleaning brush and hot soapy water clean all the parts, taking care with the grating sieve, which has sharp edges. The motor housing may be wiped with a damp cloth, and some washing-up liquid. For stained plastic use a damp cloth and a mild bleach solution.

KETTLES

Over half of British people live in hard-water areas, so limescale can be a problem.

Chrome kettles get coated all over the interior as well as the element. Most plastic kettles are made of polypropylene, which doesn't attract scale, but the elements do.

Built-in filters stop pieces of limescale from being poured into your drink but do not stop limescale build up. They too need descaling.

There are different chemical descalers, some designed specifically for metal kettles, others for plastic models. Check carefully before you buy. These come in liquid or sachet form.

For very light scaling try covering the element with a solution of vinegar and water (equal parts of each). Bring to the boil, then leave overnight.

TIPS FOR DESCALING

- Descale frequently: every four to eight weeks.
- Don't let scale build up as it will then be more difficult to remove.
- Expect to treat heavy deposits twice.
- Don't over-fill the kettle when descaling as the solution may effervesce over the side.
- Rinse the kettle thoroughly, and boil up with fresh water after treatment.
- Use a kettle protector: a stainless-steel wire ball which attracts deposit away from the element. Rinse and squeeze each month to clear the scale.

KITCHEN SURFACES

UNITS

Aim to clean the inside of food cupboards every few months. Remove all items and wipe the surfaces with a damp cloth using an anti-bacterial cleaner or a washing-up liquid solution. Do not rinse the surface. Replace items when the surfaces are thoroughly dry. Take care not to soak exposed chipboard and around hinge joints where water can seep through to chipboard.

DOORS

Coloured/wood effect

Wipe with a damp cloth and a washing-up liquid solution. Take care not to over-wet the surface. Stains can be rubbed carefully with a slightly abrasive cream cleaner (except glossy surfaces). High-gloss surfaces can easily be scratched, so use a soft cloth and make sure it is free from grit. Wipe thoroughly with a dry cloth to prevent smearing. Use a neat solution of washing-up liquid on stains and rub gently with a soft cloth.

Wood/wood veneer

Wipe with a damp cloth and a washing-up liquid solution. Use a neat solution of washing-up liquid on stains and rub along the grain with a soft cloth.

WORK SURFACES

Laminates

Include Formica and Duropal.

Daily care: After use wipe the surface with a washing-up liquid solution. Alternatively use an all-purpose cleaner with spray application for ease and speed. Choose one with an anti-bacterial agent and do not rinse.

Thorough care and stains: At least once a week remove all items from the work surface and clean with neat multi-surface liquid cleaner, or cream cleaner, using a damp cloth. Rinse with clean water and allow to dry. For stubborn stains use a slightly abrasive cream cleaner or diluted bleach. On textured surfaces use a nylon bristle brush to get into the grain.

Solvents will not damage laminates so stains such as felt-tip pen can be treated with methylated spirits, white spirit or some nail polish remover.

Maintenance: Chips and scratches can be repaired with ColorFill, a purpose-made laminate repairer and sealer. It requires patience because, like any filler, several thin layers are preferable to one thick layer.

Synthetic solid surfaces

Include Corian, Silkstone and Avonite.

Daily care: See Laminates.

Thorough care and stains: See Laminates.

Maintenance: Solvents can damage the surface after prolonged contact but can be used on stains such as felt-tip pen if thoroughly rinsed after application. Stubborn stains can be rubbed gently with an abrasive cream cleaner.

Cuts and scratches can be sanded away using medium-grade sandpaper followed by fine-grade. This removes some of the surface so you need to buff well afterwards to restore the shine. For severe damage contact the manufacturer to sand down the area.

Natural, solid surfaces

Includes Granite.

Daily care: As for Laminates. Pay particular attention to any joins in the surface. Wipe thoroughly with a dry soft cloth.

Thorough care: At least once a week, remove items from the work surface and give the surface a thorough clean with a solution of washing-up liquid. Buff with a soft cloth to maintain the shine. This sort of surface is difficult to stain and neat washing-up liquid should be sufficient to remove marks.

Maintenance: For severe damage contact the Stone Federation (020 7608 5094) for details of a specialist who can repolish the surface. This may not be advisable because the colour of the surface may well alter.

Ceramic tiles

Daily care: See Laminates.

Thorough care: See Laminates. For stains, use a slightly abrasive cream cleaner on work-surface tiles, which are matt finished and therefore less likely to show scratches than glazed tiles.

Maintenance: If grouting becomes dirty, clean with a solution of bleach (one part bleach to four parts water). Use an old toothbrush to get between the tiles. Wipe over with a damp cloth and allow to dry. Do not use a grouting whitener on matt tiles. Chipped tiles on work surfaces must be replaced as bacteria can collect there.

SINKS

Many sink manufacturers sell their own cleaning products and will send you instructions for care of your sink.

Stainless steel

Daily care: Wipe with a damp cloth and a washing-up liquid solution or an anti-bacterial spray cleaner, but do not rinse.

Thorough care: Give the sink a really good clean using a neat multi-purpose liquid or cream cleaner. Pay particular attention to the area near the taps. If you live in a hard water district use a limescale cleaner on this area once a week.

Coloured sinks

Polycarbonates are less expensive to buy and less heat resistant than blended composite sinks (see below). Brand names include Prima and Riva by Astracast, and Resan by Resopal.

Daily care: See Stainless steel. Tea, coffee and fruit juices will stain the sink if they are left to dry, so clean it every day. Use neat multi-surface liquid or non-abrasive cream cleaner, rinse and dry.

Thorough care: See Stainless steel. Stubborn stains can be soaked with a solution of biological washing powder or well-diluted household bleach.

Blended composites

Mix an acrylic substance with minerals such as silica, quartz or granite for a very hard and heat-resistant finish. Brand names include Franke Fraquartz, MFI Quartzite, Carron Silquartz and Astracast Supersinks.

Daily care: See Coloured sinks, above.

Thorough care: See Coloured sinks, above.

Blended composites containing granite, such as Blanco Silgranit, Carron Phoenix Granite and Franke Fragranite, are more hard wearing and you can rub stains gently with an abrasive cleaner.

Du Pont's Corian, Silkstone and Avonite are even more hard wearing and you can use any cream cleaner, abrasive powder or scourer on stains in the sink that are proving difficult to shift.

Enamel

Daily care: See Stainless steel.

Thorough care: As for Stainless steel. Look for a product with the Vitreous Enamel Association's logo.

Limescale removers are not recommended to use on enamel surfaces. See Enamel Baths, page 57, for how to deal with limescale.

TAPS

See Bathroom Surfaces, page 59

WALLS

Ceramic wall tiles

Wipe with a damp cloth and a solution of washing-up liquid. Buff dry. Stains can be rubbed with neat washing-up liquid.

Paintwork

As for ceramic wall tiles. For heavy soiling, wash with a solution of sugar soap and rinse with clean water.

Washable/vinyl wallpaper

Sponge over with a solution of washing-up liquid. Take care not to over-wet the surface. Remove grease marks immediately as they are more difficult to remove if left.

FLOORS

See Flooring, page 65

LAMINATED SURFACES

See Kitchen Surfaces, page 76

LAMPSHADES

FABRIC SHADES

Clean with a vacuum cleaner that is fitted with a dusting brush, but don't forget to reduce the strength of the suction if possible so that you don't damage it.

Treat spots with a solution of washing-up liquid at your own peril: it is possible to remove the surface finish and cause water marks, or to dissolve the glues holding the shade together.

GLASS/PLASTIC SHADES

Can feature delicate finishes and surface effects. Dust regularly or use a clean cloth and a solution of washing-up liquid.

PAPER/PARCHMENT SHADES

Brush often with a feather duster. When dirty, buy a replacement.

RAFFIA AND STRAW SHADES

Vacuum with adusting brush.

LAUNDRY BASKETS

See Basketware, page 56

LEATHER

For cleaning, see Leather furniture, page 112. If an item needs repair contact the British Antique Furniture Restorers' Association (01305 854822). If you want to tackle leather desk-top repairs yourself contact Artisan Brighton Regency Leathers (01273 557418) or Just Desks (020 7723 7976).

LIMESCALE

See Bathroom Surfaces, page 57, Kitchen Surfaces, page 76 and Kettles, page 75.

Products to prevent and remove limescale vary in toxicity and formulation.

Limescale removers/general-purpose cleaners

For regular use:
- Oz Limescale Remover for Bathrooms and Kitchens (liquid).
- Oust Surface Limescale Remover (liquid).

For heavier deposits:
- Limelite Thick for Surfaces (gel).

For encrustations:

- Manger's Stainex (thick gel) applied with a brush. It is particularly suitable for vertical surfaces such as toilet bowls.
- Descalite Lift Off (liquid).

Appliance descalers

- Limelite for Kettles and other Appliances
- Descalite Kettle Scale Remover
- Oust All Purpose Descaler (in sachets)
- Oz Kettle Descaler and All Purpose Descaler Powder (sachets)
- Quickshine Descaler Bag. (Sachets like teabags that you drop in the kettle.)

MARBLE

Marble needs special care to prevent it from dulling. For regular cleaning, wipe over with a solution of washing-up liquid. Polish once or twice a year with a proprietary marble polish to bring back the shine. Be prepared to use elbow grease and repeat the process if necessary. Bell marble polish gives a matt finish whereas HG Marble Polish gives a high gloss.

Treat stains with HG Marble Stain Colour Remover, available in an easy-to-use spray bottle, or Bell Special Marble Cleaner, which is mixed to a paste and left to dry on the marble.

For severe chipping and marking call in a professional: contact the Stone Federation (020 7608 5094).

METALS

COPPER AND BRASS

Brass is an alloy of copper and zinc. It's easier to polish if first washed in a warm solution of washing-up liquid. Brush gently with a soft brush (stiff bristles can scratch) then rinse and dry with a soft cloth.

Copper and brass polishes come in two forms and most include anti-tarnish agents.

Creams/liquids These quickly break down the grease and tarnish without hard rubbing and buff well to leave a good shine. The majority of creams/liquids are applied with a cloth and polished off before the polish has completely dried. Some polishes can be rinsed off with water and buffed dry to leave no residue. These are ideal for intricate pieces.

Wadding For heavier tarnishing, use copper or brass wadding impregnated with polish. It's easy to apply but messy to use and does require some elbow grease. It moulds well into

CLEANING METALS

- Work in a well-ventilated room.
- Protect your work surface with newspaper as some cleaners can leave marks on laminates and stainless-steel surfaces.
- Wear cotton or rubber gloves to prevent your hands from getting messy, and to also prevent grease from hands getting on to the polished metal.
- Have plenty of soft cloths for buffing. They soil quickly.
- Use a soft, old toothbrush or cotton buds to get into and clean intricate areas. But if working on expensive silver, buy a silver-cleaning brush, which is a much softer texture.
- After cleaning cutlery wash thoroughly before use.
- Always follow the manufacturer's cleaning instructions.

BRASS AND COPPER AFTER-CARE

- After brass or copper has been cleaned, use a transparent lacquer, such as Rustin's Transparent Lacquer for Metal, to protect against re-tarnishing, especially on intricate items that are awkward to keep clean. Apply two coats to ensure the item is fully covered.
- For valuable pieces and a more durable finish it may be preferable to have the lacquering done professionally. For more information contact the Metal Finishing Association (0121 236 2657).

ornate sections but is also quite abrasive so don't use it too frequently.

TIP   Reseal metal-cleaner containers firmly after use to stop them drying out. If polishing wadding dries out, it can be moistened again with white spirit.

Verdigris

For really heavy, green corrosion (verdigris) use Rustin's Rust Remover. Apply with a paintbrush and gently rub the surface with fine steel wool. Then clean with a proprietary metal polish.

DIY polish

If you only have one or two small pieces to clean and don't want to buy a proprietary cleaner, use the following DIY method. Rub the surface with half a lemon that has first been dipped in salt. The lemon cuts right through the grease and then the salt acts as a mild abrasive. Don't leave the mixture on too long as it will pit the surface. Rinse and buff dry with a soft cloth. This cleaning method tends to lighten copper items and bring out the orange colour.

Lacquered brass and copper

Many copper and brass pieces are lacquered by the manufacturer, especially door furniture which will be touched a lot and pieces that are subject to weathering. These types of lacquered items do not need much care, only regular dusting and occasional washing in a soapy, warm solution.

Over a period of time the lacquer can wear, usually unevenly, allowing the brass or copper underneath to tarnish. The lacquer should then be removed with a proprietary paint remover in order to clean the brass or copper underneath with a proprietary polish.

Either reapply the transparent lacquer or have the item professionally lacquered (see Brass and Copper After-care box, above). Unfortunately, lacquers you apply yourself are not as durable as those applied by manufacturers, and may need reapplying every 9 to 12 months.

PEWTER

Pewter is a grey-coloured alloy made almost entirely from pure tin. Small amounts of other metals give strength and harden the tin. It is a soft metal so should not be subjected to harsh polishes. Many people prefer their pewter to look quite dull, although it can be polished up like silver. Wash in warm soapy water and dry well with a soft cloth about once a year. If your pewter is more heavily tarnished use a proprietary silver polish.

For cleaning antique pewter contact the Association of British Pewter Craftsmen (0121 454 4141).

SILVER

Silver is the metal that is most prone to tarnishing. The tarnishing process is caused by hydrogen sulphide that is present in the atmosphere acting on the surface of silver.

Several things encourage silver to tarnish including certain foods such as salt, eggs, peas (especially mushy), olives, salad dressings, fish, vinegar and fruit juices, mainly because of their acid content. Acid etches into the silver and can cause pit marks. Cutlery and salt cellars are particularly prone, so it is important to rinse and wash them as soon as possible after use.

To reduce cleaning keep silver away from open coal or gas fires.

Don't mix silver and stainless steel cutlery in a dishwasher as the silver will turn black. Also, don't allow dry dishwasher detergent to come in contact with silverware as it will cause black spots to appear.

Regular cleaning

Wash silver promptly after use, using a warm solution of washing-up liquid and a soft cloth. Rinse in hot water and dry. In between polishing and when dusting use an impregnated silver polishing cloth or mitts. Metal cleaning products come in five types and most include an anti-tarnish agent:

Creams/liquids These are the largest group. Allow them to dry to a fine powdery deposit, then buff with a dry cloth to bring up the

CLEANING TIPS

Silver is a soft metal. A very fine layer of silver is removed every time tarnished items are cleaned, so keep polishing to a minimum. The abrasive action can, over a period of time, remove fine detail and wear silver plate.

Don't rub too hard since it can scratch the surface; use straight even strokes. Do not rub silver crosswise or with a rotary movement.

shine. Some require rinsing in water so are ideal for ornate and engraved pieces and cutlery that will need to be washed after cleaning anyway. Manufacturers of fine silver services recommend this type of cleaner. They are good at cleaning medium tarnishing.

Foaming silver pastes These are a good choice for cleaning ornate and engraved pieces and for covering larger areas such as a platter. They are easy to use and require little effort. The paste is applied with a damp sponge and lathers to a foam. The item is then rinsed in water. Particularly good for cutlery, which has to be washed after cleaning anyway.

Sprays Liquid polish in a spray formulation. A good choice for covering larger areas such as a silver platter.

Wadding Thick cloth impregnated with polish. Use for items with heavier tarnishing. It's easy to apply but messy to use and requires a degree of elbow grease. It moulds well into ornate sections but is quite abrasive, so don't use too frequently.

Dips A less arduous method of cleaning as items are just immersed in the solution and buffed dry. The dip solution converts the film of tarnish (silver sulphide) back to silver by removing the sulphide and leaving the silver

STERLING SILVER

Pure silver is rarely used as it is too soft so sterling silver is used instead. Sterling silver means that the metal contains at least one-quarter silver to three-quarters copper. The copper is added to give strength, making the silver more resistant to wear and to the effects of polishing. Unlike the different qualities of gold (where copper and zinc is added to 'dilute' the purity), sterling silver is not necessarily cheaper than pure silver.

TIPS FOR PROPRIETARY AND DIY DIPS

- Don't leave items in the dip solution for too long, especially silver plate. Always follow the manufacturer's time limits.
- Avoid getting dip solution on stainless steel knife blades as it can stain or even etch the surface. Rinse off any drops immediately.
- Don't use dips on very heavily tarnished items. They can produce a dull white finish.
- Don't ever use on damaged silver-plate items.

behind. Not recommended by experts as it leaves the silver duller with less lustre. Best for small items such as jewellery (do not use on pearls, corals or opals) and heavily embossed designs. Only suitable for light tarnish.

DIY dip

To make your own silver dip line a plastic washing-up bowl with aluminium foil. Fill with very hot water and add a handful of washing soda. Immerse the tarnished silver, making sure it is in contact with the foil.

This method of cleaning involves an electrochemical reaction by which the silver sulphide is removed from the silver and deposited on the aluminium foil.

If you have a large item that comes above the water line, turn it after five minutes. When the foil darkens, it has lost its effectiveness and needs replacing. Leave items in no longer than ten minutes.

Silver teapots

Remove tarnishing, water scale and tea stains using a silver dip. Pour the contents of the dip into the teapot and swirl around. The hydrochloric acid in the dip will dissolve the water scale and get rid of the tarnish. Rinse well before using.

Lacquered silver

See Lacquered brass and copper, page 80

Storage tips

- To store silver, wrap in acid-free tissue paper to protect against tarnishing. Don't use newspaper or brown paper as they will accelerate tarnishing. Press out the air as you wrap the silver and never secure any wrapping with rubber bands as the rubber will corrode the silver, even through several layers of cloth.
- Use cutlery rolls and storage bags impregnated with anti-tarnish agents.
- Use tarnish-inhibiting capsules in the back of a display cabinet, such as Tarnprufe's Carosils from department stores and jewellers.
- Cabinets and cutlery drawers should be lined with cotton felt. Woollen felt contains sulphur, which may tarnish silver.

Repairs

It is always best to seek professional advice before attempting to repair or restore silver yourself. Contact your local retail jewellers who are a member of the National Association of Goldsmiths. For more specialist enquiries you can contact The Worshipful Company of Goldsmiths (020 7606 7010), who can suggest silver restorers that are near to you.

SILVER PLATE

Silver plate consists of a coating of silver applied on top of another metal, nickel, by a chemical process called electroplating. Hence silver plate is marked EPNS: electroplated nickel silver.

The majority of household silver items are silver plate which is more affordable than sterling silver. There are various qualities of silver plate, depending on the thickness of the silver coating. The thickness is measured in microns (one micron equals one-thousandth of a millimetre). Good-quality silver plate will be 30 microns plus.

Silver plate is cared for in exactly the same way as sterling silver. However, it should be polished with less vigour and without excessive pressure. This is because the plating is made from solid silver, which is a softer substance than sterling silver (see Sterling Silver box, page 81).

Cleaning precautions

• Don't use dip solutions to clean silver plate that is wearing in patches since they can attack the base metal.

• Never leave silver-plated items in the dip for more than ten seconds.

• Avoid using abrasive cleaners, such as wadding, too frequently.

Worn silver plate

If silver plate has worn, exposing the base metal, you can have items re-silvered.

This can be expensive. (Most companies will need to see the item in order to quote a price, so consider if the cost is justified by the value of the item.)

Contact the British Cutlery and Silverware Association (0114 266 3084) for companies who offer a re-plating service.

MICROWAVES/ COMBINATION OVENS

Always disconnect before cleaning.

Those with an acrylic interior should be wiped out with a cloth and a hot solution of washing-up liquid. Alternatively, use a branded microwave cleaner. Never use anything abrasive.

Some ovens with a stainless-steel interior can be cleaned with a normal oven spray-cleaner, but spray on to a cloth first to avoid spraying into the vents.

Spillages cook on to the glass plate, so this should be wiped after use and occasionally cleaned in a hot solution of washing-up liquid, or in the dishwasher.

To avoid spattering, particularly of fatty or liquid foods, cover while cooking with a paper towel, an upturned plate or special plate covers. Joints of meat can be cooked in roasting bags loosely tied with string and pierced so steam can escape.

TIP To clear lingering smells, switch off at the wall and leave the door open, particularly if you are going away on holiday. Alternatively, put several slices of lemon into a basin of cold water. Bring to the boil in the microwave, uncovered, then simmer for ten minutes so that the steam passes through the vents. Wipe the interior dry.

MIRRORS

Glass mirrors can be cleaned in the same way as windows, using a proprietary window cleaner according to the directions and buffing up with a soft cloth.

For bathroom and kitchen mirrors it is possible to reduce misting. Wipe the mirror with neat washing-up liquid and rub vigorously with kitchen paper, or use an anti-mist product such as Holts Anti-mist spray or cloth, obtainable from cycle and car accessory shops.

TIP Don't let any liquid run between the glass and the backing or under the frame as this could eventually cause spots on the silver surface, behind the glass.

OVENS

See Cookers, page 61

PAINTBRUSHES

Water-based paints need cleaning only in water, or in a warm solution of washing-up liquid and water.

Lacquer needs a lacquer thinner or acetone; oil-based paints, varnishes and enamels need a proprietary paintbrush cleaner.

Cleaning tips
• If soaking is required do not stand the brush directly on its bristles as this will splay the hairs and weaken them.
• To stop the hairs from splaying on small brushes, wrap the bristles in kitchen towel as they are left to dry naturally.
• If a brush has splayed out at the tip during cleaning, when storing slip a small elastic band over the tip to hold the bristles close together.
• If a brush has set hard with paint on it, soak it in a brush cleaner and restorer. When the paint has softened, scrape it out of the brush with an old kitchen knife.

PAINTED SURFACES

See Kitchen Surfaces, page 76

PICTURES AND PAINTINGS

If your paintings need cleaning or restoration this should always be carried out by a professional conservator. Contact the Institute of Paper Conservation (01886 832323).

PORCELAIN

See Crockery, page 63

PRESSURE COOKERS

Available in aluminium or stainless steel (see Saucepans, opposite).

Care tips
• Remove food as soon as possible or pitting of the metal may occur.
• Never immerse the timer in water or put it in the dishwasher.
• Don't put trivets and separators in the dishwasher.

If food has boiled up and the inside of the lid is soiled, remove the gasket and wash the lid in a hot solution of washing-up liquid, then wipe the lid and gasket with a damp cloth. Wash the pressure control, and if blocked use a piece of wire or the end of a wire coat hanger to unblock it. Check that the Rise'N'Time and Ready to Serve indicators move freely.

RADIATORS

It is important to clean radiators regularly, especially in the winter months, as heat carries dust up and spreads it over the paint and wallpaper above.

To clean, use a duster or a vacuum-cleaner radiator brush or dusting head, then wipe over with a cloth wrung out in a solution of washing-up liquid. For bad soiling use a heavy-duty household cleaner.

Remember to cover the floor below the radiator while cleaning.

Rinse thoroughly and wipe dry.

To remove odour from the fridge, wipe with a solution of 1tbsp/15ml bicarbonate of soda to 1.7 pints/1 litre warm water. Alternatively, either buy a fridge deodoriser or put some bicarbonate of soda in an open container and leave in the fridge for six months approximately. Any stubborn deposits can be removed using baking powder and a damp cloth. This is a very light abrasive, but take care when applying.

REFRIGERATORS

Modern fridges have automatic defrost. They should be cleaned occasionally, however, to maintain their hygienic condition.

Wipe over all the inside surfaces except for the metal sections, and dry well with a soft cloth. Alternatively, use a branded fridge cleaner which removes grease and inhibits the growth of mould and algae.

Clean the outside with a solution of washing-up liquid. Wipe metal parts with a damp cloth.

Non-automatic fridges need to be defrosted and cleaned regularly. Use a bowl of hot water to help loosen the ice. Once it has all melted, empty the drip tray and wipe the frozen food compartment dry.

SAUCEPANS

ALUMINIUM

Uncoated, plain aluminium Cookware is best washed by hand. Never put in the dishwasher as the aluminium will react with the alkalinity of the detergent and will tarnish. If it develops a black tarnish this can be removed by boiling up acid foods such as rhubarb or a cut lemon in water. Then wash out the pan thoroughly.

Hard-anodised aluminium has a chemically treated surface to produce a hard finish. You can use metal utensils (but don't be too boisterous as it has been known for the metal from the utensils to leave marks on the surface of the pan). The hard-anodised surface itself is stick resistant so shouldn't be too difficult to clean in a hot solution of washing-up liquid. Some pans also have a non-stick coating to further enhance their cleanability.

Never put hard-anodised pans in the dishwasher. If a brownish film starts to develop on the surface, use a mild abrasive cleaner to remove it.

CAST IRON

Cast iron rusts easily on its own, so it usually has a non-stick interior coating or thin layer of vitreous enamel to protect it.

Wash uncoated cast iron in a hot solution of washing-up liquid and take care to dry it thoroughly. Brush with a thin layer of vegetable oil to prevent rusting. Never put uncoated cast-iron pans in a dishwasher as they will rust.

COPPER

Most copper pans are lined with another metal, usually tin or stainless steel, since unlined copper will react and discolour with certain foods such as eggs and vinegar due to their sulphur or acidic content. For this reason, always keep unlined copper pans for display only. Wash pans in a hot solution of washing-up liquid. Remove any tarnish that appears with a proprietary metal polish, and then give the pan a thorough wash after you have cleaned it.

ENAMELLED

Enamel is usually applied to steel, aluminium and cast-iron pans. Its main benefit is that it won't pit in reaction to foods or scratch easily. But, be warned, it can chip if knocked.

Wash in a hot solution of washing-up liquid and dry immediately to prevent a whitish film forming on the surface. If the enamel coating is very thin, you may experience problems with food sticking and burning, in which case simply soak the pan and use a nylon scourer to remove deposit. For severe burnt-on deposits, see Tip, below right.

Worn enamel may stain, particularly with curry-based foods. Marks can be removed with proprietary stain removers. Soak overnight and rinse thoroughly.

GLASS-CERAMIC

Glass-ceramic pans tend to retain heat well so can suffer from sticking and burning if used at too high a temperature. For burnt-on food, soak the pan in a warm solution of washing-up liquid before using a nylon scourer. For severe burning, see Tip right.

For general cleaning, wash in a hot solution of washing-up liquid.

NON-STICK COATINGS

Non-stick coatings are applied to most types of cookware these days from aluminium and steel to cast iron and stainless steel. The coatings themselves have become far more durable over the last ten years and many now come with a five- or ten-year guarantee.

Before using a new pan, wash, rinse and dry it. The non-stick coating may need to be lightly 'seasoned' by brushing the interior with a thin layer of vegetable oil. Don't forget to re-season after dishwashing.

Remove burnt-on food deposits with a scourer specifically for non-stick surfaces. Never use metal utensils or abrasive scourers.

STAINLESS STEEL

Stainless steel is very durable and is not prone to pitting or etching by acidic foods. Hot soapy water or dishwashing should suffice. For burnt-on deposits, see Tip, below.

Over a period of time, stainless steel can develop rainbow markings inside. This is not a fault of the pan, just a chemical reaction with the minerals in the water. Marks are easy to remove with a proprietary stainless steel cleaner, or Bar Keepers Friend, which is particularly effective. Always wash thoroughly after cleaning.

Pans which are subjected to too high a heat may develop brown marks on the exterior. These may come off with a proprietary cleaner.

TIP For severe burnt-on deposits try boiling, in the saucepan, a solution of biological washing powder (1tbsp/15ml powder to 2 pints/1.1 litres water). Boil for ten minutes, repeat the process if necessary then wash thoroughly afterwards.

SILVER

See Metals, page 80

SINKS

See Kitchen Surfaces, page 76

SHOES

See Shoes and Handbags, page 112

SHOWERS

See Bathroom Surfaces, page 57

SHOWER CURTAINS

See Shower Curtains, page 116

SLATE

See Flooring (stone floors), page 68

STEREO EQUIPMENT

The exterior of a stereo should only be cleaned using a duster or damp cloth. Avoid using any type of polish as this will damage the casing. To remove finger marks, use a small amount of washing-up liquid diluted in water.

The internal workings of a cassette-tape recorder require regular cleaning (every 50 hours of play) to ensure good sound. There are a number of specialist tape cleaners, such as TDK, on the market. These look like normal tapes but clean the heads while they run. Alternatively, the heads can be cleaned using a cotton bud moistened with a little methylated spirits. Absorb any remaining moisture with the dry end of the bud.

As tapes are magnetic, the tape player should be de-magnetised. You can buy de-magnetising tapes for this job. To use, always switch off all the stereo apart from the tape player and run the de-magnetising tape according to instructions.

The stylus on a record player should be cleaned using a very fine paint brush and alcohol. To avoid damage always brush from back to front.

To keep compact discs clean avoid fingering them. Always hold them around the edge and put them back in their case after playing. If they do require cleaning use some felt and lightly wipe from the inside out, not in a circular motion.

SUEDE

See Suede, page 117

TAPS

See Bathroom Surfaces, page 59

TELEPHONES

Dust a telephone when doing other furniture. If it is really grimy clean with a damp cloth and a solution of washing-up liquid. To untangle the flex, hold in your hand with the receiver dangling down and leave it free to unwind.

TUMBLE DRIERS

The most important part to keep clean is the filter, which is removable and usually situated in the front of the appliance. A build-up of lint in the filter impairs efficiency so it must be cleaned after every use. The easiest way to do this is to moisten your fingers before collecting up the fluff into a ball.

If a condenser dryer is not plumbed in you must regularly empty the water drawer where the condensed water is collected. Clean the exterior by wiping with washing-up liquid.

UPHOLSTERED FURNITURE

See Upholstery, page 119

VACUUM CLEANERS

Many vacuum cleaners have a plastic casing which can become statically charged and attract dust back on to the cleaner. To avoid this happening, use an antistatic polish.

Remove any hair or threads caught up in the brush head.

To ensure the best performance, filters should be changed frequently and the dust bag replaced when it is full. Follow the manufacturer's instructions on how you should clear blockages.

VACUUM FLASKS

Clean the inside with hot water and washing-up liquid. Don't immerse in water as it may become trapped in the casing.

To remove any odours use a solution of bicarbonate of soda and then rinse thoroughly. When storing the flask, always leave the top off so that you allow the air to circulate. If it is stained by tea or coffee, you can clean it using a proprietary stain remover that you would use on a teapot.

VENEERED SURFACES

See Furniture, page 69

VASES

See Limescale page 78, and Decanters and Carafes, page 64

WASTE BINS

Use a disinfectant spray such as Dettox or a solution of Milton and a damp cloth for regular cleaning. If the bin is soiled and stained, wash out with a mild solution of bleach and rinse with clean water.

WICKER

See Basketware, page 56

WINDOWS

Take down net curtains and blinds as they could be damaged if they got wet. Remove any ornaments from the window sills.

Always clean the frames before cleaning the glass. Because of condensation, mildew grows on the frames. It can be cleaned off with an old rag dipped in a fungicide such as Polycell Mould Cleaner or Rentokil Mould Cure. This stops the black mould from growing back. Alternatively, try a solution of bleach.

Avoid cleaning windows on a sunny day. The heat from the sun dries the glass too quickly and causes it to smear. Make sure the window is dry before cleaning.

Proprietary window cleaners come as a liquid or a trigger-operated spray so are easy to apply. They are quite expensive, so an alternative is 2tbsp/30ml vinegar or methylated spirits to 7 pints/4 litres of water. For grimy exteriors of windows use the same dilution of ammonia.

Always use a lint-free cloth, or chamois leather, to clean windows. For a really good shine, buff the dry window with a crumpled pad of newspaper: the printer's ink really gives the glass an extra sparkle. Alternatively, rub with a dry chamois leather or a soft cloth.

A window cleaner incorporating a rubber blade and a cleaning reservoir is a quick way of removing the water plus dirt on large panes of glass. Only use this on the exterior windows to avoid water dripping on to carpets. Wipe the blade after each stroke.

WOOD

See Furniture, page 69

WASHING MACHINES

Before cleaning the machine, always check the manufacturer's instructions.

The detergent dispenser drawer can get clogged up with unused detergent and fabric conditioner. Choose a powder or liquid that is used in a ball and placed directly in the drum on top of the clothes. Otherwise remove the drawer and rinse out in a bowl of warm water. Detergent can also accumulate inside the drawer recess so wipe out with a damp cloth. Once done, replace the drawer.

Always check the drain filter, usually on the front of the machine, if it has one. This collects coins, buttons, cuff-links and other small objects that are often left in the clothes. Make sure the machine is disconnected when emptying, and place a shallow bowl underneath to collect any surplus water. Replace the filter securely after you have cleaned it.

When the machine is not in use, keep the door open to allow air to circulate, but if you have a cat, check before switching on that it has not crept inside.

The outside of the machine can be easily cleaned with a warm solution of washing-up liquid and water. Then wipe with some clean water and dry well.

WASTE DISPOSAL UNITS

Put a slice of lemon in the waste disposal unit to help reduce any odours, and avoid using any drain-cleaning chemicals as these are caustic and may damage the unit.

WATER FILTERS

Whether you have a jug water filter or a plumbed-in unit beneath the sink, it is essential to keep a check on how old the filter is as there is no way of telling when the filter cartridge has reached the end of its life. (Activated carbon filters are the most common type available.) Manufacturers suggest you watch out for a slower flow rate or an inferior water taste and then change the filter in accordance with their instructions or recommendations.

Jug filter cartridges should be changed every 100–180 pints/60–100 litres, or roughly once a month. The frequency depends very much on how often you use the filter.

It's also a good idea to wash the filter jug and housing (not the cartridge) regularly in a warm solution of washing-up liquid. Rinse thoroughly, and drain.

The lifetime of plumbed-in filter cartridges varies considerably depending on the model: from six months up to three years, or a certain number of litres. As this is less easy to calculate over a longer period of time and easy to forget about, reputable manufacturers will send out reminders when the filter is due for changing. But it's still a good idea to make a note in your diary of the date when it should be changed. There is very little else you can do in the way of cleaning a plumbed-in unit as they are usually completely sealed.

WASH-DAY WISDOM

Laundry habits have changed dramatically over the past 20 years. Long gone is the tradition of washing on a Monday; wash-day blues can last all week with some of us washing around five loads. Not only do we wash much smaller loads, but with the increase in man-made and synthetic fabrics, gone is the boil wash and in many cases the pre-wash. As well, lower-temperature wash programmes are making new demands on detergents.

GETTING THE BEST OUT OF YOUR WASH

Whether washing by hand or machine, it's important to match the correct washing procedure to the type of fabric. Depending on how dirty your washing is, you need to consider water temperature, type of detergent, fabric and wash type; whether any special treatments are needed and how you are going to dry and iron afterwards.

WATER TEMPERATURE

It's vital to choose the correct water temperature because this can affect various aspects of successful washing:

WASHING-MACHINE PROGRAMMES

Even though the average washing machine has over fifteen programmes to choose from, as many as 23 per cent of us use only one programme; 35 per cent use two programmes; and 26 per cent use three programmes.

Colour: too high a temperature will cause non-colourfast fabrics to fade.

Creasing: some fabrics, such as polyester, will crease more at high temperatures.

Cleaning efficiency: too low a temperature will not remove some types of stains. With the increase in synthetic fibres, 100°F/40°C and 120°F/50°C washes are the most popular. However, the colder the water the more difficult it is to get a really clean result because detergents traditionally work better at higher temperatures. The latest detergents have been specially formulated to include enzymes and bleaching systems which work effectively between 100–140°F/40–60°C.

Fabric finishes: easy-care finishes, for example, can be broken down by too high a temperature.

Fibre type and construction: delicates and synthetics generally prefer lower temperatures, whereas cotton and linen wash better at higher temperatures.

Energy consumption: in low-temperature washes less energy is required to heat the water, making them more economical. Most UK machines are hot and cold fill. It is often more economical to use water that is heated by the domestic boiler than by the heater in the machine.

WHICH DETERGENT?

Ten years ago, buying a washing powder or detergent was simply a matter of deciding between the brands and choosing a box size. Now you have to choose between shelves of different products after deciphering the descriptions on the packaging. From powders to liquids, micros to ultras, refill pouches to powders just for coloureds, it's not surprising that a trip to the supermarket can baffle the best of us.

Conventional powders

These are for machine or hand washing and can be biological and non-biological. Dispense through the detergent drawer.

Concentrated powders

Similar to conventional powders, but in a concentrated form and should be used with a dosing ball provided by the manufacturer.

They are worth considering because they:
• Use less packaging – an important environmental issue. Many brands also use recycled cardboard.
• Are more convenient to carry home.
• Are more free-flowing than conventional powders and so less likely to cake in the box.
• Are very slightly cheaper to use per wash than conventional powders.

Powders for coloureds

Use these for washing coloured items to reduce fading and dulling. Unlike standard powders they don't contain bleaches and fluorescers. However, once fading has occurred, colour cannot be restored.

Liquid detergents

When using in the machine dispense through the drawer (without the problems of clogging) or in a dosing ball.

Bottles are more practical to store and some brands use recycled plastic. To save money make full use of refill packs or pouches.

Concentrated liquids can also be used for pre-treating stains. If using in your machine dispense only via a dosing ball.

Environmentally-friendly detergents

These can be powders or liquids and usually do not contain phosphates, fluorescers or perfume. However, you may have to compromise on performance.

Soap flakes

More gentle products, specially formulated for hand washing delicate items and woollens, and should not be used in the machine.

Pre-wash detergents

Useful for removing heavy soiling. Put in a pre-soak prior to machine or hand washing, or use with the pre-wash programme on your machine. Because they don't contain bleaches, use for whites, coloureds and most delicates – but always check the fabric can be soaked.

Fabric whiteners

If your whites are looking grey and dull, try a speciality product for whitening wool, cotton and some synthetics.

Fabric conditioners

After washing you'll find most fabrics begin to lose their natural softness and texture as the fibres become entangled and matted. Use a fabric conditioner to:
• Help untangle the fibres and restore some of the lost softness and texture.
• Coat the fibres to reduce creasing and make ironing easier.
• Reduce static which builds up, particularly after tumble drying.

In normal or concentrated forms, conditioners can be used in the washing machine or for hand rinsing. Follow the manufacturer's dosing instructions and always use in diluted form on fabrics.

Special impregnated sheets are available for use in tumble driers.

TIP Clean the fabric-conditioner drawer of

INTERNATIONAL TEXTILE CARE LABELLING

Always use the recommended care label advice to achieve the best results and help make your clothes look good and last longer.

Labels on clothes should correspond with programmes on your washing machine.

The wash-tub number shows the most effective washing temperature.

Cotton wash (no bar) 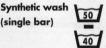 Articles which will withstand normal (maximum) washing conditions at quoted tub temperature

Synthetic wash (single bar) Synthetic articles, easy-care cottons and blends which will withstand reduced (medium) washing conditions at quoted tub temperature

Wool wash (broken bar) Machine-washable wool and wool blends which require much reduced (minimum) washing conditions

OTHER SYMBOLS USED OUTSIDE THE UK

Synthetic wash (single bar) White nylon and white polyester/cotton mixtures. Wash as for 50 (single bar)

Cool wash (single bar) Short cool wash often found on washing machines as a hand-wash option.

See manufacturer's manual for details. If your washing machine does not have this programme, cool hand wash gently

Hand wash only Do not machine wash

Bleaching Chlorine bleach may be used

Tumble Drying May be tumble dried

If dots appear:

 Highest heat setting

 Low heat setting

Ironing Hot iron: Cotton, Linen, Viscose

 Warm iron: Polyester mixes, Silk, Wool

Cool iron: Acrylic, Nylon, Polyester

Dry Cleaning May be dry cleaned. Where letters appear in the circle (eg, P) or it has a bar underneath, these are special instructions for the dry cleaner.

Any symbols appearing with a cross through them mean DO NOT (eg, do not iron).

As a general guide you can combine:

- All items without the bar symbol, and wash at the lowest quoted temperature.
- Items with the same bar symbol, and wash at the lowest quoted temperature.
- Wash labels with and without a bar, provided that you wash at the lowest temperature, but you must also reduce the washing action.

- Always follow any special instructions shown on labels, particularly 'wash separately', which means what it says. Heavily soiled goods should be washed according to the care label, and not included in mixed loads.

Compiled by the Home Laundry Consultative Council.

the washing machine regularly to avoid clogging. If undiluted fabric conditioner does come into contact with fabric, rub the affected areas with soap and re-wash normally.

TIPS ON POWDERS

• For good, all-round stain removal and cleaning efficiency choose a biological powder.
• For a coloured wash load use one of the specially formulated coloured products.
• For delicates, hand washing and light soiling choose a non-biological formulation, or one specifically targeted at certain fabrics such as Woolite for wool.
• All-in-one detergent and fabric conditioners are available for extra convenience.

DECIPHERING THE PACKAGING

Biodegradable

This is a word we're always coming across with the increase in environmental awareness, but what does it have to do with detergents?

Basically, it's what happens when you rinse them away. They are broken down into harmless ingredients, naturally, by micro-organisms. When detergents first came into widespread use, they contained ingredients which were not very biodegradable, and were held responsible for widespread foaming on rivers. Now EC Regulations stipulate that detergents must be 80 per cent biodegradable. Most UK detergents are around 95 per cent.

Biological

These detergents contain enzymes that help improve wash performance at lower temperatures (100–140°F/40–60°C). This means we can wash using less energy.

Their job is to break down stains, namely proteins, fats and starch, commonly found on clothing. Once they have been broken down by the enzymes it's easier for the other ingredients in detergents to remove the dirt.

Some people with sensitive skin are allergic to certain enyzmes, so if a reaction occurs use a non-biological detergent.

TIP If you have a lot of greasy stains, look for a biological detergent which contains lipase. This enzyme, which works best at low temperatures, is good for tackling grease on collars and cuffs and helps prevent yellowing of whites.

Bleach

Bleaching agents in detergents help to keep fabrics looking bright and clean. They also remove stains caused by coloured foods and drink such as tea, coffee and wine. The most common is sodium perborate or oxygen bleach, but if you're concerned about their effects on the environment look out for sodium percarbonate. The latest bleaches work well at low temperatures, giving a boil wash hygiene at 100–120°F/40–50°C.

Builders

These ingredients hold the dirt in the water and stop hard-water salts forming scale.

Fluorescers

Also known as optical brightening agents, they have a whitening or brightening effect on fabrics. They make whites appear whiter and coloureds brighter.

Phosphonates

A bleach alternative, generally found in liquid detergents and powders for coloureds.

Phosphates

Help soften water and prevent soiling from re-depositing on the clothes in the wash. More environmentally-friendly alternatives are zeolites, found in most concentrated powders.

Surfactants

These are the ingredients which do all the hard work to remove soiling.

CHOOSING THE CORRECT WASH

Always read garment labels thoroughly before washing. These have been included by the manufacturer to give you information about the fabric and how to care for it. The labels may not be immediately obvious, so look at the neck, hem or in a side seam. Furnishing fabrics often have the instructions printed on the selvedge, so keep a section back when sewing. If you find garments more comfortable without labels make sure you keep them safe so you can refer to them when necessary.

The label should include details of:

COUNTRY OF ORIGIN

This isn't a legal UK requirement but a manufacturer can be prosecuted under the Trades Description Act if he's deliberately set out to deceive the consumer. Country of origin refers to the country where the last major process in manufacturing the garment was carried out.

FIBRE CONTENT

This tells you exactly what the garment is made from – whether it's pure cotton or a blend, for example – and is a legal requirement. However, if there is less than 15 per cent of a fibre included it doesn't have to be listed as long as the bulk of fibres are. You may come across 'mixed fibres', which means mixed waste or reclaimed fibres have been used, which are difficult to analyse.

WASHING AND CARE INSTRUCTIONS

International Textile Care Labelling (ITCL): although only voluntary in the EC (compulsory in the USA), most garments in this country have washing instructions as promoted and recommended by the HLCC (Home Laundry Consultative Council); see the chart on page 92.

These instructions include washing recommendations, whether by hand or machine, suitability for certain treatments such as bleaching, plus drying and ironing procedures. Dry-cleaning instructions are also provided.

As a general rule, the wash-tub symbol represents washing, the triangle is about bleaching, the square is about drying, the iron about ironing and the circle about dry cleaning.

OTHER DETAILS

Information about sizing, distributor's or manufacturer's name, and flammability should be included.

PREPARING THE WASH LOAD

- Empty and turn all pockets outwards.
- Brush off any surplus mud, dust or fluff.
- Remove tissues from sleeves.
- Close zips and do up buttons.
- Make all repairs before you wash not after. Washing will make any damage worse.
- Turn pile fabrics, jeans and corduroy fabrics inside out.

SORTING THE LOAD

- Identify any items which must be washed separately.
- Sort out hand-wash only items.
- Group together items with the same wash

symbol, but don't mix whites and non-colourfast fabrics.

• If you have to machine wash mixed loads, always wash them according to the instructions for the most delicate fabric. Whites, however, will benefit from washing every few washes at their correct recommended temperature.

PRE-WASH SOAKING

• Use when items are very heavily soiled or stained.

• As a general rule, don't soak silk, wool, leather (including trimmings), elastanes, fabrics with special treatments such as flame retardancy, easy-care, non-colourfast dyes and items with metal fasteners.

• Soak in a plastic bucket or bath with plenty of water and check detergent is thoroughly dissolved before adding the clothes.

• Water should be cool for protein-based stains, such as egg, blood and milk; and hand hot for others.

• Leave to soak for several hours, or overnight for whites.

• For persistent marks, rub detergent or a stain-removal bar directly on to the stain.

• Treat collars and cuffs before washing. Dampen and rub soap along the marks. Leave for an hour and then scrub with an old toothbrush.

• To reduce colour run, soak the fabric in a solution of salt and water using 1tbsp/15ml of salt to 1pint/500ml of water.

MACHINE-WASHING TIPS

• Before loading, shake items out, and load one at a time to reduce tangling.

• Load evenly with small items, then large, taking care not to over-fill.

• Follow care label instructions and do not over-dose with detergent, especially if washing small loads.

• If colours do run place the dyed item back in the machine and re-wash.

• Wash tights and stockings in a pillowcase or cotton bag.

• Don't leave damp items in the machine or clothes basket as mildew can develop.

• To eliminate fluff, add 1 cup/7fl oz/190ml of white vinegar to the final rinse; or put some netting in the tumble dryer to catch the fluff.

HAND-WASHING TIPS

• Sort according to colour and temperature.

• Make sure the detergent is thoroughly dissolved.

• Rinse in cold water until free of scum. Add a little vinegar to the final rinse to remove all the scum.

• Don't rub wool or it will matt. Gently squeeze the water through the fabric.

• Do not lift items out of the water as they will stretch.

WASHING THE GREEN WAY

• Most manufacturers have at least one environmentally-friendly machine in their range (see Washing Machines, page 28). They may cost a little more to buy, but because they feature a range of energy-saving options, running costs can be less. Performance isn't sacrificed either.

• If you have to wash small loads use the half load option, which many machines now have. This uses less water, energy and detergent but not half the amount as you might expect, so always wash maximum loads if you can.

• Use a ball-dosing device if this is applicable to your type of detergent (see Which Detergent? page 90). This ensures all the detergent stays in the drum of the machine rather than escaping into the pipework.

TIP   Look out for washing machines with special devices or locks to prevent detergent escaping from the drum. Alternatively, some machines have detergent regeneration systems which recycle the detergent through the pipework back into the drum.

• Use lower temperatures for lightly soiled loads.
• Always rinse in cold water when hand washing.
• Make use of off-peak electricity if you have the option.
• Use high spin speeds before tumble drying (except for synthetic fabrics).
• Use refill packs of detergents and fabric conditioners. Use correct dosages, don't guess.
• Use concentrated products.

SPECIAL TREATMENTS

BLEACHING

• Always wear gloves.
• Bleaches, particularly chlorine, should be diluted or they will rot fabric.
• Do not bleach wool, silk, viscose, fabrics with special finishes, and deep colours.
• Check the care label and try on a hidden area first.
• Avoid bleaching damaged or discoloured items as they won't bleach evenly.
• Rinse thoroughly or residual bleach will damage the fabric.
• Check container you use is colourfast.

STARCHING

• Mostly used for stiffening cotton or linen.
• If you want a very stiff result, use a powdered starch. Vary the concentration depending on the application.
• Liquid starches such as Dip are easier to use.
• Use a basin or bucket for powdered starches, rather than the washing machine.
• Starch after washing, spin, and finally rinse to remove excess starch.
• Spray starches often contain silicones for easier ironing.

DYEING

Home dyeing is an inexpensive way of adding a new lease of life to sad-looking clothes. However, it's not suitable for all fabrics and there are a few basic rules to bear in mind and choices to make:

Machine dyes for natural fibres – cotton and linen – but not for silk, wool or viscose.
Hand dyes for natural fibres, including wool and silk.
Multipurpose/universal dyes for natural fibres and polyamide.
Cold water dyes for natural fibres, including wool and silk.
     Remember you can't:
• Dye acrylics.
• Cover patterns with dye.
• Cover stains and marks with dye.
• Dye anything a perfect black.
• Remove colour from polyesters before dyeing them.

Ten golden rules for home dyeing

1 Wash and remove all stains so the fabrics will take the colour evenly.
2 You'll get better results if you remove the original colour first. Proprietary colour

removers will strip non-colourfast dyes (natural fibres and some synthetics) to neutral.

3 Follow the manufacturer's recommended instructions carefully. Don't skimp on dye or else the colour won't match the colour card.

4 Wear gloves and always wipe up spills immediately.

5 Machine dyeing will produce more even results than dyeing by hand, and is less messy.

6 Specialist machine dyes won't leave the drum of your machine dirty, but wipe any spills off the outside or window immediately. If using multi-purpose dyes in the machine you will need to dissolve the dye in a container beforehand and to clean the machine after use.

7 Smaller items, such as T-shirts and shirts, dye the best. Anything bulky or expensive should be professionally dyed.

8 If you have to dye over the original colour remember the basic rules: blue on yellow goes green, blue on pink equals mauve, red and yellow will make orange or red, etc. For best results, dye within the same colour spectrum from pale to dark, for example pale blue to navy or black over grey.

9 Use a proprietary colour fixer which helps to keep colours brighter after dyeing. Also stops dye bleeding on to other items.

10 Polyester does not dye well and blends containing this are pale and may be slightly mottled where the different fibres are. Obviously, the more polyester in the blend the paler the result will be.

TIP Add very dark blue dye to black dye to give a darker result.

DRYING TIPS

First spin dry the wash load, if possible, to remove any excess water.

When spinning delicates, such as tights and stockings, place them in a pillowcase first. Otherwise wring them gently or roll them carefully in a towel to soak up the water.

LINE DRYING

Do

- Wipe the line before use.
- Line dry whites: the sunlight will bleach and freshen them.
- Hang pleated garments on a hanger.
- Hang drip-dry skirts by the waistband.
- Turn coloureds inside out to prevent fading.
- Fold sheets in half and hang by the hem.
- Hang striped garments vertically.

Don't

- Dry silk, wool or polyamide outside because sunlight will cause them to yellow and weaken considerably.

FLAT DRYING

Do

- Flat-dry knitted and jersey fabrics to avoid stretching.
- Pull into shape when damp.

Don't

- Dry near a direct heat source such as a fire or radiator.

TUMBLE DRYING

Do

- Make sure to always check care labels. Do not tumble dry wool, knits, delicates and elastanes.
- Choose the correct heat setting for the type of fabric. Synthetics must be dried using the cool cycle or else the fibres could melt, crease or shrink.
- Tumble dry harsh towels – it should help to soften them.
- Clean filters regularly.

Don't

• Over-load, or drying will be patchy and uneven.

• Dry very large and small items together or results will be uneven.

• Over-dry, as the fibres can become brittle, more difficult to iron – and it's also a waste of energy.

WASH-DAY BLUES: TROUBLESHOOTING

FABRIC HARSHNESS

This applies particularly to towels.

Cause

• Over-drying natural fibres.

• Continual under-dosing with detergent, allowing mineral salts to build up.

• Inadequate rinsing of the wash load.

Cure

For under-dosing, soak in a solution of water softener (eg Calgon) using 2tbsp/30ml of softener to 7 pints/4 litres of water. Also run the machine empty using the hottest programme with the recommended dose of detergent containing a bleaching agent to remove any calcium build-up within the washing machine.

For inadequate rinsing, wash the fabrics at as high a temperature as possible without any detergent. Add 1 cup/7fl oz/190ml of white vinegar to the drawer dispenser of the washing machine.

Prevention

Follow the manufacturer's pack recommendation for dosage. Increase this if the items are very heavily soiled.

If drying natural fibre garments on a radiator or in a tumble drier, remove them before they are fully dry to prevent removal of the natural moisture within the fibres. Over-drying these clothes will lead to harsh and brittle fibres, and this makes them much more difficult to iron.

GREYING OF WHITE COTTONS

Cause

Dirt and soiling removed during washing has re-deposited on to the clothes as a very thin uniform layer making whites appear slightly grey and coloureds dull. It occurs if insufficient detergent is used to suspend the soiling in the water.

Cure

Re-wash using the maximum dose of detergent and wash temperature.

Prevention

Follow the manufacturer's recommended dosing instructions and wash programme. Don't overload the machine.

PATCHY COLOURS OR STAINING

Cause

Chemicals in the wash water. Light patches on bedding and nightwear can be caused by some skin creams and acne treatments; or because of neat, heavy-duty powders that have been in direct contact with a damp fabric that is not colourfast.

Cure

Re-washing may remove some types of staining. If the dyes have been affected the problem is permanent.

Prevention

Avoid fabrics touching offending chemicals or neat detergents.

DYE TRANSFER FROM OTHER GARMENTS

Cause

Non-colourfast items have been washed with paler items at too high a temperature. Excess dye from dark-coloured items has leached to other items in the wash load.

Cure

Re-wash in as hot a wash as possible. It may be necessary to soak whites and colourfast items in a proprietary colour-removing product.

Prevention

Sort your load carefully and test for colour-fastness (see Ten Golden Rules for Successful Stain Removal, page 122). Always wash dark colours separately at first and do not use too high a temperature for non-colourfast items. Do not mix whites and coloured items.

WHITE/GREY SPECKS OR STREAKS

Cause

Hard water deposits that are present in the local water supply.

Cure

Re-wash using maximum dosage of detergent. It may be necessary to soak the load in a water softener.

Prevention

Increase the dosage of detergent. In very hard-water areas, carry out an idle wash periodically with just detergent and no load, to help reduce scale build-up.

EXCESSIVE CREASING

Cause

Incorrect wash programme, over-drying or overloading machine.

Cure

Reduce temperature, or wash with smaller loads. Use the specific synthetics programmes which have reduced drum agitation and shorter spin cycles at lower speeds.

Prevention

Follow care labelling. Creasing of synthetics occurs if too high washing and drying temperatures are used.

SHRINKING AND FELTING OF WOOL

Cause

Too high wash temperatures, excessive agitation, and tumble drying.

Cure

None. It is irreversible.

Prevention

Only machine wash if the label states it is machine washable. If in doubt, hand wash. Never tumble dry wool.

CLINGING AND RIDING UP OF SLIPS AND SKIRT LININGS

Cause

Build-up of static electricity in synthetic fibres.

Cure

Use fabric conditioner in the final rinse of the washing programme. Alternatively, use an antistatic spray before or while wearing the relevant garment.

Prevention

Wear a natural fibre garment between two synthetic ones, for example, try wearing a cotton slip between a polyester skirt and polyamide tights.

BOBBLING ON COTTON AND SOME SYNTHETIC BLENDS

Cause

Abrasion of the fibres from normal wear.

Cure

Pick off the bobbles by hand or with some sticky tape. Alternatively, use a safety razor or specific de-fuzzing gadget.

Prevention

This is difficult to prevent, but you can try washing garments inside out and using a fabric conditioner.

RUCKING OF COLLARS AND SHIRT FRONTS

Cause

Collars and bands have facings with layers of different sorts of fabrics to stiffen them. These can shrink at different rates when washed, causing puckering of the top fabric. Alternatively, using cotton thread to sew synthetic fabrics can cause puckering as the cotton shrinks.

Cure

This rucking or puckering may unfortunately be irreversible. However, you can try steam ironing the garment while it is damp and then carefully pulling the offending layers back into shape.

Prevention

Dry clean items or wash them in cool water to avoid any shrinkage. If home dressmaking, ensure that you don't over-stretch the facings when you are fitting and sewing them. Always match the thread content to the type of fabric that has been used.

IRONING

All irons have at least three heat settings, each suitable for certain fabrics, depicted by one to three dots on the iron: • •• or •••. These dots relate to specific temperatures recommended by the HLCC (Home Laundry Consultative Council).

Cool: one dot   •   250°F/120°C
Acrylic, Silk, Polyamide, Acetate, Polyester
Warm: 2 dots   ••   320°F/160°C
Polyester blends, Wool
Hot: 3 dots   •••   410°F/210°C
Cotton, Linen, Viscose, Denim.

Most irons have a steam setting.

TAKING THE STRESS OUT OF IRONING

• Always allow the iron to heat up thoroughly. This will give the thermostat time to settle down. Leave the iron for several minutes when changing temperatures as it does take time to adapt. This is particularly important when going from hot to cool.
• Start with the items needing the coolest settings, and work up to the hottest.
• If in doubt about temperature, start at the lowest and work your way up, ironing a small hidden area of the garment.
• When using a damp cloth you will need a higher temperature setting because the cloth will cool the soleplate.
• Move the garment away from you as you iron, supporting large items to avoid the fabric distorting.
• Use a plant sprayer to dampen really dry cottons and linen.
• Sleeves: avoid creasing down the sleeve by

IRONING TIPS

- Iron pile fabrics on the reverse side, on a thick cloth or towel, using minimum pressure.
- When ironing pleated items, tack the pleats down first; this will be quicker in the long run and will avoid double lines. Alternatively, hold pleats down with some paper clips.
- If the fabric has a special finish, iron on the wrong side.
- To avoid shine, iron fabrics on the wrong side. Steam pressing with a damp cloth may remove slight shine.
- Don't iron over zips. Close the zip and iron lightly down each side of it, avoiding the teeth.
- Don't put clothes on immediately after ironing as it will encourage creasing.
- To remove bagginess, from skirt seats for example, lay the baggy area flat and work from the outer edge of the bagginess towards the centre, pressing it repeatedly with a damp cloth, on the right side, until it flattens. Remove the cloth, place a piece of brown paper on the area and iron all over. This will absorb the moisture from the cloth and the shape will therefore hold better. Allow to cool.

---

inserting a rolled-up towel and ironing gently.
- Shirts: start at the top and work down. Iron all the double sections first on the wrong side (collars, cuffs, front bands); then do shoulders and sleeves, back and front.
- Sheets: fold lengthwise twice.
- Trousers (with a centre crease): iron pockets, waist; fold trousers lengthways so seams are in the middle and creases at outside edges. Repeat with other leg.
- Gathers: press on the reverse side, working with the point of the iron towards the gathers.
- Belts: iron on the wrong side first.
- Hems: iron from the wrong side.
- Seams: press flat from the inside.

DRY CLEANING

WHY DRY CLEAN?

Always dry clean items:
- If specified on their care label.
- If instructions are not available.
- With leather trim, pleated skirts, tailored wool suits, wool, jersey, hand-painted silk.
- Anything old, valuable or delicate.

Either use a coin-operated dry cleaning machine or a professional dry cleaner.

Coin-op machines use a system similar to a professional cleaner, but you don't get the personal care, advice and finishing. However, it is cheaper, because several garments can be treated at once.

These machines use different solvents so only use if the item is labelled with an A. If you are in any doubt, or the item does not have an A, it is best to have it professionally treated.

TIP Always air items thoroughly before wearing to remove any toxic fumes.

Professional cleaners have the edge on stain removal because they have a whole range of cleaning solvents which are not available on the domestic market. Choose a dry cleaner who is a member of the Textile Services

Association. They should display a blue and white logo in their window with the current year's date on it. These cleaners agree to observe a code of practice to guarantee high standards of service, and to protect you should anything go wrong.

Taking a garment to the cleaners

• Draw their attention to any specific stains or unusual fabrics.

• Avoid treating a stain yourself first, because this may fix it. However, if you have tried to remove it, inform the cleaner of the treatment.

• Remove unusual and ornate trimmings.

• Point out any dry-cleaning symbol which is underlined because this tells the dry-cleaner that a special treatment is required.

• You may find that some stains, such as colourless spills that contain sugar-lemonade or alcohol, only show up after dry cleaning because they have been brought out by the solvents used. These will need re treating.

IF THINGS GO WRONG

1 Make a formal complaint, in writing, to the manager of the company explaining the problem, keeping copies of all correspondence.

2 If you don't hear anything after ten days, or are not satisfied with the response, ask for help from your local Citizens' Advice Bureau or Trading Standards department.

3 If you don't seem to be getting anywhere, contact the Customer Adviser of the TSA. If the cleaner is a member, the adviser will help sort out the problem. If the cleaner is not a member, the adviser will then suggest your next step.

4 If the problem is difficult to resolve you may want to have the garments analysed by an independent test laboratory. You will be charged for this service, but should the cleaner be found to be at fault you will be reimbursed and compensated.

5 If the cleaner is not a member, under the terms laid out by the Office of Fair Trading, they still have a legal duty 'to provide their service with reasonable care and skill and in a reasonable time'. If this duty is not followed you are entitled to part or all of your money back from them.

CARING FOR CLOTHES

A little time taken to care for clothes is time well spent. The suggestions below will help to prolong their life and keep them looking their best.

1 Always follow the care instructions found on clothes labels.

2 Before you put clothes away give them a good brush down to remove any loose hairs and dust. Never put them away dirty. Clothes with stains – especially wool – attract destructive clothes' moths.

3 Avoid wearing the same garment two days running. Fabrics need time to recover. Hang them up while still warm from the heat of the body, to help creases drop out.

4 To help garments keep their shape close all zips and fasten buttons and hang or fold them away carefully.

5 Don't fill the wardrobe too full, or clothes will crease and natural fibres cannot breathe. If short of space only hang items worn frequently.

6 Pack summer clothes away in winter and vice versa.

7 Wet clothes, such as swimsuits and sportswear, should be allowed to dry naturally before being put away.

8 Don't allow clothes to become over dirty; clean regularly.

9 Repair hems and replace buttons, etc, straight away.

10 Cover hanging garments that are only occasionally worn with a plastic bin liner or dry cleaning cover. This will protect them from dust and unwarranted creasing.

11 Don't leave silk items in direct sunlight as they could fade.

12 Line drawers with wallpaper or self-sticking plastic.

CLOTHES-CARE TIPS

• Swimsuits: After a swim don't just wring out your swimsuit. Rinse it thoroughly in tap water and then dry flat. Salt water, perspiration, suntan lotions or chlorine from swimming baths can rot the fibres. Wash by hand rather than the machine, and avoid wringing, tumble drying and ironing especially if it has bra cups. Never leave damp swimwear in a plastic bag, for even a short time, or the fabric may rot.

• Trousers should be folded along the vertical crease line and stored on a solid coathanger (not wire).

TIP To avoid getting a crease across the legs of trousers, place a piece of cardboard or foam rubber along the bar.

• Hang evening dresses inside out to keep them as clean as possible. Sew loops on the waist so hems do not trail.

• Hang skirts by loops on the waistband, or if storing don't fold pleated skirts. Instead, cut the feet and top off an old pair of tights, roll up the skirt lengthwise and pull it through. Store flat.

• Shirts: Hang up on a coathanger, if possible, or store in a drawer. When folding, after fastening all the buttons, lay it face down. Turn both sides to the middle, with sleeves lying flat down the back. Turn the tail up about three inches and then take the bottom fold up to the collar.

• Knitted/woollen items: Don't hang or they will stretch. Fold, and put in a drawer. To fold place face down, fold one side and arm to the middle. Fold the arm back on itself and repeat with the other side. Fold in two, taking the top down to the bottom.

• Jackets: Use a wooden coathanger which spans the width of the shoulder. Never hang by the loop as it will pull the shoulders out of shape.

• Shoes: Wipe wet shoes, stuff with newspaper or a shoe tree and dry away from direct heat.

• Hats: Stuff with tissue in boxes. Felt and velour hats need to be brushed, and if they become misshapen hold them in some steam, press them to shape again and let them cool supported by crumpled paper. Straw hats can be brushed and scrubbed with lemon juice and left in the sun if they become dingy.

• Ties: hang over expanded curtain wire, or a wire coathanger hung on the inside of the wardrobe door.

• Belts: hang by the buckles from hooks on the inside of the wardrobe door.

• Linens: rotate the use of sheets to prolong their life. Store duvets in a large bag, on top of a wardrobe or under the bed.

• Remove fluff or hair from clothes by dabbing with a piece of sticky tape. Wind a length round the back of your hand, sticky side out.

- Stop clothes falling off hangers by sticking a piece of foam rubber at each end.
- Store black items inside out to stop them from picking up fluff and dust.

MOTHPROOFING

Moths attack natural fibres, particularly wool. Synthetics are mothproof, but if blended with natural fibres they can be attacked.

When storing clothes at the end of the season, make sure they are washed; then pack in plastic-lined cases or boxes, or hang in mothproof bags.

Hang an insecticidal strip in the wardrobe or put moth-repellent crystals between blankets and woollens. Natural substances such as lavender and cedar wood are sometimes used to repel moths.

PACKING CLOTHES

When going away, first make a list of the things you need to take with you: clothes, cosmetics, first aid kit, shoes, books, etc.

- Collect together all items and discard non-essentials.
- Avoid over- and under-filling the case.
- Do up all fastenings on clothes before folding, and pack everything face down to minimise creasing.
- Place tissue paper between the folds.
- Place heavy items, such as shoes, books, etc, at the bottom and fill gaps with underwear and socks.
- Pack heavy garments next, followed by woollens and breakables.
- Lay trousers with the waistband at one end of the case and the legs overhanging at the other. Pack shirts, sweaters, etc, on top and then fold the legs over to reduce creasing.
- Finish off with dresses and blouses covered over with a towel or tissue paper. Fold dresses horizontally, as these folds drop out quicker than vertical ones.
- Unpack as soon as you can when you arrive, and hang up any creased garments in a steamy bathroom.

A–Z OF FABRIC CARE

These guidelines must not be used instead of care labels. Read the labels thoroughly and match up with care symbols in the chart on page 92. If there isn't a label, follow these guidelines, or dry clean only. When washing and ironing try on a small, hidden area first.

ACETATE

Man-made fibre which has a silky appearance so often made into synthetic silk-like fabrics such as satin, taffeta and brocades. Often used for linings, which can shrink.

- Wash in warm water using a delicates programme as hot water will soften and damage the fibres.
- Do not spin.
- Iron using a cool setting.
- Some acids and solvents can dissolve acetate, therefore avoid acetone (nail-varnish remover) and vinegar when removing stains.

ACRYLIC

Made from petrochemicals and solvents as an alternative to wool. Often used for knitwear because it is soft, warm, shrink resistant and inherently mothproof. However, it does not have the same warmth as wool.

- Use a warm wash using a synthetics programme with a short spin.
- Fabric conditioner in the last rinse will reduce static.
- Do not wring and use a cool iron, not the steam setting.
- Acrylic knitwear has a tendency to become baggy, so pull it back into shape when wet, and dry flat.
- Dry clean curtains and soft furnishings.
- Pile fabrics should be ironed carefully on the wrong side. Then brush the pile with a soft brush.

ANGORA

Soft rabbit wool used for jumpers, mohair fabrics and knitting yarns. Sometimes mixed with nylon.

- Always hand wash, and treat as for wool.
- To prevent moulting store in the fridge!

BLANKETS

Usually made from wool, but cotton and synthetics are available.

- Rest blankets periodically to help prolong their life.
- When not in use, wash, clean, air and store sealed in a polythene bag in a cool cupboard, to avoid any crushing. If you've forgotten to wash them and they've become infested with moths, check whether they are worth keeping.
- Check the care label for cleaning details; most wool blankets should be dry cleaned. Some laundries and dry cleaners operate special blanket washing and cleaning services. Local addresses of these specialists are available

from the Textile Services Association (020 8863 7755).

- Synthetic and cotton blankets can generally be machine washed but always check the label first. Make sure the dry blanket will fit in your washing machine. If hand washing, use the bath and remember the blanket will get heavier when wet and become bulky to handle.
- Dry naturally away from direct heat.

BLINDS

Austrian/Festoon

Vacuum with the upholstery tool. Occasionally wash or dry clean.

Roller

Vacuum with the upholstery tool or use a soft brush. If spongeable use an upholstery shampoo but avoid over-wetting. Alternatively, try a proprietary blind cleaner, available from department stores or specialist curtain shops.

Re-hang while still damp. If it doesn't wind properly, re-tension by pulling down the blind halfway. Remove from the brackets and rewind by hand. Pull down and repeat if necessary.

Venetian

Special brushes are available, or, alternatively, wearing cotton gloves, run your hands along both sides of the slats. Wash in the bath, avoiding immersing the operating mechanism, using a nylon scourer and a dilute detergent solution. Line the bath with a towel to prevent scratching. Rinse, shake off excess water and hang to dry.

BROCADE

Heavy, stiff fabric with a raised pattern on a

plain background. Can be made from cotton, viscose, silk, acetate or a combination. Often used for soft furnishings and upholstery.

- Dry clean only.
- Iron on the reverse side with a cool iron.

BRODERIE ANGLAISE

Traditional open-work embroidered fabric or lace. Available in cotton or polyester cotton.

- Wash according to fabric type.
- Wash delicate pieces by hand or in a muslin bag in the machine to avoid other garments catching the embroidery.

CALICO

Plain, closely woven cotton. Generally unbleached and coarse.

- Wash as for cotton.
- To whiten unbleached calico, add a little white spirit to the first wash. Rinse thoroughly.

CAMBRIC

Traditionally a fine linen from France but now generally cotton. Often used for table linen and handkerchiefs.

- Wash as for cotton.
- To crispen its texture, use a spray starch when ironing or a liquid starch such as Dip, after washing.
- Easier to iron when damp; use the steam setting.

CANDLEWICK

Patterned, tufted fabric of cotton, nylon, polyester or viscose, used for bathmats, dressing gowns and bedspreads.

- Wash according to fibre type.

- Do not iron as this will flatten the pile.
- Shake frequently to maintain the appearance of the pile.

CANVAS

Stiff, coarse cotton used for strengthening tailored garments, and making tents, handbags and shoes.

- Sponge or scrub soiled areas with a stain-removal bar of household block soap. Rinse with cool water.

Shoes

Some will withstand washing in the machine. Use a low-temperature synthetics programme.

- If they become muddy, allow the mud to dry before brushing off.
- Use an upholstery shampoo or proprietary cleaner for fabric shoes.

CARPETS

(For specific stains look under the stain: see A–Z of Stain Removal, pages 124–135.)

Most carpets are now supplied with care instructions. If you buy one that is not, contact the National Carpet Cleaners' Association (0116 271 9550) for advice.

- Vacuum regularly to remove embedded dust and grit which could damage the fibres, and keep the pile in good condition.
- Tackle stains and spills immediately.
- For spot cleaning use the lather from a solution of dry-foam shampoo, or use a carpet-spotting kit available from hardware and department stores.
- For all-over cleaning use:
– a carpet shampooer, manual or electric (can be hired) that dispenses dry-foam shampoo which forms a powder when dry, absorbing dirt. This is then vacuumed away.

– a steam cleaner (can be hired) that sprays hot water and a cleansing agent under pressure into the carpet and then extracts it immediately together with any dirt.

– a three-in-one-type cleaner. These will vacuum, shampoo and pick up water spills. Water and a cleansing agent are sprayed on to the carpet and immediately sucked back up together with any dirt. All these machines can be hard work to use and results are variable.

• For stubborn staining it's worth having a carpet professionally cleaned. Choose a cleaner who is a member of the National Carpet Cleaners' Association (NCCA). Members have training in all the different techniques of carpet cleaning and will advise on the best cleaning method for your problem. However, do get several quotes and compare advice. If you have a problem with the cleaner, the NCCA operates an arbitration scheme. Contact the organisation and it will then put you in touch with their Standards and Fair Trading Officer.

• Raise the pile of crushed carpet by covering the area with a damp cloth, then apply a hot iron carefully. When it is dry, brush up to lift the pile.

CASHMERE

Light, soft and warm wool made from the Kashmir goat.

• Always hand wash this fabric, treating it in the same way as wool.

CHENILLE

Heavy fabric of cotton, viscose, wool or silk with soft velvety pile. Often used for furnishing.

• Wash according to the instructions for the fabric type or dry clean.

CHIFFON

Finely woven sheer fabric from cotton, silk or man-made fibres.

• Wash according to fibre type, or dry clean.
• Handle with care and do not wring or spin.
• Iron gently while damp using a cool iron.

CHINTZ

Tightly woven cotton, generally with a flowery design used for furnishing fabrics. Some chintzes have a chemical glazed finish.

• Avoid using glazed chintz in any areas very prone to dirt because continual cleaning will remove the glaze.
• Dry clean only. The finish can wash off and fade. Once this goes it cannot be re-built. Some companies offer special cleaning for chintz. Contact the Textile Services Association (020 8863 7755) for details of cleaners offering this service.

COIR MATTING

Slightly hairy fibre from the coconut husk used for natural floor coverings. Some floor coverings can be treated with a stain inhibition treatment which slows down the penetration of spillages.

• Vacuum regularly with a suction-only-type cleaner (cylinder) to keep it dust free.
• Treat stains immediately. Spills on treated flooring can be mopped up with absorbent paper or a sponge, and wiped over with clean warm water.

CONTINENTAL QUILTS

See Duvets, page 109

CORDUROY

Includes needlecord and jumbocord.

Cotton or synthetic-mix woven ribbed fabric. Used for garments and upholstery.

- Wash using a synthetics programme with minimum spin.
- If washing garments such as trousers, turn inside out.
- Iron on the reverse side, while damp, using the steam setting.
- Brush up the pile gently.

CREPE DE CHINE

Lightweight, slippery fabric traditionally made from silk but now mostly from synthetics such as polyester.

- Hand wash according to fibre type. Cold rinse and roll in a towel to remove moisture.
- Iron on a cool setting.
- If washing pure silk, always soak in cold water first.

CURTAINS

The type of cleaning and treatment required depends on the type of fabric. Some can be washed; others must be dry cleaned. Often, though, it's not just the fabric type but the weight and size which will make washing impossible. Remember that whatever the fabric, dirty curtains will eventually rot and need to be replaced.

- Brush down monthly using the upholstery nozzle of the vacuum cleaner or a soft, long-handled brush.
- Curtains should be thoroughly cleaned every few years.
- As a general rule the following fabrics should be dry cleaned only: velvet, velours, chenilles, tapestries and brocades, all fabrics containing wool or silk, and all interlined curtains.
- Remove all hooks and curtain weights and loosen the heading tape. Let down the hem if the fabric is likely to shrink. Shake them first to remove dust.
- Soak curtains made of washable fabrics in cold water first. Then wash carefully, according to the type of fabric. Make sure, if you are hand washing, that the detergent is thoroughly dissolved before putting the curtains in.
- Do not rub or wring. Rinse thoroughly. Squeeze out as much water as possible, or use a short spin.
- If machine washing, use a programme specifically for delicates.
- Iron the curtains while they are still damp. Work lengthways, on the wrong side, stretching the fabrics gently to avoid puckering of the seams.
- Clean curtain tracks, windows and sills before re-hanging.
- For care of net curtains, see Net, page 114.

DAMASK

Heavy woven fabric with shiny thread. Silk, cotton, viscose or a combination. Used for table linen, soft furnishings and upholstery.

- Wash according to fibre type.
- Dry clean heavier items.

DENIM

Hard-wearing, twilled cotton fabric.

- If not pre-shrunk, use a cool wash.
- Turn inside out and wash separately, as the colour runs even after several washes.
- Iron using the maximum or steam setting while still damp.

DRALON

Trade name for an acrylic-fibre, velvet-type, furnishing fabric.
• Brush or vacuum upholstery and soft furnishings regularly. Brush against the lay of the pile to raise it, then in the other direction.
• Curtains should be dry cleaned at temperatures below 120°F/50°C. Do not iron, but hang immediately to avoid creasing.
• Do not over-wet Dralon upholstery, because this is often woven on to a cotton or cotton/synthetic backing which could shrink and distort the surface.
• Clean using a dry-foam upholstery shampoo.
• Remove water-based stains by immediate and thorough blotting, followed by sponging with a weak solution of biological detergent. Work in the pile direction. Rinse and blot dry.
• For other stains, try acetone applied with cotton wool.
• If in doubt, have it professionally treated.
• Do not apply heat as the fibres will melt.

DUVETS

These can have natural feather and down fillings, or polyester, eg hollowfibre.
• Should not require frequent cleaning.
• Air frequently in order to keep the filling fluffy and dry.
• Shake occasionally to redistribute the filling.
• Store in a cool place; on a spare bed is ideal, but if it must be put away, fold it loosely.
• Mop up spills immediately to avoid them soaking through the filling. If the casing has become stained, ease the filling away from that area and tie it off from the rest of the cover with an elastic band or string. Sponge this area first with cold water and then with a mild detergent solution. For stubborn marks, soak in a biological detergent solution.
• Unless specified, washing is recommended over dry cleaning, whatever the filling. Before washing, check there are no holes or weak points in the casing. Repair and patch the casing where necessary.
• Use a launderette machine, as domestic ones are too small even for single duvets. Dose with one-third the usual amount of detergent.
• Wash children's smaller duvets using a wool programme with a short spin. Line dry or dry in a launderette-sized tumble drier on the cool setting.
• Dry thoroughly and leave to air for a day.
• For companies offering commercial cleaning of duvets contact the Textile Services Association (020 8863 7755).

ELASTANES/LYCRA

These are a synthetic alternative to rubber. They keep their elasticity well and resist attack from perspiration and suntan lotions. Often in blends with other fabrics, between 2 per cent and 20 per cent.
• Machine wash at low temperatures using a delicates programme.
• Alternatively, hand wash in warm water, rinse, and use a short spin or roll in a towel.
• Do not iron or tumble dry.

ELECTRIC BLANKETS

There are only a few companies who still manufacture under- and over-blankets. They carry out servicing and may offer cleaning services.
• Always check the manufacturer's instructions first.
• Some may be washable. Use a little

washing-up liquid and water on a sponge, avoiding over-wetting.

• Dry completely. To freshen up, use a little talcum powder and then brush it away with a clothes brush. Never re-use the blanket until completely dry.

• Never have them dry cleaned as this may well damage or disturb the internal wiring of the blanket.

• Clean and service every three years.

• Dreamland Appliances Ltd offer a repair service for their own models of electric blanket only (0161 628 8018).

• Warmabed Ltd service their own and other manufacturers' – under-blankets only (01977 67 2051).

• Warmalux service and repair their own under-blankets only (01422 37 4801).

• Johnson and Calverley will repair and service any make of over- or under-blanket and electric duvet (01422 37 6320).

EMBROIDERY

• The silks and wools that are used for this type of work are frequently not colourfast. To check if they are, start by firmly pressing a wad of white cotton fabric against the stitches and then ironing over it gently, in a hidden area so that you don't cause any damage.

• Dry clean if not colourfast, otherwise hand wash and treat as wool.

• If the piece is valuable, contact the Royal School of Needlework (020 8943 1432), who offer a special restoration service.

FELT

Thick, non-woven material made from matted wool fibres.

• Dry clean, as it shrinks and it is not always colourfast.

FLANNEL

Woven wool or wool and cotton blend. Mainly used for suitings.

• Dry clean tailored and expensive garments. Otherwise, treat as wool.

FUR

Includes natural and synthetic.

Natural

• Have cleaned regularly by a professional.

• Put expensive furs into cold storage during warm weather.

• Do not cover in polythene: store in a cotton bag in the wardrobe.

• Hangers should be padded.

• Allow air to circulate between the fur and other garments in the wardrobe.

• Shake before wearing.

Synthetic

Made from polyamide, viscose, cotton, acrylic or polyester.

• Cotton and viscose should be dry cleaned.

• Wash others as polyamide, and shake well before allowing to dry naturally.

• For light soiling, sponge the area with a warm solution of non-biological washing powder, rinse and towel dry.

• Brush straight-pile fabric while damp. Curly pile should never be brushed while damp.

• Between washings, brush the pile with a medium to hard brush.

GABERDINE

Made from wool, cotton or either of these, blended with man-made fibres. The woven fabric has fine diagonal ribs.

Often used for suits, coats, trousers, etc.
- Dry clean only.

GEORGETTE

Fine, sheer fabric from cotton, silk, wool or man-made fibres.
- Dry clean natural fabrics.
- Wash man-made fabrics according to fabric type.

GINGHAM

Checked or striped fabric typically made in bright colours and white, from cotton or polyester-cotton.
- Wash according to fibre type after testing for colour fastness.
- Steam iron while damp.

GOATSKIN

Rugs should always be professionally cleaned because the hairs become brittle and break away from the base if washed. Coats are specially treated to avoid this.

GROSGRAIN

Fine, ribbed fabric of silk or man-made blends.
- Wash according to fibre type, or dry clean.

JERSEY

Stretchy knitted fabric of wool, silk, cotton or man-made fibres.
- Wash according to fibre type or dry clean.
- Short spin.
- Dry flat and pull to shape while wet.
- Steam iron on the reverse side to avoid the surface becoming shiny.

LACE

Cotton, polyester, polyamide or a combination.
- Wash according to fibre type.
- Use a gentle non-biological powder.
- If washing in a machine, first place in a muslin bag or a pillowcase.
- Iron while damp, on the wrong side, pulling to shape.

Antique lace
- Wash by hand, using a mild detergent which does not contain fluorescers, and dry flat.
- Delicate pieces should be pinned on to a padded board covered with cotton sheeting, sponged with a mild detergent solution and then rinsed with cold water.
- Precious items should always be dry cleaned; or consult the Royal School of Needlework (020 8943 1432).

LAMBSWOOL

See Wool, page 121

LEATHER

Chamois
- Hand wash in a warm soap-flake solution and then squeeze the item in the water to release the dirt.
- Rinse once in a warm water solution to which 1 tsp/5ml of olive oil has been added, to retain a soft texture.
- Squeeze out moisture and pull to shape.
- Hang to dry, away from direct heat. Scrunch up the leather during drying to maintain its flexibility.
- Store damp in a polythene bag.

Leather clothing

Leather clothing described as washable can only be sponged, so do not immerse it in water.

• New or newly cleaned clothes should be treated with a waterproof spray such as Meltonian Protector.

• A scarf around the neck will prevent grease marks on leather collars.

• All leather clothing should be professionally cleaned every three to four years, including re-tinting and re-oiling. Contact the Textile Services Association (020 8863 7755) for details.

• Skins are stretched during manufacture so will contract with cleaning. These should stretch out when worn again but don't buy a very tight-fitting garment just in case.

• If it does get wet wipe over with a clean cloth and allow to dry naturally.

• Remove surface soiling from washable leathers with a soapy sponge (use glycerine soap or soap flakes). Then wipe with a clean damp cloth and hang to dry.

• When not in use store in a cotton cover, not plastic, in a cupboard, using a padded hanger.

• Treat the garment occasionally with an application of hide food.

Leather furniture

Always check manufacturers' care instructions first because some leather should not be wetted.

Dust leather furniture regularly and give it an accasional application of hide food (available from specialist outlets or department stores) to prevent the leather from drying out and to protect against stains. Try to site furniture away from direct heat, such as radiators, which can encourage cracking. Remove all-over grime by wiping over with a soft damp cloth. If there is very obvious staining have the item professionally cleaned.

Leather gloves

• Wash in a warm soap-flake solution whilst on your hands. Rub together gently. Remove and allow to dry naturally.

• When nearly dry, pop them back on to restore their shape.

• Do not rinse doeskin gloves as the soap keeps them supple. After washing, press between two towels to remove excess moisture and dry naturally.

Reptile skin

• Dust shoes and handbags regularly.

• Occasionally, apply a special reptile dressing or hide food, rubbing it in the direction of the scales.

Shoes and handbags

• When new, apply a waterproof protector spray.

• Before polishing these items, wipe the leather over with a Mars Oil NonScratch Cleaning sponge.

• Clean shoes regularly with recommended shoe polishes which will clean and maintain the dye colour. They will also cover scuff marks.

• If shoes get really wet, allow them to dry out at room temperature in a well-ventilated spot. Stuff them with paper to help retain the shape or use a shoe tree. Never dry in front of a radiator as it could crack the leather.

• Handbags need similar care, but less often. Do not use pigmented polishes as they will rub off on to clothing.

• To remove grease and oils from speciality leathers use a rubber adhesive which will absorb the grease. Coat the stain with a thin layer and leave on for 24 hours, then roll the adhesive off. Treat with hide food.

Alternatively, try Meltonian Grease and Tar Remover.

Patent leather

- If patent leather becomes very cold it will crack.
- Dust with a soft cloth and apply patent-leather dressing when looking dull and lifeless.
- If the item is only used occasionally, apply a thin layer of petroleum jelly or Vaseline all over and wipe off before use.
- Always use shoe trees or stuff with a wedge of paper.

LINEN

Woven fabric from flax fibres. The sign of good linen is creasing.

- Hot wash and spin dry. Hang drying is preferable because it will remove some of the creasing.
- Some garments have special finishes applied to minimise creasing, and these should be dry cleaned.
- Iron while still damp on the reverse side, to prevent shining. Use a hot steam iron.
- Stored table linen can become soiled along the crease marks. Rub a stain-removal bar along the dampened lines before washing.

LYCRA

See Elastanes, page 109

MATTRESSES

It's worth buying separate mattress covers which are removed for washing.

Spring interior

- Turn over or swing round to reverse head and foot frequently when new, then quarterly

after several months. This helps settle the filling.

- Occasionally, brush the mattress and base to remove fluff and dust. Don't vacuum or it may dislodge the filling.

Foam

- Foam mattresses with a layered construction should never be turned.
- Single-layered mattresses should be turned monthly.
- Use the crevice tool on the vacuum cleaner.

METALLIC YARN

Includes lamé and woven brocade-type fabrics which contain a metallic thread.

- Dry clean.

MICROFIBRES

These are fabrics made from ultrafine polyester or polyamide yarns. Air pockets become trapped between the fibres making the fabrics soft with good draping characteristics.

- Follow care-label instructions.
- Machine wash using a 100°F/40°C wash programme. Minimum spin.
- Warm or steam iron.

MILIUM

Metallic-coated fabric used for its insulating properties, particularly in curtain linings and ironing boards. If making curtains the metallic side should face inwards.

- Dry clean.

MOHAIR

Light woven fabric made from hair of the Angora goat, often mixed with other fibres.

- Hand wash and treat as wool.

MOIRE

Traditionally made from silk, but now often from synthetics. Heavy weights are used for furnishings and lighter weights for ball gowns.
• Watermarked surface is easily damaged by water, so dry clean only.
• Do not use a steam iron.

MUSLIN

Open weave, loosely woven, sheer cotton.
• Hand wash in warm water.
• Do not spin and dry flat.
• Iron carefully while damp with a medium setting.

NET

Loosely woven mesh fabric made from a variety of fibres such as polyester, cotton and polyamide. Mostly used for curtaining or underskirts.
• Wash net curtains frequently because they tend to hold on to dirt once soiled.
• Wash separately in hot water (but do not exceed the recommended washing and drying temperatures or they will become permanently creased), followed by a cold rinse.
• Use a proprietary whitener, for greying polyester, available from department or hardwear stores. Alternatively, try soaking in biological detergent.
• Hand wash dress net in warm water. Rinse, drip dry and iron with a cool iron.

NUBUCK

Made from cow leather like suede but is buffed to a finer velvet pile.
• Use specialist nubuck and calf-leather cleaners which are solvent based, eliminating the need to brush as they evaporate.
• Do not use suede shampoos (which are water based) or brushes as they will damage the pile.

NYLON

See Polyamide, below right

PATENT LEATHER

See Leather, page 340

PERCALE

A finely woven cotton or cotton-polyester blend, often used in bedding. Can be glazed.
• Wash according to fibre type.

PILLOWS

Natural filling
• Air regularly outside in summer.
• Do not have them dry cleaned as it is difficult to remove all the toxic fumes from them.
• Can be washed in a washing machine. Check first that the machine will take the weight as pillows can be heavy when wet. Must be spin dried to remove as much moisture as possible.
• Dry thoroughly, or the pillow will start to smell and the feathers will be damaged. Hang outside and shake occasionally. It may take several days to dry.
• Air thoroughly before re-using.
• If it is possible, have them professionally cleaned. All the feathers are removed from each pillow. They are then sterilised with ultraviolet light and the old pillowcase is replaced with a new one.

Polyester/Hollowfibre

- Machine wash using the wool programme and about a third of the normal quantity of detergent.
- Spin, then tumble dry.

Foam

- Sponge in warm soapy water, about once a year.
- Rinse well and remove excess water with absorbent towel.
- Do not wring, and dry away from direct heat and sunlight.

POLYAMIDE

Used to be known as nylon.

Lightweight and non-absorbent man-made fibre; elastic and strong even when wet; flame resistant.

- Wash in hand hot water, or 100°F/40°C delicates programme; cold rinse, short spin and drip dry.
- It absorbs dye very easily so wash separately from coloureds if possible.
- Whites become grey quickly, particularly if washed in water that is too hot.
- Wash pleated and delicate items after each use because once soiling occurs it is difficult to remove.
- Use fabric conditioner to reduce static.
- Do not bleach or expose to direct heat or sunlight.
- Inherently crease resistant, but if it does need ironing use a cool setting. Do not iron pleated nylon.

POLYESTER

Versatile synthetic fibre. Will not shrink, stretch, fade or crease. Often combined with cotton because of its easy-care properties.

- Wash using the 100°F/40 or 120°F/50°C synthetics programme with a short spin.
- Can be tumble dried.
- Prone to static, so use a fabric conditioner in the final rinse.
- Grease stains are very difficult to remove from polyester so treat immediately by soaking in a biological powder.
- Do not wash over 120°F/50°C as it will then crease badly when it is plunged into cold water.
- Whites have a tendency to go grey or yellow in time.
- Cannot be home dyed successfully, but can be professionally treated.
- Hand wash pleated items and drip dry.

POPLIN

Closely woven cotton, viscose, silk or wool.
- Wash according to fibre type.

PVC

Polyvinylchloride: a strong plastic material or coating. Used for upholstery, tablecloths, shower curtains, etc.

- Sponge any marks off upholstery with some warm water. Use a dilute solution of washing-up liquid if there is noticeable all-over soiling on the item.
- Where applicable, hand wash in warm water and drip dry.
- Do not apply heat as it will soften and melt.
- Do not dry clean.
- Shoes should be wiped clean and dried away from direct heat.

QUILTS

See Duvets, page 109

RAINWEAR

Includes garments that are completely impermeable to slightly showerproof cotton coats.
- Check care label as some items can be machine washed.
- Bulky items and those with protective finishes should be dry cleaned only. Some dry cleaners offer a re-proofing service: contact the Textile Services Association (020 8863 7755).
- Rubberised macs such as riding coats should be scrubbed with a soft brush and detergent solution. Wipe with a damp cloth and dry with a towel.

RUSH MATTING

Hand-plaited strips of rush which are sewn together.
- Vacuum as regularly as carpet.
- Treat any stains with a solution of warm water and washing soda. Occasionally scrub over the matting with some soap and warm water.
- Lift occasionally and then vacuum the floor underneath.

SATIN

Lustrous, smooth fabric with a short nap made from silk, cotton, polyester, polyamide or acetate. Used for dress fabrics, linings and lingerie.
- Wash lightweight satins according to the fibre type.
- Iron while still damp until dry, on the reverse side.
- Acetate satin will spot if sprinkled with water so do not dry clean.
- Dry clean heavier weights.

SEAGRASS MATTING

Seagrass is grown in paddy-like fields and needs a flooding of seawater during the crop cycle. It is spun into strands. It is naturally stain resistant and dye resistant so excellent for tough natural floor coverings.
- Vacuum regularly.
- Sponge up any spills.

SHANTUNG

Originally a term for slubbed Chinese silk; now also made from acetate or polyamide.
- Wash according to fabric type.

SHEEPSKIN

Coats
- Have professionally cleaned regularly.
- When new, or just after cleaning, apply a protective spray to help prevent marking.
- Wear a scarf around the neck to prevent grease marks. If these do occur the wool side can be freshened by using a dry shampoo for hair.
- To clean small areas of the skin use a suede cleaner. Test first.

Rugs
- Can be washed at home if the wool pile is quite short.

SHETLAND WOOL

See Wool, page 121

SHOWER CURTAINS

- To prevent the build-up of soap deposits,

clean down after use by spraying with water.

• Leave the curtains drawn so air can circulate freely.

• If machine washable use the wool programme, adding detergent and bleach. Bulk out the load using old white towels.

• Add one cup of white vinegar to the final rinse water.

• Do not spin or iron.

• To remove mildew, see Mildew, page 131.

SILK

Lightweight, resilient, luxury fibre made from the cocoon of the silk worm. Weakened by sunlight and perspiration.

• Dry clean taffetas and brocades.

• Avoid biological detergents, heat and washing soda, which can damage silk fibres. Preferably, use a mild liquid detergent designed for hand washing.

• Do not rub or wring the fabric or the fibres break and produce a white, chalky effect.

• Wash garments after each wear or perspiration stains may become impossible to remove.

• Have other stains professionally removed. However, for fatty stains try a detergent designed for coloureds which contains lipase.

• Iron while still damp with a warm iron. Do not use a steam iron on silks as the water will leave marks.

• Silk is not very colourfast so after washing coloureds, to preserve the colour, soak the item in a solution of 2tsp/10ml vinegar to 5 pints/3 litres water after the final rinse. Leave for three minutes. Dry.

• Use the special detergents for coloureds with care because they weaken silk fibres.

• Printed silks should be dry cleaned.

• Never hand wash a garment labelled dry clean only. Some silks have a resin applied to

give texture and body which may watermark if hand washed.

• Two-piece garments should be cleaned or washed together to avoid differential fading.

• Use a fabric conditioner in the final rinse to add softness.

• After rinsing, roll up in a clean dry towel and squeeze lightly to remove surplus water before ironing.

SISAL MATTING

Sisal is a fibre produced from the leaves of the *Agave sisalana* bush. It is soft and tough and available in a range of different weaves.

• Vacuum regularly except when wet or muddy.

• Lift occasionally to clean underneath.

• If necessary, clean very occasionally with a dry-foam shampoo, avoiding over-wetting.

• Dry naturally.

• Treat stains immediately as dried stains are difficult to remove. Some manufacturers will pre-treat with a stain inhibitor.

SOFT TOYS

• Wash frequently to avoid permanent soiling.

• Hand wash using a mild detergent solution. Rinse thoroughly.

• Wrap in a towel to soak up excess moisture, but avoid squeezing, to keep their shape.

• Hang by the feet to dry and air.

SUEDE

Clothes

• Washable suede does exist but is more expensive than ordinary suede.

• New or newly cleaned suede should be treated with a waterproof spray to prevent the colour rubbing off, and to provide a protective coating. Test first.

• Dirty or rain-spotted suede should be wiped over with a clean damp cloth and allowed to dry naturally.

• Brush up frequently with a wire brush or suede block.

• Proprietary suede cleaning cloths or blocks are useful for removing soiling along wear creases.

• For serious discoloration have the item professionally cleaned to restore both colour and oil.

Shoes

• Treat new shoes with a protective suede spray.

• Fading can be improved with an overall application of coloured suede dressing, generally available only in brown, navy, black and neutral.

• When necessary, clean with a nailbrush and clean soapy water. Rinse and blot dry.

• Proprietary cleaning products work well, but follow instructions carefully.

• If they get wet allow them to dry naturally, then use a rubber or nylon suede brush to remove dust and raise the pile.

• Scrape off mud while still wet and blot with a damp cloth.

TACTEL

See Microfibres, page 113

TAFFETA

Crisp, closely woven shiny material, made from a variety of fibres, including silk, acetate, viscose, polyester or polyamide.

• Dry clean.

• Iron on the reverse side.

TAPESTRY

• The Royal School of Needlework will restore valuable tapestry. Ring them for an appointment (020 8943 1432). Otherwise someone in the textile department of a museum may be able to advise.

TIES

Most are polyester, wool or silk.

• Stains on these fabrics are quite difficult to remove without leaving a ring mark, so spray new ties with a fabric protector. Try on the back first and leave to dry before doing the front.

• If stains do occur try a dry-cleaning spray, otherwise get professionally cleaned as laundering is rarely successful.

• To iron, position the tie wrong side up on the ironing board. Make sure the interlining is lying flat.

• Slip a cardboard shape inside the wide end of the tie so you press it without causing an imprint of the seam on the right side. Press over a damp cloth to avoid scorching.

TOWELLING

Looped pile fabric, usually made from cotton.

• Machine wash using a cotton programme.

• Dark colours should be washed separately.

• Nappies should be washed on a very hot wash. Add fabric conditioner to the final rinse.

TRAINERS

These are made from a multitude of materials, including plastic, leather, latex, canvas and other synthetic fabrics.

• After use, check the sole for thorns and grit,

which could penetrate and damage the mid-sole.

- Rinse off mud after use, using the back of an old knife in the tread. Pack with newspaper and let them dry naturally at room temperature.
- Clean according to the manufacturer's advice; only machine wash if specifically recommended. Most should only be wiped over with a soft cloth soaked in a detergent solution.
- Don't leave shoes in bright sunshine or keep damp shoes in a bag.
- Occasionally, remove the in-sock and wash it in warm soapy water. Rinse and dry naturally.

TREVIRA

Trade name for polyester fabric (page 115).

TULLE

Fine, sheer net-like fabric of silk, cotton, viscose, polyamide or other fibres. Used on evening and bridal wear.

- Dry clean silk.
- For other fibres, hand wash following the instructions for fibre type.
- If cotton tulle becomes limp, starch it in a weak starch solution, such as Dip, or use spray starch when ironing.
- Nylon and viscose tulle can be stiffened with a gum arabic solution available from health food stores.

TWEED

A woven woollen fabric available in different weights. Imitations are also made in polyester and acrylic.

- Dry clean.

UPHOLSTERY

- All upholstery should be thoroughly dusted every week, using the brush attachment (on pile fabrics) and crevice tool of the vacuum cleaner.
- Upholstery should be positioned away from sunlight to avoid fading.
- Removable cushions should be turned weekly to ensure they get even wear and soiling.
- Clean all upholstery before it becomes heavily soiled, following the manufacturer's advice.
- Loose covers should be washed or dry cleaned according to the fabric type. Take care because they often shrink.
- If washed, place them back on the furniture before completely dry to re-shape and prevent shrinkage.
- Iron while they are in position, using a cool iron on foam furniture.
- If covers cannot be removed, have them professionally cleaned or clean them with an upholstery shampoo and spotting kit. Try on hidden areas first.
- Avoid over-wetting, particularly on Dralon (see Dralon, page 109).
- Always dry clean chenilles, tapestries, velours, velvets and fabrics containing silk, wool or viscose.

Leather
See Leather Furniture, page 112.

VELOUR

Pile fabric similar to velvet usually made of acrylic but may be other man-made fibres, cotton or silk.

- Dry clean or wash the item according to the fibre type.

- Iron with a cool iron on the reverse of fabric.

VELVET

Originally a silk or cotton cut-pile fabric. Now many velvets are made from viscose, polyamide, polyester, etc.
- Treat according to the fibre, or dry clean.
- Curtains, particularly cotton velvet, should be lined as they fade readily in sunlight.
- Dry clean curtains.
- Shake periodically while drying and smooth the pile with a soft cloth or velvet brush to restore the pile.
- Use steam to remove between-wear creases, eg hang over a bath of steamy water.
- Iron velvet with pile face down on a soft cloth or towel.

VISCOSE

Also known as rayon, this is a cellulosic fibre made from the pulp of eucalyptus and spruce wood which is reacted with certain chemicals. It is used on its own, or in blends. Drapes well but creases easily so is sometimes treated with an easy-care finish.
- Wash with care at low temperatures because fibres are weak when wet. High temperatures will affect finish.
- To discourage creasing, use a short spin when washing, and do not wring.
- Iron on the steam setting while damp.

VIYELLA

Brand name for lightweight wool-and-cotton blend fabric.
- Hand wash in hand-hot water.
- Do not spin; remove water by squeezing gently or rolling in a towel.
- Warm iron on the reverse side while damp.

WAXED JACKETS

- Some brands can be cleaned by specialist companies, eg Nikwax. They will clean and re-wax jackets, trousers, hoods and waistcoats.
- Barbour branded jackets can be re-waxed, repaired and re-proofed by the manufacturer, J Barbour. Barbour does not recommend dry cleaning.

WEDDING DRESSES

This information also applies to accessories such as the veil and other special, occasional clothes such as christening gowns.

A wedding dress should be professionally dry cleaned before storing. Contact the Dry Cleaning Information Bureau (020 8863 8658), who can give you specialist dry cleaners in your area. This should be done, even if the gown is not visibly dirty, since colourless stains such as alcohol, perfume and perspiration can develop and discolour as they react with the air. The discoloration cannot be removed.

FOLDING A WEDDING DRESS

- If practical, detach bulky or stiff underskirts and store separately.
- Line the base and sides of the box with overlapping layers of acid-free tissue.
- Start from the hem and work upwards.
- Fold in a concertina fashion, interleaving with layers of acid-free tissue.
- Place rolled layers of tissue along each of the folds.
- Insert tissue inside bodice, sleeves, shoulders and inside any bows.
- Finish with layers of tissue and cover with lid.

Never use ordinary plastic bags, PVC zip covers or cardboard boxes to store a wedding dress. Chemicals within these packaging materials can leach out over a period of time and cause the fabric to discolour. This reaction is accelerated if there is little air movement. Storing the dress in a wooden chest of drawers can have a similar effect. The yellow discoloration is permanent and cannot be removed.

For long-term storage, use an acid-reduced cardboard box and interleave the dress with acid-free tissue. These are available from Harry Berger (0161 485 3421), although acid-free tissue is sold by department stores. Unlike conventional tissue or cardboard, the acid-free has been specially treated and doesn't contain harmful chemicals. Don't be tempted to use an ordinary cardboard box with acid-free tissue paper since the chemicals from the cardboard can still leach through the tissue.

Place the box in a cool cupboard, away from damp, indirect heat or sunlight. Inspect the gown every 18 months to two years, re-folding the dress along slightly different lines to help prevent permanent creasing.

Vacuum packing: Another option is to have the dress vacuum packed. Jeeves of Belgravia offer a vacuum-packing service. The process involves storing the gown in a polythene bag which has had all the air removed and replaced with nitrogen, a bit like shrink wrapping ham. This prevents the oxidisation of stains and discoloration. Vacuum packing should 'preserve' the gown for at least 25 years.

However, bear in mind that you won't be able to remove the dress from the bag, since once the seal is broken, the preserving properties will be lost. The other disadvantage is that you leave the dress in this fixed position for so many years it can cause permanent creasing.

WOOL

Natural, versatile fibre used to manufacture woven fabrics and knitting yarns.

- Wash with care as it is easily spoiled. Wool has a coating of scales which work against each other if rubbed while wet, causing the fibres to shrink and felt. It stretches when wet but will never unfelt.
- Only machine wash if the label specifies that the item is machine washable wool. If so, use the special woollens programme, which has reduced agitation and has a very short spin programme.
- Hand wash in warm water using a gentle detergent. Do not rub, wring or twist. If your washing machine has the option for washing woollens, a very short spin will not harm the fabric.
- Dry flat between two towels. Pull gently to the correct shape while still damp.
- Never tumble dry wool.
- Oiled wool such as Guernsey sweaters should be washed in warm water using well dissolved soap flakes as detergents will remove the oil. This type of sweater can be re-oiled, but you will need to check with the manufacturer first.
- If you have washed a woollen garment and it has slightly shrunk. It is sometimes possible that by giving it a gentle wash in hair shampoo you will soften the fibres which will allow you to pull it back to shape.

HOW TO TREAT STAINS

In these days of sophisticated cleaning substances, stains need not be an insoluble problem. With prompt and careful attention – detailed in the following pages – they can usually be readily removed.

TYPES OF STAINS

ABSORBED STAINS

These include liquid spillages such as tea, coffee, milk or beer which have been absorbed into a surface. Fresh stains can generally be removed from washable fabrics by rinsing out with warm water and washing as normal. If you can't wash immediately, leave to soak.

Treat stubborn stains with a proprietary stain remover or bleach.

Sponge non-washable fabrics with warm water and blot dry.

BUILT-UP STAINS

Such as grease, nail varnish and paint. They do not normally penetrate the surface. Treat immediately to remove as much deposit as possible and then according to type.

COMPOUND STAINS

These penetrate the surface *and* leave a deposit, such as blood. Treat first as a built-up and then an absorbed stain. These sorts of stains will require a final laundering.

TEN GOLDEN RULES FOR SUCCESSFUL STAIN REMOVAL

1 Use stain-removal products with care and always read the instructions thoroughly. Wear rubber gloves if you have sensitive skin.

2 Before using any solvent or cleaner, check on a hidden area first. This is particularly necessary on synthetic fibres.

3 Test fabric for colourfastness by rubbing a white damp cloth repeatedly on a hidden area of the fabric. If the dye rubs on to the white fabric it is not colourfast.

4 Some fabrics react better to stain removal than others. Wool, for example, is very absorbent, so marks can become embedded and difficult to remove. Polyester, on the other hand, does not dye readily so colours from stains do not penetrate the fabric.

Delicate fabrics should always be professionally treated.

5 If you can't launder at once, try interim measures:
- Sprinkle talc on fresh, greasy stains.
- Sprinkle salt on coffee, fruit, wine and beetroot, to absorb the colour and moisture (but not on carpets).
- Rinse non-greasy stains with cold water.

6 Washable fabrics should be machine washed using as high a temperature as the fabric will allow.

7 Protein stains should be soaked in cool water first to avoid setting the stain.

8 Small repeated applications work better than totally saturating the stain.

9 If coloured traces remain after treating a stain, dab with methylated spirits (except on acetate fabrics) until clear.

10 Dry clean-only fabrics should be professionally treated, or for small areas follow the directions for upholstery.

TREATING STAINS

Whatever the stain, act quickly to prevent permanent staining and odour. Blot up any excess, using absorbent paper, or scrape off with a palette knife.

Work from the outside inwards to avoid spreading the stain, holding white absorbent paper on the top side. Dab rather than rub, using a white cloth or cotton wool.

Several small applications are better than totally soaking the stain.

STAIN-REMOVAL KIT

It's worth keeping a few essential remedies at the ready. Label clearly and do not decant into different containers, such as squash bottles, which could encourage children to open them.

The following are the most useful items to help with stain removal. Most are available from chemists, hardware or department stores.

Absorbent materials

Include a selection of clean white cotton cloth, cotton wool, paper towels, cotton wool buds, soft brush and sponge.

Ammonia

Will remove certain water-based stains and neutralise acid marks. Always use diluted with cold water, and in a well-ventilated room. Test on coloured fabrics because dyes can bleed.

Biological detergent

These contain enzymes which break down specific stains such as protein (blood, egg, milk, etc) and fat. They have improved so much in recent years that many stains will be removed just by normal washing.

Use as a pre-wash for soaking heavy stains. Ensure detergent is thoroughly dissolved

SOLVENT SAFETY

- Wear rubber gloves.
- Always ensure solvents are kept away from children because many of the substances are toxic and highly flammable.
- Never smoke or use solvents in a room where an open fire or radiant heater is burning. Turn off any pilot lights.
- When using solvents, always open a window if possible or leave the door open, because some give off toxic fumes.

before immersing fabrics.

Do not use on protein fibres such as wool and silk, or on non-colourfast or flame-resistant fabrics.

Glycerine

Used for lubricating and softening stains, making it easier to remove. Dilute with equal parts warm water and rub into the fabric. Leave for about an hour and then rinse or sponge with warm water.

Hydrogen peroxide

Mild oxidising bleach. For fabric stain removal use the 20-vol strength and dilute this with one part to six parts of cold water. Soak fabrics for around 30 minutes.

It will fade coloured fabrics. Do not use on polyamide or flame-resistant fabrics.

Methylated spirits

Used for removing oil-based stains and dyes. Use neat, dabbed on to the area with cotton wool. If using on coloured fabrics always try on a hidden area first. Not recommended for use on acetates, but check first.

Other solvents

For grease use a spirit, eg vodka, surgical spirits, turpentine, lighter fluid or white spirit.

For water-based stains use caustic soda, sodium bicarbonate, Milton, or dilute hydrochloric acid.

Pre-wash products

These proprietary products are designed to be used on heavily soiled and stained areas, on washable white and colourfast fabric. They either break down or soften soiling ready for washing, and eliminate the need for pre-soaking and scrubbing.

They are most effective on grease stains but less so on protein- and dye-based stains.

Proprietary stain removers

These can be general or very specific. Always follow the manufacturers' instructions very closely. Recommended brands include Stain Devils, Mykal De-Solv-It, Dabitoff and The Stain Slayer.

Spotting kits, available for upholstery and carpets, include a selection of chemicals for removing different stains.

White vinegar or acetic acid

Good for removing water-based stains. Always wash out thoroughly after applying.

A–Z OF STAIN REMOVAL

ADHESIVES

Work quickly and scrape off any excess deposit. Stain-removal advice is generally given on the packaging, or contact the manufacturer direct. Several have products for glue removal.

ALL-PURPOSE HOUSEHOLD

Carpets and fabrics

Dab area with acetone until glue is dissolved. Launder where possible.

CONTACT ADHESIVE

These harden on contact so speed is essential. Treat as all-purpose adhesives.

EPOXY RESIN

These consist of two parts: a glue and a hardener, and once mixed and hardened they are nearly impossible to remove. Before they set, use acetone or methylated spirits to remove any residue.

Carpets and fabrics

Before it dries, dab with cellulose thinners, methylated spirits, or lighter fuel on synthetic fibres. Once dry the glue cannot be removed except by cutting away the pile.

PAPER ADHESIVE AND LATEX

Carpets

Pick off any residue before treating. Dab area with a dilute detergent solution, and avoid over-wetting if possible. Rinse and dab dry.

Fabrics

Remove as much residue as possible. Dried adhesive will wash out as normal. If any greasy marks remain try Stain Devils Glue and Chewing Gum Stain Remover.

SUPER GLUE

Skin

Use special remover from manufacturer, eg Bostik's Skin Release Agent or Loctite's

Detach, or immerse in hot soapy water to soften it.

Carpets and fabrics

Try dabbing with acetone or use one of the proprietary glue removers as above.

WATER-SOLUBLE ANIMAL AND FISH GLUES

Carpets and fabrics

Usually soluble in cold water. If not, try dabbing with household ammonia. Rinse thoroughly. If not removed, apply liquid detergent and rinse.

ANIMAL STAINS

BLOOD

See Blood, page 126

EXCRETA, VOMIT AND URINE

Carpets

Scrape away or blot up excess carefully to avoid spreading further. Flush the area with a solution of sodium bicarbonate or sponge with warm water. Blot dry. Clean and deodorise the area with a proprietary pet stain remover such as Bissell 'Not on the Carpet' Accident Cleaner, Secto Enz Stain (from hardware and pet stores), Shaws Pet Stain Remover (from pet stores and mail order: 01296 630121). Shampoo the carpet if necessary and blot dry.

Fabrics and upholstery

Scrape away any deposit and blot dry. If it is not possible to remove the area, isolate and gather up the area by tying string tightly around it. Rinse under some cold running water or treat with a proprietary pet stain remover such as Shaws Pet Stain Remover or Secto Enz Stain.

BALLPOINT PEN

Fabrics and upholstery

Dab gently with cotton wool moistened with hydrogen peroxide solution (one part 20-vol peroxide to six parts cold water). Machine wash if possible. If it is unsuccessful contact the manufacturer for advice, or dry clean.

Suede

Rub gently with abrasive paper or a suede-cleaning block such as Swade Aid. Alternatively, seek professional advice.

Vinyl upholstery, wall coverings and bags

Must be treated immediately or cannot be removed. Scrub with warm detergent solution using an old nail brush.

BEER

Carpets

Clean with proprietary carpet shampoo or carpet spotting kit available from department stores. Alternatively, try a proprietary stain remover such as Carpet Devils No 3 followed by a carpet shampoo. On old stains try dabbing with methylated spirits.

Washable fabrics

Should be removed by machine washing with a biological detergent. For dried stains soak in a warm washing soda or a proprietary pre-wash detergent solution.

Upholstery and non-washable fabrics

Blot and wipe with warm water. Dried stains can be treated with a white vinegar solution (one part vinegar to five parts water) and then with clear water. Blot to dry.

BEETROOT

Table linen

Sponge immediately with cold water and soak overnight if possible. Then wash using a biological detergent. For stubborn dried stains try Stain Devils Fruit and Wine Stain Remover or Mykal De-Solv-It 2.

BIRD DROPPINGS

Washing on the line

Scrape off the deposit and then wash the items again, as normal.

If stains persist on white or colourfast fabrics (not polyamide) immerse all the items in a hydrogen peroxide solution (one part 20-vol peroxide to six parts cold water). Wash and then rinse thoroughly.

Canvas and awnings

Allow to dry thoroughly and then brush off with a stiff brush. If marks remain, dip brush in a biological detergent solution and rub area. Hose down and rinse well.

BLACKCURRANT JUICE

Also applies to other dark berry fruits.

Carpets

Blot up as much as possible, while still wet, with absorbent paper. Rub with a stain-removing bar and shampoo the area. Remove any remaining stain with Carpet Devils No 3 and then shampoo.

Fabrics

Rinse under cold water. Pre-soak in a solution of washing soda followed by machine washing at 120°F/50°C using a biological detergent. Treat dried stains with Stain Devils Fruit and Wine Stain Remover followed by washing. If stubborn stains persist on whites, try bleaching with dilute household bleach, then rinse.

Upholstery

Sponge with cold water and blot dry. Dab dark, dried stains with a hydrogen peroxide solution (one part 20-vol peroxide to six parts water).

BLEACH

Carpets and fabrics

Neutralise with soapy water. Blot up excess with a sponge, and rinse. Blot dry. Wash if possible.

BLOOD

Carpets

Sponge fresh stains with cold water and blot dry. If staining remains, shampoo the area. Dried stains will need professional treatment: contact the National Carpet Cleaners' Association (0116 271 9550) for recommended cleaners in your area.

Bedding and washable fabrics

Sponge with cold salt water. Machine wash using a biological detergent and a wash temperature of at least 120°F/50°C. Pre-soak dried stains using a pre-wash detergent or washing soda followed by washing as above.

Mattresses

Dried stains are difficult to remove. Tip the mattress on its side to prevent penetration and sponge with cold salt water. Blot thoroughly. Treat with the foam from a carpet or upholstery shampoo. Rinse and blot dry.

Non-washable fabrics and upholstery

Brush away surface deposit and sponge with cold water. Rinse and blot to dry. For stubborn stains try an upholstery spotting kit or have professionally cleaned.

CANDLE WAX

Carpets

Scrape off excess deposit. Remove the remainder by placing a sheet of brown or absorbent kitchen paper over the area and iron gently. Do not let the iron touch the pile as it may scorch and melt. Continue until all the wax has been absorbed. Keep moving the paper around for maximum absorption. Clear any remaining colour or stain using methylated spirits or Carpet Devils No 1.

Table linen and washable fabrics

Scrape away surface deposit using the back of a blunt knife. Place clean absorbent paper on both sides of the stain and melt out remaining wax using a warm iron. Launder as normal using a hot wash if possible.

Upholstery

Melt out using a moderately hot iron and white absorbent paper. Remove any remaining colour by dabbing with methylated spirits. On pile fabrics try removing the deposit by rubbing lightly with a cloth, or melt out by placing the absorbent paper on the pile and ironing the reverse side if possible.

Wooden surfaces

Chip away at the wax, when it is hard, using a fingernail or a plastic spatula. Remove any remaining film with a duster and then polish the area as normal. If heat marking has occurred rub firmly along the grain using a metal polish.

CHEWING GUM

Carpets

Hold a plastic bag of ice cubes on the area to harden the gum. Pick off as much deposit as possible. Remove any remaining marks using a proprietary stain remover such as Mykal De-Solv-It 1 or The Stain Slayer.

Fabrics

Harden the deposit as above or place in the freezer and pick off the deposit. Remove any remains with The Stain Slayer, rubbing in gently until the stain dissolves.

Upholstery

Remove excess deposit and treat with Stain Devils Glue and Chewing Gum Stain Remover. For greasy residues, try Dabitoff.

CHOCOLATE AND COCOA

Carpets

Blot or scrape up any excess deposit using a blunt knife. Treat the stained area with carpet shampoo or a carpet spotting kit.

Treat any remaining stain with a proprietary stain remover such as Dabitoff or Carpet Devils No 2. Follow by shampooing the carpet in the normal way.

Fabrics

Scrape off excess deposit using the back of a knife blade. Soak in a solution of washing soda or proprietary pre-wash detergent, followed by machine washing at 120°F/50°C using a biological detergent.

Upholstery

Blot or scrape up any deposit with the back of

a knife. Use a proprietary stain remover such as Carpet Devils No 2, rinse and blot to dry.

COFFEE

Carpets

Flush fresh stains with cold water and blot well to dry. Dried stains should be treated with Bissell Carpet Shampoo or Mykal De-Solv-It 2.

Fabrics

Soak in a warm solution of washing soda or pre-wash detergent followed by washing at 120°F/50°C using a biological detergent.

Upholstery

Sponge with cold water followed by treating with Carpet Devils No 4 or 1001 carpet spray, and then shampoo.

CURRY

Carpets

Small areas can be treated with Carpet Devils No 1 followed by shampooing. Large stains should be professionally cleaned.

Fabrics

Fresh stains will respond to sponging with a detergent solution before and after dabbing with Dabitoff. Machine wash. Treat dried stains on white and colourfast fabrics with a hydrogen peroxide solution (one part 20-vol peroxide to six parts water). Machine wash. Non-washable fabrics should always be dry cleaned.

Upholstery

Dampen the stain and treat with a stain-removing soap bar. Alternatively, have professionally treated.

DYES

Carpets, upholstery, non-washable fabrics

Should be professionally treated.

Washable Fabrics

Soak in a cold-water solution of washing soda or proprietary pre-wash detergent to avoid setting in the dye. Machine wash using a biological detergent. Alternatively, on whites, try Beckmann Colour Run Remover or Dylon Colour Run Remover (also suitable for colourfast fabrics). Beckmann In-wash Colour Run Remover can be used in a washing machine on a 140°F/60°C wash and therefore eliminates soaking.

EGG

Carpets

Scrape to remove as much deposit as possible. Treat with Carpet Devils No 2 followed by shampooing.

Fabrics

Rinse through with cold salt water. Soak and wash using a biological detergent.

Upholstery

Scrape off surface deposit and sponge with cold salt water, then clear water. Blot dry. Treat with Stain Devils Blood and Milk Stain Remover.

FATS, GREASE AND OIL

Carpets

First, using an iron, blot up as much as possible. Treat with a stain remover such as

Mykal De-Solv-It 1 or Carpet Devils No 1 followed by shampooing.

Fabrics

Wash in a hot wash if possible using a biological detergent containing lipase. If a hot wash cannot be used, try Mykal De-Solv-It 1 followed by washing.

Upholstery

Spread French Chalk or talcum powder over small marks on pale fabrics. Leave for several hours and then brush off. If marks remain, try Mykal De-Solv-It 1. Sponge with water and blot dry.

FELT-TIP PEN

Fabrics and upholstery

Blot up as much as possible while still wet with absorbent paper. Treat with Stain Devils Felt Tip Pen Stain Remover followed by washing or sponging.

FOUNDATION CREAM

Fabrics

Clear away any surface deposit. Soak using a pre-wash detergent and then machine wash at 120°F/50°C with a biological powder containing lipase. Stain Devils Grease and Oil Stain Remover will remove light markings. For stubborn stains wash in a detergent solution, treat with Dabitoff and re-wash.

Upholstery

Wipe away wet deposits or brush away dried stains. Sponge with a detergent solution and treat with Dabitoff. Finish by sponging again with the detergent solution and rinse with clear water. Blot well to dry.

GRASS

Fabrics

Before washing treat with Stain Devils Grass Stain Remover then machine wash using a biological detergent. Use as high a temperature as possible. Dry clean non-washable fabrics.

GRAVY

Fabrics

Pre-wash or soak using a proprietary product and machine wash using a biological detergent. Use a hot wash if possible.

Upholstery

Treat as for Foundation Cream.

ICE-CREAM

Carpets

Scrape away deposit and wipe up as much excess as possible. Shampoo area. If any staining remains use Carpet Devils No 2 followed by a carpet shampoo.

Fabrics

Soak and then wash in a biological detergent using as hot a wash as possible.

Upholstery

Sponge with warm water and then treat with The Stain Slayer or a hydrogen peroxide solution (one part 20-vol peroxide to six parts cold water). Rinse and blot dry.

INK (WASHABLE)

Carpets

Tackle immediately. Remove as much ink as possible by dabbing with absorbent paper soaked in cold water. Keep blotting to avoid over-wetting. Soak a clean pad in soap solution and leave for 15 minutes. Repeat until clear, blotting between applications. If stains remain, try a carpet spotting kit or have professionally treated.

Fabrics and upholstery

Ink is easier to remove from some fabrics such as polyester-cotton but more persistent in pure cotton. Act quickly! Sponge or hold under cold running water until excess ink is removed. Machine wash if possible using a high temperature and a biological detergent.

If staining remains, rub area with lemon juice and rinse thoroughly. Keep repeating until clear. Or soak in a hydrogen peroxide solution (one part 20-vol peroxide to six parts cold water), followed by laundering. Treat dried stains on white cotton and linen with a dilute solution of household bleach. Other whites and coloureds may respond to Stain Devils Mould and Ink Stain Remover. Non-washable fabrics should be professionally cleaned.

Treat upholstery with an upholstery spotting kit or upholstery shampoo.

IRON MOULD

Fabrics

Rub with lemon juice, cover with salt and leave for at least an hour. Rinse and wash as normal. Treat stubborn stains with a proprietary stain remover such as Stain Devils Rust and Iron Mould Stain Remover.

KETCHUP AND BOTTLED SAUCES

Carpets

Carefully remove excess, taking care not to spread the stain further, or soften dried stains by rubbing in a glycerine solution. Sponge gently with warm water and blot to avoid over-wetting.

Apply foam from a carpet shampoo or spray such as 1001. Alternatively, treat with Carpet Devils No 2. Rinse and dry thoroughly.

Fabrics

Pre-soak followed by washing with a biological detergent.

Upholstery

Sponge the affected piece with cold water followed by a detergent solution. Rinse well and blot dry.

If marks persist use Mykal De-Solv-It 2 followed by rinsing.

LIPSTICK

Carpet

Scrape away any deposit, then treat with a stain remover such as Stain Devils Grease and Oil Stain Remover, or Carpet Devils No 1, followed by shampooing.

Fabrics

Difficult to remove on natural fabrics. Soak in a detergent solution then dab with Dabitoff. Wash off with a detergent solution followed by ordinary laundering.

Upholstery

Have professionally treated.

MAYONNAISE

Fabrics

Sponge with warm water (avoid hot water as this will set the stain). Soak and wash in a biological detergent.

Upholstery

Remove excess, taking care not to spread the stain. Treat with Mykal De-Solv-It 1 or Stain Devils Grease and Oil Stain Remover. Rinse and blot dry.

MILDEW

Upholstery

Brush away spores and spray with a proprietary fungicide to kill the bacteria. Dab marks with Milton, and be prepared to be persistent. Sponge with cold water to rinse. Mattresses also respond well to treating with Milton. Start with a dilute solution and then get more concentrated until it is cleared.

Before treating items of value consult the Victoria and Albert Museum (020 7938 8500).

Plastic shower curtains

To prevent mildew growth see page 116.

Soak in a solution of bleach (one part bleach to four parts water). Rinse thoroughly by hand, or if possible, wash in a washing machine to prevent the fabric from being damaged by bleach residue. However, bleach will not inhibit future mould growth, so after bleaching apply a mould killer or inhibitor such as Cuprinol Interior Mould Killer, Rentokil Mould Cure or Fungo.

Walls

Wash down with a mild detergent solution followed by wiping over with a mould killer or inhibitor as above.

Fabrics

Fresh mildew marking should be removed by normal washing procedures. For old stains on whites, cotton and linen, soak in a solution of household bleach. Treat white and colourfast fabrics (except acetates) with Stain Devils Mould and Ink Stain Remover. Regular washing will reduce marks.

MILK

Carpets

Treat quickly to stop penetration and drying, as the smell lingers. Flush the area with warm water and blot to dry. Use a carpet stain remover such as Carpet Devils No 2 or 1001 carpet spray.

If any odour persists try Neutradol Carpet Deodorizer, which neutralises any smells rather than just masking them with a pleasant perfume.

Fabrics

Rinse through in lukewarm water and then wash as normal. You may need to soak dried stains first in a biological detergent solution. If any odour persists try XO. This product can be sprayed directly on to fabrics.

Upholstery

Sponge with lukewarm water and blot dry. If a stain remains, use a spray stain remover or Dabitoff. If any odour persists try XO as above.

MUD

Carpets

When the mud is completely dry, brush it all off the carpet and then vacuum it well. Use a carpet spot cleaner or shampoo to remove any other staining.

Fabrics

This is quite difficult to remove, especially if they are dried-on stains. Pre-wash in a biological detergent solution or pre-treat with a stain-removal bar.

Upholstery

Lightly brush when mud is completely dry. Sponge remaining marks with a warm, mild detergent solution. Sponge with clear water to rinse and blot dry.

NAIL VARNISH

Carpets

Treat with Carpet Devils No 1 followed by shampooing. If marks remain, have them professionally cleaned.

Fabrics

Treating with acetone will fade the mark, but probably not totally remove it. Dry cleaning may be effective but, if not, try to disguise the mark by adding a motif or brooch.

Upholstery

Have professionally treated.

PAINTS

WATER BASED

For example, emulsion: rinse out or flush fresh marks with cold water followed by laundering. Dried marks are difficult to remove. Treating with Stain Devils Tar and Paint Stain Remover may fade it, but don't expect total removal.

OIL BASED

For example, gloss: marking is usually permanent. Dabbing with turpentine may help fade it. Professional cleaning may help.

PERFUME

Non-washable fabrics

Lubricate with a glycerine solution (equal parts glycerine and water), leave for up to an hour and then sponge clean, avoiding over-wetting. Blot dry. Expensive items and silk should be dry cleaned.

Washable fabrics

Rinse through immediately. Lubricate dried stains as above or use Stain Devils Fruit and Wine Stain Remover before washing as normal.

PERSPIRATION

Non-washable fabrics

Dry clean heavily stained areas, particularly on tailored items. On lightly soiled areas try a solution of white vinegar (using 1 tbsp/15ml vinegar to 250ml warm water) to clean and deodorise the area.

Washable fabrics

To tackle a build-up of staining on shirts use Beckmann Stain Salts. Immerse colourfast items and soak overnight. Scrub affected areas with a nail brush and then wash with a biological detergent. For stubborn stains try White Wizard.

POLLEN

Fabrics

Treat stain with Stain Devils Grass Stain Remover. Wash as normal.

SALT AND WATER MARKS

Leather and suede shoes

White tide marks occur when water leaches out of the salt used to preserve the leather (involved in the tanning process) or when leather comes into contact with sea water or salt used to grit roads. Try moistening the stain and rubbing with a soft cloth, or try a proprietary product such as Meltonian Stain Remover and Cleaner. After treating, spray the shoes with a water-repellant spray protector which will help prevent any further stains from occurring.

Nubuck
Cow leather similar to suede but with a finer velvet pile. Use special nubuck and calf-leather cleaners which are solvent based and evaporate (no brushing required). Do not use suede cleaners or brushes as they will flatten the pile.

SCORCH MARKS

Carpets
These cannot be removed, but if it's only a small mark, trim the tufts or loosen any fibres using a stiff-bristled brush. Some carpet manufacturers will re-tuft or patch a small area but it is expensive. Contact the British Carpet Manufacturers' Association (01562 747351) or look in your local Thomson Directory for companies who offer this service.

Fabrics
Impossible to remove heavily scorched marks because the fibres, particularly synthetics, will be permanently damaged. You may be able to fade but not remove light marks by soaking in Beckmann Stain Salts. If possible, try disguising the offending area with motifs or brooches.

SHOE POLISH

Carpets
Carefully scrape away excess, avoiding spreading deposit further. Dab with Carpet Devils No 1 followed by carpet shampoo to dissolve remaining residue.

Upholstery
Scrape away the deposit. Sponge the upholstery with warm water to rinse and blot dry. Sponge with biological detergent, avoiding over-wetting and scuffing the surface. Rinse and blot dry.

Fabrics
Scrape away any deposit and treat with Mykal De-Solv-It 1 before rinsing and laundering.

SOOT

Carpet
Do not brush as this will spread the mark. Use the nozzle attachment of your vacuum cleaner to pick up any residue. Try absorbing the stain with talcum powder. Rub in lightly and then vacuum away the deposit.

If stains remain, try Carpet Devils No 1 followed by shampooing.

Fabrics
Vacuum up the residue to avoid spreading it further. Washing will gradually fade the stain.

SOY SAUCE

Fabrics
Launder using a biological detergent.

Upholstery
Sponge with cold water and then with a biological detergent solution. Rinse and dry thoroughly.

TEA

Carpets
Sponge the area with cold water. Treat with the foam from a carpet shampoo or try 1001 carpet spray. Rinse and blot dry.

Fabrics

Rinse fresh stains in warm water and then wash as normal, using a biological detergent. Loosen dried stains with a pre-wash treatment before machine washing.

Upholstery

Rinse with cold water and then apply a biological detergent solution. Rinse thoroughly and blot dry. On stubborn stains try Carpet Devils No 4, but do not leave on for too long or it could affect the dye.

TYPING CORRECTION FLUID

For example, Tipp-Ex fluid, Liquid Paper.

Carpets and upholstery

Allow to dry and pick off as much of the deposit as possible, taking care not to snag the fabric. Treating with turpentine will fade but not remove the mark. The remainder can only be cleared by professional treatment.

Fabrics

Try acetone or turpentine followed by repeated washing. However, professional treatment is recommended.

URINE

Carpets

Flush the area with cold water and blot until nearly dry. Sponge with carpet shampoo solution such as 1001 Trouble Shooter Stain Remover with deodoriser or Carpet Devils No 3. Rinse well with cold water to which a few drops of disinfectant have been added. Blot to dry. If any odour persists you can try using a deodorising product such as Neutrodol Carpet Deodorizer.

Mattresses

Hold the mattress on its side while the treatment is being carried out. Sponge with a cold solution of washing-up liquid or upholstery shampoo. Wipe with cold water to rinse to which a few drops of disinfectant, such as Milton, has been added. Alternatively, you can try using an upholstery spotting kit which can work well.

Non-washable fabrics

Fresh stains can be removed with a vinegar solution (1tbsp/15ml vinegar to 1 pint/500 ml warm water). Dried stains should be professionally treated.

Washable fabrics

Rinse and then soak in a biological detergent solution overnight. Then machine wash, as normal.

VOMIT

Carpet

Scoop up as much of the deposit as possible and flush through with a bicarbonate of soda solution. Blot well. Rub in the foam from a carpet shampoo solution such as 1001 Trouble Shooter Stain Remover containing deodoriser. Repeat until the stain has cleared. Rinse with warm water to which a few drops of antiseptic has been added. Blot well.

If any odour persists you can try using a deodorising product such as Neutrodol Carpet Deodorizer.

Fabrics

Remove any deposit and rinse well with cold water. Machine wash using a biological detergent if possible. Dry clean expensive or non-washable fabrics.

If any odour persists, try XO.

Upholstery

Scoop up the surface deposit and sponge the area with warm water. Blot dry. Try an upholstery cleaner or foam from a carpet shampoo. If any odour still persists you can try using XO.

WINE

Carpets

Sponge with sparkling water and blot to dry. Treat with a carpet shampoo and rinse well. If stains persist try a carpet spotting kit or Carpet Devils No 3 followed by shampooing.

Fabrics

Sponge fresh stains with white wine or sparkling water. Then follow with normal laundering.

Treat dried stains with Stain Devils Fruit and Wine Stain Remover or a hydrogen peroxide solution (one part 20-vol peroxide to six parts cold water). Follow by washing as normal.

Upholstery

Sponge the area with warm water and blot well. Treat with an upholstery shampoo or The Stain Slayer.

CREATIVE DIY

PAINTING & DECORATING

I t's never been easier or more fun to do your own decorating. All you need is a little imagination and some basic know-how to transform your home, help protect it – and save money too.

WHICH PAINT?

Every year sees the introduction of new, sophisticated paint finishes, such as solid emulsion, one-step gloss, environmentally-friendly 'green' paints, and tough sheens for kitchens and bathrooms.

With all these different and confusing products on the market, it may be a relief to know that there are only two main types of house paint: water based; and solvent based, which is traditionally, if not always accurately, called oil-based paint.

Water-based paints include emulsion, quick-drying eggshell and water-based gloss, while solvent-based paints range from traditional eggshell and gloss to durable sheen finishes and specialist lacquers or paints for metal. Some paints may have added ingredients such as vinyl, acrylic or polyurethane – to make them more durable or to increase coverage – but that doesn't alter their basic composition.

Water-based paints are ideal for walls and water-based eggshell or gloss can be used for most interior woodwork, while solvent-based paints are perfect for areas of hard wear: exterior as well as interior wood, and metal.

TIP Find out if a paint is water-based or solvent-based by reading the instructions given for thinning. If water is recommended, the paint will be water-based; if white spirit is advised, it's solvent-based.

PREPARATORY COATS

PRIMER

Primer seals absorbent surfaces and provides a key for the subsequent coats. Use it before painting bare timber, and when using gloss on bare metal. (Check the instructions to see if a special metal primer is required.) It's also possible to buy universal primer, for treating wood, plaster or metal.

Primer, undercoat and liquid gloss form the traditional three steps for painting wood but they are not always necessary today because you can buy combined primer/undercoat, which reduces the steps to two. Water-based primer (quick-drying primer or primer/undercoat) dries in around two hours. It's ideal for use indoors.

Plaster primer (primer/sealer) and stabilising solutions are used for walls that are porous or liable to flake.

Solvent-based primer can be used outside. In white or the traditional pink, it needs 12 hours to dry before you can apply undercoat.

Aluminium primer is ideal for resinous woods. For added protection, apply two coats, thinning the first with 10 per cent white spirit.

UNDERCOAT

Undercoat provides a smooth, solid-coloured base for liquid gloss. It's a solvent-based paint that is attractive in its own right, but has limited colours. It can chip, so if using without a gloss top coat, protect with clear varnish.

TIP For the best effect, buy the same brand of primer, undercoat and gloss. They're designed to be used together.

EMULSION PAINT

Emulsion is the first choice for walls. It's a water-based paint, and normally contains vinyl, which makes it durable and easy to clean. It can be used on most sound, already painted surfaces.

If the area to be painted was previously covered with a different kind of paint, it may need some preparation. Sand gloss or eggshell surfaces lightly to provide a 'key' for the new coat. Varnish must be stripped completely.

Old-fashioned treatments like distemper and whitewash must be washed off before you can start. You're unlikely to encounter these today but you'll know if you do because new paint won't adhere to them.

DESIGN TIPS

'Warm' colours (red, yellow, orange) appear to bring surfaces closer. Use them for cool north- or east-facing rooms, high ceilings (especially effective if you continue the paint down to picture rail level), and the end wall in a long passage.

'Cool' colours (blue, green, lilac) make surfaces look further away. Use them in warm, south- and west-facing rooms and in small areas.

Depth of colour can be used to modify the effect of warm and cool tones. Dark shades, which absorb light, seem to advance, while pastels, which reflect it, appear to recede.

Lose unwanted features such as cupboards, radiators and pipes by painting them the same colour as the wall. If you want to highlight features, use a contrasting colour.

COLOUR AND LIGHT

Artificial light can alter the effect of the colours you choose, so it's worth looking at samples at night as well as in daylight.

Standard tungsten light bulbs emphasise red tones but reduce blue and green, making colours look yellower than by day.

Fluorescent light can bring out blues and reduce shadows. Look for 'warm' fluorescents, which are much closer to natural light.

Halogen lamps have a bright white light and colours may look harsher.

Reflected light is softer. Try using uplighters or spotlights that bounce light off the ceiling or wall.

Emulsion paint can be applied directly to new plaster or plasterboard, but it's best to first apply a 'mist' coat diluted with water to improve coverage. Modern emulsion is quick-drying: allow two to four hours between coats.

TYPES OF EMULSION

There is a range of different consistencies and finishes for a variety of purposes.

Consistencies

Roller or solid emulsion paint (rather a misnomer, because it's more like cream cheese) is sold in trays for use with a roller. As it's virtually spatter-free, it's perfect for ceilings and stair-wells but more expensive than buying paint in tins.

'One-coat' emulsions are opaque enough to cover in a single application.

Flexible emulsion is designed to cover any hairline cracks.

Finishes

Matt finish gives a soft, velvety look, and is ideal for concealing flaws in plaster or uneven walls. It will wipe clean, but take care, because if you rub too hard it starts to shine.

Silk finish has a delicate sheen that can highlight patterns on textured wall coverings but may also emphasise flaws.

Soft sheen is easier to clean than matt but is less shiny than silk finish.

Textured emulsion gives a random rippled effect. Like flexible emulsion, it will conceal flawed plaster, though it won't cover wide cracks, and it can be difficult to remove.

TIP Use emulsion paint rather than solvent-based paint or wallpaper on new plaster. Emulsion allows water to pass through as the plaster dries out.

PAINTS FOR WOODWORK

GLOSS PAINTS

Gloss paint is the traditional choice for wood and metalwork.

All solvent-based gloss has a high shine but for a truly mirror-like finish, it's best to opt for the liquid paint used over undercoat, a system favoured by professional decorators, especially for outside use. The one-coat non-drip formula designed for DIY use is much easier to apply, but sometimes brush marks are difficult to avoid. Self-undercoating gloss has added colour, and can be used over primer or paint.

Water-based acrylic gloss has more of a sheen than a shine. It's often recommended for use in children's rooms, because it's not toxic – completely lead and solvent free. Some acrylic gloss can be used outside, but check the tin before using it.

EGGSHELL PAINTS

Eggshell is a versatile sheen finish usually sold for indoor woodwork, though it can also be used on walls for a uniform look.

Solvent based

Traditional eggshell is solvent based but because it can be difficult to apply, it's sometimes re-formulated for domestic use and sold under another name: 'Satinwood' is one common example.

It has a rich sheen but is less shiny than gloss paint. It's ideal for metal, interior woodwork and walls in areas of hard wear or condensation, because it can virtually be scrubbed clean and seals the wall from damp. (Before painting bare plaster, apply a plaster primer.)

There are drawbacks, however, because it's expensive over a large area and the sheen will emphasise every possible irregularity in the wall. Traditional solvent-based eggshell can also produce troublesome fumes, but this is less of a problem now than it used to be with new, low-odour varieties.

PAINT SAFETY

- Solvent-based paint is flammable, so store it outside the house, but protected from frost and damp.
- Fumes from solvent-based gloss and eggshell are unpleasant so make sure the room is cool and well ventilated before you start painting.
- Lead is no longer added to paint, although a tiny amount exists naturally in gloss, solvent-based primer and undercoat. If you want to avoid it entirely, use water-based paints.

Water based

Newer 'quick-drying', 'green' or 'kitchen and bathroom' eggshell paints are water based and are effectively emulsions.

It may be best to use water-based eggshell on walls, as it has less shine and doesn't give off fumes like solvent-based paints.

Water-based eggshell is ideal for most purposes indoors, but shouldn't be used on wood outdoors.

WOOD STAIN AND VARNISH

WOOD STAINS

Wood stains designed for use indoors are more decorative than protective, so cover them with two or more coats of clear varnish. Some products offer a degree of protection, but will still need varnishing in areas of heavy wear, such as skirtings, chairs or table tops.

Wood stains are designed to penetrate the wood and can only be removed with bleaching and sanding, so test the colour on an offcut or in an inconspicuous place before you start.

Stains for exterior use often contain a preservative to protect the timber and may not need varnishing. They include alternatives to creosote for use on rough-sawn wood such as fences and sheds, and mid-sheen finishes for planed wood on doors and window frames.

VARNISH

Varnish provides a clear, protective coating for paints and stains. It's available in matt, satin (mid-sheen) or high gloss finishes and in liquid or non-drip consistency. (Liquid varnish is difficult to apply so non-drip is much better for beginners.) A solvent-based product, it may have acrylic or polyurethane substances added for extra durability.

Yacht varnish is one of the most weather-resistant, but not all varnishes are suitable for use outside, or on floors, so check the label carefully before you buy.

Coloured varnish is available, usually in timber shades or occasionally in translucent tints, but when the top coat is chipped, the colour is removed too.

TIP Add a trace of white gloss paint to clear varnish, to stop it yellowing.

PAINTS FOR SPECIAL PURPOSES

Anti-condensation paint is an emulsion which insulates the wall, reducing the contrast in temperature that can cause condensation. It may contain glass particles and usually has a fungicide to prevent mould.

Anti-damp and anti-stain paints do not cure damp, but create a thick synthetic barrier that prevents damp marks and stain marks (from felt-tip pens, for example) from bleeding through to the surface. These paints are usually solvent based.

Bituminous paint is tar based. It will waterproof concrete and metal gutters but should not be covered by any other paint.

Enamel is a durable gloss available in smooth or hammered finishes and may contain metal particles. It is corrosion resistant and can be used on bare metal, though you may need to use a metal primer before applying it over existing paint.

It is ideal for household appliances, painting over tiles, or on china and glass, but you will need heat-resistant enamel for cookers and fireplaces and a special enamel for baths.

Enamel is expensive, which limits its use to small areas. Colours (such as hobby tins) are often bright, though the heat-resistant enamel sold for radiators is usually white or magnolia.

Flat oil paint, available from decorating specialists, is designed for use on walls, but because it is solvent based, should be used over undercoat. It has a matt, velvety effect but marks easily and is difficult to clean.

Floor paint is usually solvent based, though some designed for indoor use may be emulsions. These are relatively non-slip and resist abrasion.

Lacquer is a hard, gloss paint with a mirror-like shine. It's ideal for giving a colourful finish to doors, railings or furniture.

Microporous paints and stains are for outside use. They're designed to flex with the timber, keeping damp out but allowing the wood to 'breathe', but they won't work as well on previously painted surfaces. No primer or undercoat is needed, but preservative is required on bare wood.

Masonry paint is a tough emulsion for outside

walls, usually strengthened with nylon, chips of silica or sand, giving a textured effect.

Matt black paint is used for beams and blackboards. It's a solvent-based paint with minimal shine.

Stove black is a heat-resistant paint that will withstand temperatures of up to 390°F/200°C. Use it for grates and fire backs.

PREPARATION FOR PAINTING

Good preparation is essential, because paint and paper won't adhere to flaking surfaces and can magnify, rather than disguise, any flaws that are underneath. As a rule of thumb, allow two-thirds of your time for preparation and one-third for decoration. Clear the room as much as possible before you start, removing any light fittings and carpets if you can, and then covering anything that is left with several dust-sheets.

PAINT COVERAGE AND DRYING TIMES*

Type of paint	Area covered per litre	Touch dry	Re-coatable
Matt vinyl emulsion	12–14 sq m	2 hrs	4 hrs
Silk vinyl emulsion	12–14sq m	2 hrs	4 hrs
Soft sheen emulsion	13–15 sq m	2 hrs	4 hrs
Solid emulsion	11–13 sq	2 hrs	4 hrs
One-coat emulsion	10 sq m	2 hrs	4 hrs
Flexible emulsion	7–9 sq m	2 hrs	4 hrs
Textured emulsion	5–7 sq m	2 hrs	4 hrs
Water-based satin	14–16 sq m	2 hrs	4 hrs
Eggshell **	15–17 sq m	12 hrs	16 hrs
Liquid gloss	16–17 sq m	12 hrs	16 hrs
Non-drip gloss	10–12 sq m	1-3 hrs	5–6 hrs***
Water-based gloss	14–16 sq m	2 hrs	4 hrs
Self-undercoat gloss	10–12 sq m	2 hrs	4 hrs
Undercoat	15–17 sq m	8 hrs	12 hrs
Masonry paint	6–10 sq m	1 hr	4 hrs

* Coverage varies with the brand and absorbency of the surface.   ** Solvent-based
Times depend on moderate, dry conditions   *** Normally only one coat required

HOW TO FILL CRACKS

1 Open up small cracks with a putty knife or the end of a screwdriver to make them easier to fill.

2 Dampen with a small paintbrush dipped in water to clean out the crack and remove the dust.

3 Apply filler (available ready-mixed or in powder form) with a narrow-bladed filling knife, pushing it deeply into the crack so it fills it completely and leaving it raised above the level of the wall. (Deep cracks must be filled in layers, leaving each to dry before you add the next.)

4 When dry, sand the area down until it's flush with the wall and wipe clean.

Choose a flexible sealant for cracks between walls and window or door frames, which may expand or contract. If you use ordinary filler, the crack may open again.

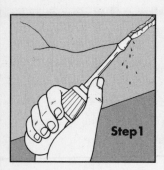 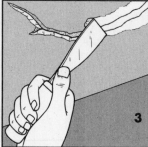 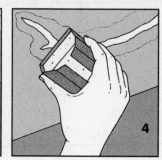

Keep a pair of old shoes for the job, and leave them by the door of the room being painted when you finish. This will help prevent treading paint and dust through the house when you leave the room.

Walls

If the walls are in good condition, simply wash them with a detergent solution, rinse and allow to dry.

If the walls are damp, you'll need to find the cause and tackle it before you decorate. Then wash any mould away with a solution of one part bleach to four parts water, leave for two days, and rinse.

TIP Wash walls from the bottom up, to prevent dirty streaks running down and making the task more difficult.

TIP To find the cause of damp, tape a piece of aluminium foil over the patch and leave for a week. After this period, if the outer surface of the foil is wet, the cause is probably condensation. If the foil is moist on the underside, the cause might be rising damp (from a faulty damp proof course) or penetrating damp, from walls that need re-pointing on the outside.

Lift off any patches of flaking plaster, fill dents and cracks, and sand until the repairs are level with the rest of the wall. Don't forget to sand any runs in old paintwork and lightly sand all over walls covered with eggshell or solvent-based paint to provide a key for the next coat. Apply a stabilising solution to powdery plaster, plaster primer to new plaster if necessary, and allow to dry.

WOODWORK

Remove all the door furniture (handles, finger plates and so on) and scrape old putty back from the window frames before you start.

If the paintwork is sound, simply sand the surface slightly to provide a key for the new coat, then clean with white spirit. Any blistered or flaking paint should be scraped back and sanded level with the surround.

New wood and bare patches must be primed before painting to seal the surface. This includes the bottom edge of new doors and any deep cracks.

Cracks should be stopped with flexible filler, but choose a wood filler and stain it to the shade you require if you intend to varnish natural wood.

Treat knots with knotting solution, to prevent resin seeping through and spoiling the new paint. If a knot does bleed through later, sand down to the bare wood, treat with the solution, and then prime before repainting.

TIP Silicon carbide sanding paper can be used dry, or wet, to keep down dust. Wrap it round a sanding block – an offcut of wood will do – for ease of use.

Stripping wood

There are several ways of stripping old paint or varnish from wooden surfaces:

Chemical wood stripper comes in liquid form; or as a paste or gel, which are ideal for ornate or vertical surfaces such as chair legs or banisters. The process takes time (from 15 minutes to 8 hours) and may need repeating.

Hot-air guns soften paint, making it easier to remove. Work from the bottom up to make the most of rising heat, and wear gloves to protect your hands.

Sanding can be done by hand, or with an electric orbital or belt sander. Drills may have disc sander attachments, which are suitable for rough work but won't give a fine finish.

Dry stripping is done with a shavehook (a small triangular, or combined straight and curved-edge scraper). You will also need a wide-bladed stripping knife to remove flaking paint. These tools are also useful to shift paint loosened by chemical or heat stripping.

Take care when stripping old paintwork. It may contain lead, which should not be released into the atmosphere. If the paint is very old and thick, take professional advice; otherwise use chemical stripper and always wear a mask.

PAINTING EQUIPMENT

BRUSHES

Brushes should have natural hog's-hair bristles, which pick up more paint than cheaper materials. Look for bristles that don't moult (run them through your hands a few times) and are tapered at the ends for a smooth finish – especially important when painting with eggshell and gloss.

Buy a range of widths (1, 2 and 3in/25, 50 and 75mm) for wood and metalwork, plus ¾in/19mm angled cutting-in brush for painting the edge of the wall and a ½in/12 mm brush for the glazing bars on windows. If you want to paint the walls with a brush, choose a 4in/100mm wall brush, but make sure it's not too tiring to use.

ROLLERS

Rollers vary in width from 7–12in/175–300mm and come with a single frame (one end attached to the handle) or double (attached at both sides). A single-frame roller is easier to manipulate, especially in corners, but a double-frame roller helps you to exert even pressure – useful when painting ceilings or using an extension handle.

Roller sleeves made from lamb's wool (real or synthetic) are good for use with most paints, especially matt emulsion. Use on rough or textured surfaces. Mohair sleeves, which have a fine pile, are ideal for smooth surfaces with eggshell, silk emulsion and solid emulsion paint. Foam rollers are available, sometimes textured to create special effects. Although they are cheap, they tend to spatter. You'll also find small rollers especially designed for painting behind radiators.

PAINT PADS

Paint pads are easy to use but a fine finish can be difficult to achieve. They're available in sizes from an extra-wide 8in/200mm to a narrow 1in/25mm sash pad for windows. Like rollers, they're best for use on walls.

PAINT RECEPTACLES

Paint trays are sold with both rollers and paint pads. Most have ribs for removing excess paint.

A paint kettle is ideal for decanting liquid paint. Line it with some foil to keep it clean and buy an old-fashioned S hook to hang it up by.

TIP Strain any lumpy liquid paint through a stocking, or tie one loosely over the top of the tin so that it acts as a filter when you dip in the brush.

TIP Jam the paint-tin lid on hard when you've finished painting and store the tin upside down, to prevent a skin forming.

WAYS WITH BRUSHES

- Hold a wide brush by the stock – the part that joins the bristles to the handle; hold a narrow one like a pencil.
- When dipping the brush into the paint, only cover half of the bristle area with emulsion, one-third with gloss. Remove the surplus by pressing the bristles against the side of the tin, not the rim, where paint may dry and lumps may fall into the tin, causing problems in the paint later.

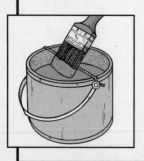

- Tie a length of string tautly across the opening of a paint kettle or paint tin, so you can wipe excess paint off the brush as you lift it out of the paint.

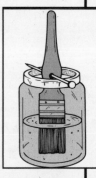

- For easy cleaning of a brush used with solvent-based paints, drill a hole through the handle of the brush and push a long nail through. Suspend it in a jar of white spirit.
- When you take a break from painting, wrap brushes in clingfilm so they don't dry out.
- As soon as you stop for the day, clean brushes in detergent for water-based paints, or white spirit for solvent-based paints. (Check the manufacturer's instructions.) Pat dry with kitchen paper.
- Store flat, or hang from a hole in the handle. Use a rubber band to keep all the bristles together neatly.

PAINTING A ROOM

ORDER OF PAINTING

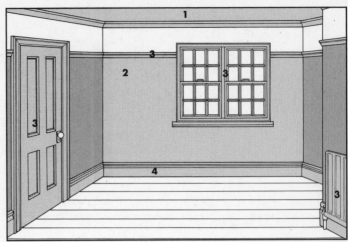

The following steps are the most orderly way to paint a room, and will avoid any drips or spills of one colour or type of paint on another.

1 Paint the ceiling. If there is a ceiling rose or other mouldings, give them an initial coat of paint and complete after finishing the ceiling.

2 Paint the walls, working away from the light source.

3 Paint window frames, picture rail (if any), radiators and doors.

4 Paint the skirting.

PAINTING A CEILING

Working with your arms above your head can be tiring, so choose a roller or paint pad for fast coverage and, if you can find the colour you want, use solid emulsion (roller paint), which makes less mess. Using extension handles makes access easier but can also affect the way you control the roller. You may find that it is better to work from a plank between two sets of step ladders, but before you start, do make sure that they are stable.

ORDER OF PAINTING

1 Paint a narrow strip around the perimeter of the ceiling where the roller won't reach, using a narrow 'cutting in' brush.

2 Paint a wider strip parallel to one edge with a wide brush, paint pad or roller, leaving a small gap.

3 When you come to the end of the run, reverse the direction and use the brush, pad or roller to fill in the gap. Go over it again lightly to blend in the paint if you find that this is necessary.

4 Recharge with more paint and then start a new line, again leaving a small gap, and continue painting until the ceiling is complete.

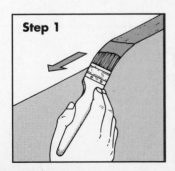

Step 1

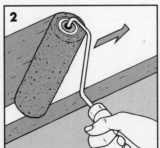

2

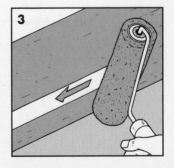

3

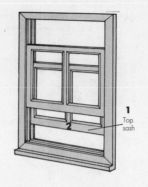

PAINTING WINDOWS

When protecting the glass with masking tape, let the paint overlap on to the glass by a millimetre to form a protective seal.

Casement (side opening) windows

1 Paint any glazing bars on the fixed window.
2 Paint the opening window, except for the outside edge which should match the exterior.
3 Paint the window frame and sill.

Sash windows

1 Open the window until the bottom sash and top sash overlap by about 8in/20cm.
2 Paint the bottom of the top sash.
3 Close the bottom sash and pull up the top sash so it's almost closed.
4 Paint the rest of the top sash.
5 Paint the bottom sash.
6 Paint the frame, taking great care to avoid getting paint on the sash cords.

PAINTING PANELLED DOORS

1 Remove door 'furniture' (eg, handles, knobs and key plates, etc).
2 Paint the mouldings, if any.
3 Paint the panels.
4 Paint the vertical strips in the centre.

5 Paint the horizontals.
6 Paint the sides, edges and frame.

For the best effect, the outside edge of the door should match the paintwork of the room it opens into.

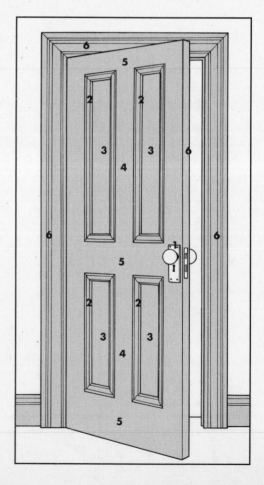

PAINTING WOODWORK

When painting wood, brush along the grain. On a narrow area, a single movement will be enough to cover it, but with wide areas, apply paint in parallel bands, reloading the brush before painting each strip. Aim for a smooth flowing movement for even coverage. After painting the second band, paint across the grain to join the two strips. 'Lay off' with light strokes along the grain for a smooth finish. Use two coats of undercoat when covering a dark base – cheaper than an extra coat of gloss.

TIP Make a 'tack rag' – a lint-free cloth moistened with a small amount of white spirit – to erase any mistakes.

VARNISHING WOODWORK

If covering a previously varnished or stained surface, sand and clean it. If varnishing bare wood or bare cork, apply a base coat thinned with 10 per cent white spirit.

Dip the brush into the tin of varnish so that half the bristle area is covered, and apply it along the grain, brushing out across the grain from the wet edge for even coverage. There's no pigment in varnish to disguise mistakes so take care to brush out overlaps and brush marks. Finish by brushing along the grain again with a single smooth stroke.

If more than one coat is needed, lightly sand with very fine abrasive paper when dry and clean with white spirit between each coat.

WHAT WENT WRONG?

Blisters are often caused by painting damp wood. Allow the paint to harden, then prick the blister. If it's wet inside, you'll need to strip back and fill the grain before repainting.

Crazing is caused by applying a second coat before the first coat is dry. Allow to dry, then rub down and repaint.

Cratering comes from too much damp in the atmosphere. Sand and repaint, keeping the room warm and dry.

Flaking paint is caused by powdery or dirty walls underneath the new coat, or gloss paint that hasn't been sanded. Emulsion paint often flakes off woodwork and radiators, so rub it down and repaint with a coat of solvent-based eggshell or gloss.

Runs come from overloading the brush. If there are only one or two, allow the paint

to dry completely and then prick, rub down and touch in with a small paintbrush. Otherwise sand and start again.

Show through of what was originally underneath needs an additional top coat (emulsion) or an undercoat plus a new top coat (gloss).

Specks and stray bristles can be avoided if both wall and paint are clean and you use quality brushes. Either sand down and start again or, in a small area, sand or pick out the pieces, rub with wet abrasive paper and touch in. This also works for insects that have been trapped in wet paint.

Uneven coverage may occur if you try to spread paint too thinly or fail to prime large patches of filler or bare plaster. These are more absorbent than the rest of the wall and so take in more paint than primed areas.

SPECIAL PAINT EFFECTS

Fashions in decorating are always changing. Plain walls will be popular one year, patterns the next. At present, the trend is towards plains, but decorative paint finishes have the advantage of camouflaging defects and adding interest without defined pattern. You can buy special textured rollers that add a design for you, but it's often just as easy to use traditional materials. Here's what to do.

WALLS

Colour washing

This treatment gives a translucent finish.

Paint the wall with solvent-based eggshell (white will give a delicate effect) and leave to dry. For the top coat, mix 30 per cent transparent oil glaze with 50 per cent solvent-based eggshell and 20 per cent white spirit. If you want solid cover and a formal effect, use it straight; for a more casual, random effect, apply with a wall brush, moving it in all directions and leaving some areas uncovered to vary the depth of colour. Repeat when dry, covering the entire wall, still using criss-cross brush strokes.

You can protect the finish with a coat of polyurethane varnish in areas of hard wear but this will need to be removed when repainting.

TIP A similar effect can be achieved with emulsion paint. Paint the wall and leave to dry, then apply two coats of emulsion thinned with water, following the instructions on the tin. Use a wall brush, not a roller, and apply the paint with a random movement.

Best for cottagey living rooms, dining rooms and bedrooms.

Dragging

This needs solvent-based eggshell for the base coat and a top coat made up of 70 per cent transparent oil glaze, 20 per cent eggshell and 10 per cent white spirit, which is applied in bands about an arm's length wide. After painting each band, pull a dragging brush through the paint from the top of the wall down.

Best for formal living rooms, studies, halls and bedrooms.

Sponging

An easy technique with emulsion paint, although solvent-based eggshell, which takes longer to dry, gives more time to create an effect. For the best results, use related colours, sponging the deeper colour over the paler one or vice versa. (Use three colours if you want a more elaborate effect.)

Pour a little paint into a saucer and apply with a natural sea sponge in a random direction, turning the sponge from time to time, until the wall is covered. You can use rags instead of a sponge if you prefer, choosing a textured cloth like stockinette or cheesecloth for greater definition.

TRANSPARENT OIL GLAZE

Also called scumble glaze, transparent oil glaze is essential for many paint treatments, especially those that take time to create, because it slows drying. It's available from specialist decorators and is often combined with solvent-based eggshell paint and white spirit as a top coat. A standard mix would be 70 per cent transparent oil glaze, 20 per cent eggshell and 10 per cent white spirit.

TIP Use solvent-based eggshell or acrylic emulsion paint in bathrooms for harder wear.

Best for bedrooms and bathrooms.

Rag rolling

This needs a base coat of solvent-based eggshell and a top coat made from 70 per cent transparent oil glaze, 20 per cent eggshell and 10 per cent white spirit. This is brushed on in vertical bands and rolled off with rags twisted into a sausage-shape, working from the top of the wall down.

Best for dining rooms and bedrooms.

Stippling

The subtlest way of producing broken colour. Paint the wall with solvent-based eggshell and, when dry, apply with a special stippling brush a top coat made from 70 per cent transparent oil glaze, 20 per cent eggshell, and 10 per cent white spirit. Keep the bristles at right angles to the wall, and wipe them from time to time so they don't become clogged.

You can also stipple walls by painting narrow (20in/50cm) strips of the top coat from top to bottom and then removing colour by using a clean, dry stippling brush.

TIP For speed, pour the top coat into a roller tray and apply with a stiff brush.

Best for all around the house.

Stencilling

Stencilling can create attractive borders and decorative motifs. Cutting your own stencils takes practice, so it's easiest to use ready-made stencils, available from most DIY superstores and decorating shops as well as specialist suppliers. Whatever you choose, start with relatively simple designs, especially if you're stencilling a border, which can be time-consuming. Add variety by reversing the stencil from time to time, but to avoid smudges, remember to wipe it clean before you turn it over.

Use a stubby stencil brush and dab colour into the stencil until the design is filled in. You can use a variety of paints, from standard emulsion or eggshell (use solvent-based on woodwork) to acrylic or spray paint; special crayons are also available.

TIP Fix the stencil in place with masking tape or spray photo-mount, not Blu-Tak, which leaves a gap between the stencil and the wall and may lead to runs.

Best for borders, ceiling decorations, and motifs on furniture.

Murals

Murals can be painted in sections using simple picture-book designs.

Draw a grid over the original picture and number the squares, then draw a similar grid, the size of the finished mural, on the wall. Copy the outline of the design into each square, using chalk or soft pencil, then fill in, using one colour at a time and working from the top down. Rub off the grid marks when the mural is dry.

Best for passages and children's bedrooms.

WOODWORK

Bambooing

This decorative effect looks wonderful on turned wood as well as on bamboo furniture that has seen better days.

Paint with three coats of yellow-brown solvent-based eggshell and mottle the top coat with a rag while the paint is still damp. When dry, draw circles of brown paint at intervals with a narrow brush. Paint a second, narrower and darker brown circle inside the first, followed by a final dark brown ring in the centre. You can also add the tiny spots and the V-shaped tail typical of natural bamboo.

Best for decorative pieces made from bamboo, cane or turned wood.

Colour rubbing

This gives a faded, weathered look. It involves brushing a milky glaze or a thin wash of water-based paint over the surface and then removing the excess before it dries, to highlight mouldings or emphasise the grain.

Alternatively, apply a base coat of solvent-based eggshell or wipe the bare wood with white spirit, and make a glaze from 75 per cent transparent oil glaze, 20 per cent solvent-based eggshell and 5 per cent white spirit. Brush this into the surface so that all the crevices are filled, and when it becomes tacky, rub along the grain with a soft cloth.

Best for doors, decorative fireplaces and floors (but not floors subject to hard wear).

Liming

Liming turns wood an attractive silvery grey. Professionals use specialist products such as white shellac and liming wax, but you can achieve a similar look in the following way.

Paint a base with white eggshell and allow to dry. Mix together 70 per cent transparent oil glaze, 20 per cent putty-coloured eggshell and 10 per cent white spirit. Brush this over the base coat, then tie a rag over a steel comb and drag over it from top to bottom. Finish by combing without a rag, using medium and fine combs. When dry, protect the finish with varnish, if needed.

TIP To vary the look, comb the sides only and leave a darker, rippled panel in the centre.

TIP For a verdigris look, paint a coat of turquoise eggshell over grey and drag the surface while still wet. Or, for a characteristic limed finish, try colour rubbing along the grain with grey-white paint.

Best for floors and doors.

Marbling

Paint with off-white solvent-based eggshell and, when dry, add a top coat made from 30 per cent transparent oil glaze, 50 per cent bone colour eggshell and 20 per cent white spirit. Dab with a rag to soften the effect and, while still wet, trace in the marble 'veins' in dark grey, using an artist's paint brush. Blur the lines with a special softening brush (or improvise with a rag) for a natural effect.

Best for table tops and floors.

Woodgraining

A way to make chipboard and pine look like oak or mahogany. Give softwood and fibreboard a coat of wood filler thinned to the consistency of single cream, and sand when dry. Repeat this step, then paint with primer, undercoat and solvent-based red-brown eggshell.

Mix several small batches of 60 per cent transparent oil glaze, 20 per cent eggshell and 20 per cent white spirit in progressively deeper shades of brown. Apply along the grain, starting with the lightest colour, using a comb or a special graining brush, and blur for a natural effect with a cloth or softening brush. Finish with button polish or polyurethane.

Best for small pieces of furniture, hand rails and panelling.

EXTERIOR PAINTING

Paint helps protect your home from wind, rain and sun. That is why the outside needs redecorating about every four years, or more often if you live near the sea or in an industrial area. It's best to paint at the end of the summer, when wood has had a long period in which to dry out.

Choose bright, still days if you can, following the sun on the house so that the paint is dried, but avoid painting in full sunlight or when it's windy. It's dangerous to use a ladder in high winds, and paint splashes on walls, caused by wind, can be very difficult to remove.

PREPARATION FOR PAINTING

- Tie back climbing plants.
- Check the state of roof and guttering and repair any leaks.
- Check for rot on fascias and barge-boards beneath the eaves, windows, doors (especially the base) and decorative wood. Replace where necessary, or repair by scraping back to sound wood, removing flaking paint and filling any cracks with exterior stopper.
- If rendering is falling apart, cut it back until you reach the part that is sound, then clean it and patch with mortar. Large areas will need professional attention.
- Clean out defective pointing and fill large cracks with ready-mixed mortar, small ones with exterior filler.
- To remove dirt on painted walls, brush with a stiff brush from the top down. Treat mould with one part bleach to four of water. Leave for two days and then brush the mould away with a stiff brush. Apply stabilising solution to flaky patches.
- Replace any cracked window panes and leave for two weeks before painting the frame,

because the putty needs time to harden. Fill gaps between the wall and window frame with flexible exterior filler.
- Scrape metal downpipes and gutters and clean with a wire brush to remove flaking paint. Apply anti-rust primer to any rusty patches that remain. Sand sound paintwork lightly to provide a key.
- Remove peeling paint from window frames and fill and prime where necessary.
- Strip peeling varnish to the bare wood, sand, and apply a sealer coat of varnish thinned with white spirit.
- Clean, sand and dust off sound paintwork.

ORDER OF PAINTING

1 Paint fascias, barge-boards and gutters.
2 Paint walls in sections, starting in a corner and working from top to bottom.
3 Paint downpipes.
4 Paint windows and doors.

PAINTING WOOD AND METALWORK

Use gloss paint or stains on wood and gloss on metal. It's important to make sure they are suitable for outdoor use. In most cases, this means using a solvent-based paint, which is

LADDER SAFETY

Ladders should be placed at ground level 3ft/1m away from the wall for every 4yds/4m of height. The top of the ladder should overlap the highest point and should be tied in place if possible. Secure at the base with a sandbag, or tie it to wooden pegs knocked into the ground. If the ground is soggy, place the ladder on a board to make sure it's secure.

A tower platform, available from hire shops, makes exterior decorating easier if your house is large, but never climb down the side, which will unbalance it. Special designs are available for chalet bungalows, wide bay windows or houses that have roofs on several levels.

more weather resistant. But although paint systems especially designed for exterior use may specify two coats of undercoat plus one of liquid gloss for maximum durability, it's often possible to use non-drip one-coat products too – check the recommendations on the tin. Start from the top and work down, placing a piece of board behind downpipes to protect the wall from the paint.

PAINTING WALLS

Before you start, wrap downpipes in polythene or newspaper to protect them from paint splatters and cover plants and paths with plastic sheeting. Start by 'cutting in' – painting a narrow strip – next to barge-boards, doors and windows. Change to a wide wall brush for small

areas, a long-pile roller for large ones, and apply the masonry paint with a criss-cross movement. Work from the top down in bands about an arm's length in width, and overlap each strip when you move on, for even coverage. Don't lean out too far when working at height.

WALLPAPER

Wallpaper is the fastest way to add texture or a floor-to-ceiling pattern to a room. In addition to traditional wallpaper, you'll find paper-backed vinyl, relief papers designed as a base for paint, and a range of textiles from silk to grasscloth. Some are much easier to hang than others, so if you're a novice at wallpaper hanging, look for a medium-weight traditional wallpaper with a random design, which is unlikely to tear and won't need pattern matching. To avoid getting paint marks or splatters on the papered wall, make sure all the painting is completed before you paper.

DESIGN TIPS

- Large patterns seem to reduce space, while small patterns on a light ground, which give a sense of 'looking through' the design, appear to increase it.
- Stripes look best on even walls and walls where a picture rail or cornice provides a break between wall and ceiling.
- Small random patterns and textured designs may help disguise poor plaster.

TIP Coat plaster walls with 'size' made from wallpaper paste (you'll find instructions on the packet) to make it easier to guide the wallpaper into place.

WHICH WALLPAPER?

Lining paper provides a smooth base for wallpaper or paint. It's available in several weights: light (for covering with paint), medium (suitable for most wallpaper) and heavy (for use beneath relief wall coverings). Ideally it should be hung horizontally, so the joints don't coincide with those of the wallpaper on top.

Textured wallpapers can act as a base for paint. They include embossed designs, such as Anaglypta; high relief wall coverings, which have a more pronounced design and are made from paper plus cotton or clay, or vinyl; and woodchip, used for disguising uneven plaster, made from sawdust and woodchips bonded on to paper.

Printed wall coverings range from expensive, untrimmed, hand-printed designs, to cheap wall coverings where the pattern is printed direct on to paper. In between come papers with a coloured ground, and vinyl wall coverings with a paper backing, which is left behind when the surface is stripped. Because the pattern is printed directly on to the vinyl layer, they're usually more water resistant than washable wallpapers, which all have a clear coating.

WALLPAPER SYMBOLS

Symbol	Meaning	Symbol	Meaning
~	Spongeable	→∣∘	Free match
≈	Washable	→∣←	Straight match
≋	Super-washable	→∣. ←	Off-set match (half drop)
▤	Scrubbable	$\frac{50}{25}$ cm	Design repeat distance off-set
☼	Sufficient light fastness	▮	Duplex (layered)
☼	Good light fastness		
⌐	Strippable	〰	Co-ordinated fabric available
⌐	Peelable (leaves backing)	∣	Direction of hanging
⌣	Ready-pasted		
▮▬	Paste the wall	∥	Reverse alternate lengths

Textile wall coverings include paper-backed cork, hessian, grasscloth and silk, and flocked wallpapers, which are made from paper plus silk, cotton or wool, or vinyl and nylon. Because they're expensive, difficult to manipulate and liable to stain if adhesive comes into contact with the surface, all but the cheapest hessians and vinyl flocks should be professionally hung.

TIP Make sure all the rolls of wallpaper have the same batch number, because colours may vary between printings.

TIP Buy an extra roll of wallpaper and keep it for future repairs.

PREPARATION FOR WALLPAPERING

Any lumps and bumps on the walls are likely to show through wallpaper just as they do through paint, so walls should be filled and sanded smooth. Old wallpaper should be stripped away because it's rarely a satisfactory surface for the new layer. Wrinkles will be repeated, colour may bleed through, and the weight of the new paper may pull it all away from the wall.

Stripping wallpaper

1 Vinyls and paper-backed wallpapers are often designed for dry stripping, which means they can be peeled away from the backing. Try lifting a corner and pulling upwards and outwards. The backing can be used as lining paper if it's in good condition, especially if you intend to paint over the top or want to cover it with heavy wallpaper.

2 To remove standard wallpaper, first turn off the electricity at the mains. Then wet the wallpaper with detergent solution, working from the top of the wall down so the water runs over the wallpaper, giving it a chance to penetrate. (Be careful not to over-wet if you're working on plasterboard.)

3 If the wallpaper is coated or overpainted, you'll probably need to scrape the surface with a wire brush before wetting it to improve absorbency. Leave it to soak before you try to remove the wallpaper.

4 It's often worth hiring or buying a steam wallpaper stripper, which can speed things up if there are several layers of paper to remove.

5 Using a scraper with a wide blade, start at the seams and base. With luck, you'll be able to remove a sizeable strip of wallpaper, but try not to damage the wall beneath, as any chips will need to be filled.

When all the paper has been removed, finish by sanding lightly to remove any small pieces of paper still stuck to the walls.

PLANNING PAPERING

Ideally you should start in a corner and work away from the light so that the joins between lengths are less noticeable. Before you start, it's

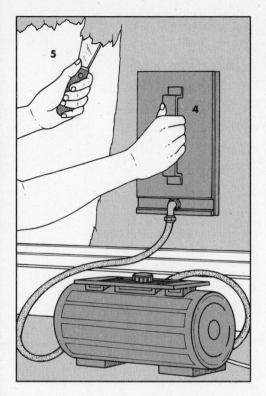

- Standard wallpaper paste (available as powder or ready-mixed) is suitable for light and medium-weight wallpapers but heavy wallpaper needs a heavy-duty paste.
- Vinyls and plastic-coated wallpapers need a fungicidal adhesive to prevent any mould forming.

- Plumb bob and line
- Ruler or tape measure
- Seam roller (to press down wallpaper edges)
- Wallpaper paste and bucket

1 Using paper-hanger's shears, cut sufficient drops for about a wall at a time, adding 2–3in/5–7.5cm to the length of each drop to allow for trimming at the ceiling and skirting, and matching the pattern as you go. (If there's a substantial pattern repeat, drops will vary in length.)

2 Roll the lengths against the curl to flatten them and then turn them over so that the pasting side is uppermost.

3 Mix the paste as instructed and brush it down the centre of the wallpaper with a pasting brush. (Tie a taut string across the bucket to remove excess paste from the brush.) Brush the paste out from the centre, first away from you and then towards you, so that the edges are covered.

worth marking where the joins will fall and adjusting your starting point if lengths meet in a prominent place. As a rule, where there are no special features, and unless you are left-handed, start at the wall to the right of the main window and work round the room. However, if there is a chimney breast, paste the first length in the middle of it. Treat each half of the room separately, working towards the door and starting at the chimney breast again to paper the other side. This way, awkward joins can be minimised.

HOW TO HANG WALLPAPER

You will need

- Copydex or similar adhesive (for repairs)
- Paper-hanger's brush
- Paper-hanger's shears
- Paste brush
- Pasting table
- Pencil

Ready-pasted wall covering simply needs soaking in water in the trough provided and can be smoothed into place with a sponge. Apply Copydex to seams and edges if they have a tendency to lift.

4 Move the paper up and gently fold the paper over so the pasted surfaces meet. When you have pasted the whole drop, fold the other

HOW MUCH WALLPAPER DO YOU NEED?

Standard rolls of wallpaper measure about 11yd/10.05m long by 21in/530mm wide, but American and continental sizes may differ. The following chart is based on standard wallpaper.
Use it to work out the number of rolls you need.

Wall height from skirting	Distance round the room (inc doors and windows)																	
	30 feet / 9 metres	34 / 10	38 / 12	42 / 13	46 / 14	50 / 15	54 / 16	58 / 17	62 / 18	66 / 19	70 / 21	74 / 22	78 / 23	82 / 24	86 / 26	90 / 27	94 / 28	98 / 30
7–7½ ft/ 2.15–2.30m	4	5	5	6	6	7	7	8	8	9	9	10	10	11	12	12	13	13
7½–8ft/ 2.30–2.45m	5	5	6	6	7	7	8	8	9	9	10	10	11	11	12	13	13	14
8–8½ft/ 2.45–2.60m	5	5	6	7	7	8	9	9	10	10	11	12	12	13	14	14	15	15
8½–9ft/ 2.60–2.75m	5	5	6	7	7	8	9	9	10	10	11	12	12	13	14	14	15	15
9–9½ ft/ 2.75–2.90m	6	6	7	7	8	9	9	10	10	11	12	12	13	14	14	15	15	16
9½–10ft/ 2.90–3.05m	6	6	7	8	8	9	10	10	11	12	12	13	14	14	15	16	16	17
10–10½ ft/ 3.05–3.20m	6	7	8	8	9	10	10	11	12	13	13	14	15	16	16	17	18	19

Ceilings:
To calculate the number of rolls required, work out the area in square metres and divide by five.

side so that the top and bottom meet in the centre. (When papering stairways and ceilings, you may have to concertina the paper to paste the longest lengths.)

5 Vinyls can be put up straight away but you should leave standard wallpaper to soak for five minutes and heavier relief designs for ten (follow any instructions supplied with the rolls), so that the paper stretches and bubbles won't occur.

6 To make sure you hang the paper straight, find the vertical, using a plumb bob and line (a small weight on a string) as a guide (A). Mark a line 1in/25mm less than the wallpaper's width if you're starting at a corner (because you'll be turning this amount on to the adjacent wall) and hang the first piece of

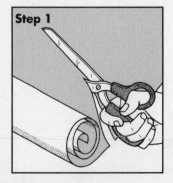

Step 1

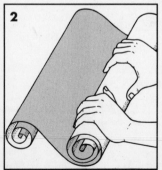

2

3

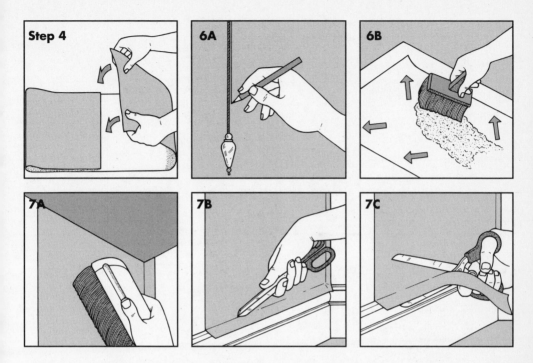

wallpaper, using this line as a guide, allowing about 2¾in/70mm to overlap on the ceiling and 1in/25mm to turn round the corner (B).

7 Manoeuvre the top half into place and smooth down with a paper-hanger's brush, pushing it well into the corner (A). Release the bottom half, lower gently (it may stretch if dropped) and smooth into place. Mark a fold at skirting and ceiling level with the shears and trim to fit.

8 Hang the next length so it butts tightly up to the first, because the paper will shrink as it dries. Leave for five minutes and then press into place with a seam roller.

TIP Use a seam roller with care on relief wallpaper as it may crush the design.

PATTERN MATCHING

Straight-match wallpapers line up horizontally.

Drop-match wallpapers require adjoining lengths to be moved up or down to match up.

Random (free-match) designs don't need to be pattern matched.

Pattern repeats can make a difference to the amount of wallpaper you need. Remember to allow extra when estimating quantity.

WHAT WENT WRONG?

Bubbles form if the wallpaper isn't pasted thoroughly or isn't given time to soak. They can also occur if the length isn't smoothed out properly. It's sometimes possible to slit air bubbles with a razor blade and paste the edges into place.

Dirty marks can usually be removed gently with a white eraser or some stale white bread.

Gaps can appear if lengths are not pushed together or if the paper has been stretched too much when smoothed out and has shrunk back when dry.

HANGING LINING PAPER

Hang lining paper horizontally, working from the top downwards and joining lengths edge to edge (butt-joining). Overlap by about ⅝–1in/15–25mm at the corners for a neat, strong finish and to take in any irregularities in the wall. Walls are rarely straight. You must do this or the paper may peel back from the wall where the edges meet.

Peeling is often caused by damp. If it's not substantial, trying lifting and re-pasting the edges with wallpaper paste or Copydex.

Tears may not be noticeable if they're stuck down carefully.

AWKWARD AREAS

Ceilings Paste the paper and fold into a concertina, then unfold as you press into place. Smooth down with a broom; this is best done by a partner walking behind you.

Corners Unless the gap between the previous length of paper and the corner of the room is very narrow, cut the last length on the wall so that it turns the corner by about 1in/25mm.

Find the vertical on the new wall and hang the first length on that wall so that it covers the overlap. External (convex) corners (on alcoves and chimney breasts for example) may need a larger overlap to make sure seams don't coincide with the exposed corners, where they will undoubtedly tear.

TIP 'Feather' relief papers to make the edge thinner by tearing the edge and press down with a seam roller to minimise bulk when overlapping a corner.

Stairways Start with the longest drop, marking the vertical by fixing a piece of chalked string from top to bottom of the stair well, and snapping it against the wall. Cut each length separately, matching the pattern and making sure that the length is sufficient to take in the angled skirting.

Window sills Pull the paper over the corner of the sill and slit it before smoothing the paper into place.

Fixings Insert matches to mark the site of screws or picture hangers and allow them to pierce through the wallpaper when you smooth it into place. Take care not to rip the wallpaper as you do this.

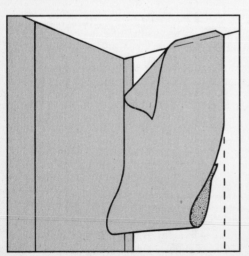

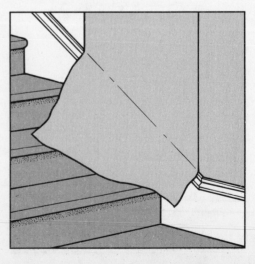

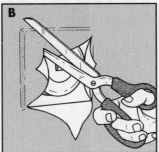
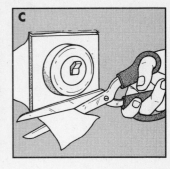

Light switches Turn off the electricity and remove the switch cover. Hang the wallpaper over the switch and smooth into place. Cut away a square of wallpaper ¼in/6mm less than the size of the switch, then replace the cover, tucking in the edges (A). If the switch projects, cut an X shape in the paper across it (B) and trim the wallpaper, leaving a small margin to overlap on to the sides of the cover (C). *Always* use this technique with foil wall coverings, which conduct electricity and must not be tucked under the switch cover.

BORDERS

Borders are available in wallpaper or ready-pasted vinyl, but though pasting techniques may differ, they are cut and fixed in more or less the same way.

You will need

Same equipment as for hanging wallpaper (page 155) plus
- Spirit-level

1 Mark the position of the border lightly in pencil, using a spirit level to find the horizontal. Then step back and see how it looks to the eye. It's sometimes better to have a border that follows the walls or ceiling than one that emphasises irregularities.

2 Cut the border, and paste or soak it.

3 Concertina the folds, matching pasted edge to pasted edge, and unwind carefully, smoothing into place as you go.

4 Butt join ends, making sure the pattern

HOW TO MITRE A BORDER

If you want to create a panelled look with wallpaper borders, you'll need to mitre the corners for a perfect right angle.

1 Find the right-hand vertical with a plumb bob and line and mark with a pencil, then paste a strip of border into place, allowing 1in/25mm more than the finished size.

2 Check the horizontal with a spirit level and smooth the border across the top of the panel into place, allowing another 1in/25mm overlap on the right-hand side.

3 Mitre the corner by placing a ruler across the diagonal from the outer to the inner edge and cut along this line with a trimming knife. Take off the surplus triangle on top, then peel back the horizontal border and remove the excess from beneath. Smooth the edges firmly into place.

OPENING UP A FIREPLACE

There are very few rooms that don't look better when a previously filled chimney breast is opened and the fireplace restored. The fireplace is the natural focal point of the room and the decorative impact it makes is well worth the sacrifice of wall space, even in quite small rooms.

Before you begin, look around for fireplaces that suit the style of your house. If you want an unusual design or one in a very small size, you may do best to look for authentic period pieces from specialists or architectural salvage firms. Alternatively, as grates and mantelpieces in good condition and a reasonable price can be difficult to find, you may find it easier to settle for a reproduction.

STEP-BY-STEP OPENING A FLUE

You will need
- Candle
- Hammer
- Bolster, or pointing chisel

1 Locate the chimney breast, which usually projects into the room but sometimes juts outside it. It may be covered by hardboard or plasterboard which are simple to remove, or it may be bricked in.

2 If the fireplace has been closed properly, you'll find an airbrick set into the wall to prevent damp. Insert the large chisel into the mortar surrounding it, and tap it with a hammer. Remove the airbrick carefully. If the fireplace has been filled with bricks and there is no airbrick, take out a few bricks about 12in/30cm from the floor.

3 Light a candle and place it the fireplace. If the flame is drawn upwards, the chimney is clear. If it goes out, ask a builder for advice.

4 If the chimney is clear, unblock the opening, taking care not to damage the lintel across the top of the fireplace.

5 Clean out the original fireplace and check that the fireback (which protects the wall from heat) is usable and not cracked, replacing it if necessary before you fit the new fireplace.

TIP   For safety, have the chimney swept before you light the fire.

WALL TILES

Tiles are waterproof, last for years and need little more care than a swift wipe over with detergent. They're ideal for walls that are likely to get wet or need protection from steam or grease, but because they last so long, it's worth while choosing colours and designs that won't date and will look good with a variety of colour schemes.

Most wall tiles are ceramic, though glass mirror tiles are available too. The most popular size is 6in/152mm square, though 4in/100mm square tiles and rectangular tiles (usually 8 x 4in/200 x 100mm, or 8 x 6in/200 x 152mm) hexagonal and Provençal shapes are also available.

Craftsman-made and continental tiles are often smaller and chunkier; that goes for borders and dados too and, as a result, it can be difficult to mix and match unless you're certain of the depth of the tiles you want to use. If you can't compare samples directly, it may be safer to choose all your tiles from the same range.

TYPES OF TILE

'Universal' tiles have at least two glazed edges so you can use them anywhere, turning the glazed edges to the outside when you reach the end of a run. Bevelled-edge universal tiles butt together leaving a space for the grout so you won't need to use spacers.

Field tiles have unglazed edges for use in the centre of a panel. They may be self-spacing, with lugs on each side.

Border or edge tiles have one or two rounded edges, to finish the outside of a panel.

Quadrant tiles are narrow rounded strips, used to top standard tiles.

TILING STEP BY STEP

You will need

- Grout
- Hammer
- Metal rule
- Nails or tacks
- Notched tile-adhesive spreader (often supplied with the tile adhesive)
- Pincers for cutting random shapes (if necessary)
- Plastic tile spacers or matchsticks (if necessary)
- Sand paper (for stripping the surface to be tiled in advance)
- Spirit-level
- Sponge
- Tile adhesive
- Tile file
- Tungsten carbide tile cutter
- Wooden battens

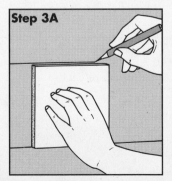

Step 3A

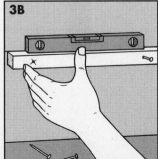

3B

4

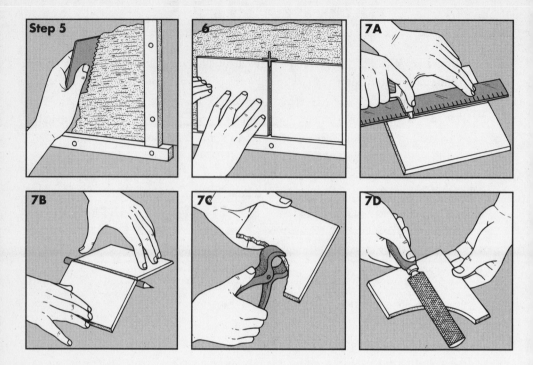

1 Wash down emulsion paint and sand solvent-painted surfaces to provide a key. Strip off all wallpaper before tiling.

TIP You can tile over old tiles if you rub down and seal with plaster primer to provide a key. You'll need a wooden strip or pieces of tile to conceal the double thickness at the top.

2 Work out where the cut tiles will fall. Have a 'dry run' and readjust if there are any very narrow pieces to cut at the end of a run. It's better to have two evenly cut tiles at each end.
3 Measure the distance of one tile up from the skirting or work-top (A) and find the true horizontal with a spirit-level (B). Mark with a pencil and nail or tack a slim wooden batten to the wall along this line.
4 Check the vertical with a spirit-level and fix a batten at the end of the last full row of tiles, to keep the tiles in line.
5 Starting in the corner where the battens meet, spread tile adhesive on to a square metre

of wall, combing it evenly with a spreader.
6 Press the tiles firmly into place without sliding them, inserting plastic spacers (to leave space for the grout) if necessary. Wipe off any adhesive on the surface of the tiles with a damp sponge as you go. Continue until all whole tiles have been fixed, checking the levels from time to time. Remove the battens when the adhesive is dry.
7 Now fix the cut tiles. Mark the cutting line

DESIGN TIPS

- Use a row of border tiles to create a frieze on a wall of plain tiles.
- Panels of patterned tiles can make long, high walls seem shorter.
- To show off the design on odd or antique tiles, set them into a window ledge.
- Tile well-used coffee tables for a water and heat-resistant finish.

CALCULATING THE NUMBER OF TILES NEEDED

Measure the area you want to tile and divide by the size of the tiles or use this ready reckoner if you are using standard sizes. Add 10 per cent for breakages.

Area	in:	4x4	6x6	4x8	12x12
	cm:	10x10	15x15	10x20	30x30
sq yd/					
sq m	**No tiles**				
1.1/1		100	44	50	12
2.2/2		200	87	100	23
3.3/3		300	130	150	34
4.4/4		400	174	200	45
5.5/5		500	217	250	56
6.6/6		600	260	300	67
7.7/7		700	303	350	78
8.8/8		800	347	400	89
9.9/9		900	390	450	100
11/10		1000	433	500	111

Per 1.1sq yd/1sq m:
Adhesive: 3⅓ lb/1.5kg/1 litre
Grout: 6oz/150g

on the tile and place it on a cutting board, right side up. Score through with a tungsten carbide cutter held against a metal rule (A). Place matchsticks or a pencil, depending on the tile's thickness, underneath the scored line and press firmly on each side. If you're lucky, the tile will snap evenly (B). For odd shapes, you will need to make a template and copy the shape on to the tile, nibbling away with pincers (C) and finishing with a tile file (D).

TIP Use pincers rather than a tile cutter to cut away a narrow strip at the edge of tile.

8 Fix cut tiles so that the smooth edge is next to the adjacent tile and the cut edge next to the work-top or skirting.
9 When tiling is complete, leave the adhesive to harden as instructed on the packet. Waterproof adhesive takes longer to dry. Mix the grout (or buy ready-mixed) and spread it over the gaps with a sponge, pushing it in well and wiping away the excess with a clean damp sponge. Neaten with your finger or a lolly stick just before the grout sets.

TIP Use flexible sealant between the tiles and bath or basin after you grout.

10 When dry, wipe with a damp sponge to remove the last traces of grout, and polish the tiles with a soft cloth.

TIP Don't rinse the sponges and cloths used for grouting under the tap. The grout residues may block the drain.

ALL ABOUT SHELVES

Shelves are the most flexible form of storage. Once you can put up a shelf, you'll have mastered the basic techniques needed for hanging everything from paintings and mirrors to wall cupboards. It's easy when you know how, as long as you make sure the shelf is absolutely level and choose suitable wall fixings so the brackets are secure.

It's wise to start by hanging a single decorative shelf rather than a floor to ceiling fitment, and if you've never used a drill before, to practise on different surfaces first, such as brick and wood.

WHICH SHELF?

Chipboard shelves can be finished with a layer of plastic laminate, like that used for kitchen cupboards, or melamine, a spray coating available in wood effect or plain colours. Plastic laminate shrugs off water and stains but melamine is less durable. It protects against damp but is easily marked.

Glass shelves must be plate glass and should have ground edges for safety.

Timber shelves range from unfinished pine, which you can paint, stain, varnish or polish, to expensive hardwoods. Most shelving for home use is made from softwoods, ready-cut or in lengths you can cut to size and then finish as you wish.

Supports can be made from pieces of wood fixed each side of a narrow alcove, individual brackets, or slotted uprights, which allow you to vary the height of the shelves. You can also buy horizontal metal supports designed to support the shelf along its entire length, which are more discreet than brackets or uprights.

SPACE SAVERS

Shelves provide an easy answer to a host of storage problems. Here are a few ideas.

• Put a shelf at the bottom of a wardrobe and store shoes underneath.

• Fit shelves in a tall cupboard and use for storing toys and games.

• A wide shelf with strong brackets can serve as a desk in a study or bedroom. Top with some bookshelves.

• Fix shallow shelves to the inside of kitchen cupboard doors or at the back of the larder or broom cupboard for extra storage.

• Line an under-stairs cupboard with shelves to keep light bulbs, plugs, small items and tools handy.

• Hang narrow decorative shelves beneath kitchen wall cupboards, for mugs or spices.

• Fit broad, widely-spaced shelves in children's rooms and use them to store toys in large plastic crates. (Make sure they're too high to be climbed or sat on.)

• Fit shelves in the garage and garden shed to hold tools and DIY equipment.

• Organise shelves in the bathroom or cloakroom: narrow glass ones for toiletries, wide wood or melamine for extra supplies and clean towels.

• Make an old-fashioned plate shelf with a slot to keep plates upright. Fix it round the room at picture rail level, to show off old china.

• Fix glass shelves across a dull window and cover with sun-loving plants; they'll thrive in the light.

WALLS AND FIXINGS

TYPE OF WALL

It's important to work out what the wall is made from, because that decides the type of fixing you use and the stability of the shelves.

TIP The dust from drilling is a guide to wall construction. Red dust indicates brick, which can take straightforward wall plugs. Grey powder is probably building blocks, which can also support conventional screw fixings. Black dust may mean breeze blocks, which need anchor fixings.

Solid walls are made from brick or building blocks. Most houses built before the First World War have solid exterior walls.

Cavity walls are made from two layers of brick or building blocks with a gap between for insulation. Houses built after the Second World War have exterior cavity walls.

Breeze blocks were sometimes used for interior walls in houses built between the 1930s and 60s. Although solid, breeze blocks do crumble easily and need reinforcement to support heavy loads.

Stud walls are made from plasterboard on a timber frame. They are often used as interior walls in recently converted flats, or where doors have been filled in, or in small added extensions, and sound hollow when knocked. Unless the load is very light, you'll need to locate the timber supports underneath the plasterboard before you can fix shelves to stud walls. Find them by making small holes with a bradawl or, if you don't want to pierce the plaster, use a special joint and stud detector which lights up when passed over wood.

Lath and plaster walls consist of plaster supported by timber slats, and are found in period homes. You usually notice this type of construction because the walls are irregular.

TIP Use a cable detector to locate the uprights in lath and plaster walls: it will light up when passed over the nails used to fix the laths.

WHICH FIXING?

If you're working on a solid wall, you can use standard wall plugs. Shelves fixed to timber uprights need strong screws which are screwed straight into the wood. If you want to fix shelving to breeze block or hollow stud walls, you'll also need cavity fixings (which open out when screwed in to provide support behind the wall) or stronger toggle bolts.

PUTTING UP A SHELF STEP BY STEP

You will need
- Bradawl
- Pencil
- Power drill
- Screwdriver
- Shelves, brackets and fixings (including wall plugs if necessary)
- Spirit-level

1 Plan the distance between the shelves. Make sure they're broad enough and far apart enough for your needs.

TIP The heavier the load, the more supports you need. Brackets should be at least 16in/ 400mm apart for bookshelves or glass shelves.

2 Check that the screws are the right size for the brackets and that the wall plugs and drill bit size are compatible.

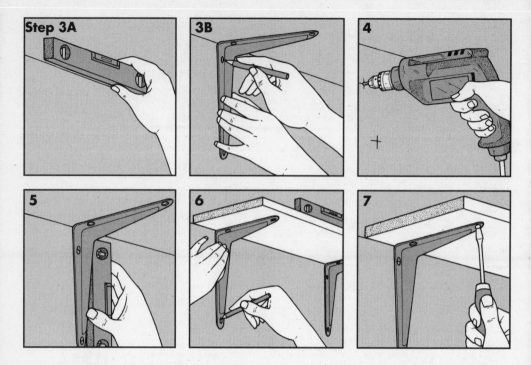

TIP 'Universal' wall plugs cover a range of common screw sizes.

3 Mark a line along the wall where the shelf will be, using a spirit-level to check that it's straight (A). Hold the brackets in place and mark the screw holes (B), before checking the horizontal with a spirit-level once more.

4 With a solid wall, use a masonry drill bit to make holes for the first bracket, about 1½in/4cm deep where marked. (Work slowly to make sure the drill doesn't overheat.)

TIP To mark the drilling depth, twist a piece of Sellotape round the drill bit marking off the first 4cm.

For breeze block or hollow stud walls, use an ordinary drill bit the correct size for the fixing. When working on wood, use a bradawl to start the screw holes as that will stop the timber splitting.

5 Push in the wall plugs until they are flush with the surface, and loosely screw the bracket into place, keeping a check that it is vertical with a spirit-level.

6 Repeat with the furthest bracket, and check both vertical and horizontal levels. Repeat until all the brackets are in place, carefully checking the levels each time, and making any adjustments as necessary.

TIP Drill and screw just one hole for each bracket, marking the others in pencil until you are sure the shelf will be level, to avoid making unnecessary holes in the wall.

7 Screw the brackets firmly in to place on the wall and put up the shelf. Mark the position of the small retaining screws that secure the shelf to the bracket. Remove the shelf and then make some small 'pilot' holes in it with a bradawl before replacing the shelf on the brackets. You can then screw into place manually or with an electric screwdriver.

MOULDINGS

Mouldings balance a high ceiling and add a decorative finish to the wall. Traditional skirtings, picture rails and cornices are available if you need to replace the mouldings in your house. To match an existing moulding, many suppliers will copy from an offcut, and make the length you want.

WHICH MOULDING?

Architrave is the moulding that surrounds a door or window frame. Popular widths are 2, 2½ and 3in/50, 63 and 75mm.

Cornices are used where the wall and ceiling meet. Made from plaster or timber, they are often elaborate in style.

Coving is the modern equivalent of cornice. Designs are usually simple, and it is made from easy-to-handle plaster or polystyrene.

Dado rails are timber mouldings fixed about a metre from the ground. Originally called chair rails, they were once designed to protect the wall from knocks by furniture but are now often used to separate decorations, such as wallpaper above and paint below.

Frieze describes the area between the picture rail (see below) and cornice.

Picture rail is the timber moulding that runs round a wall above head height and has a special slot for picture hooks.

Skirting protects the plaster at the base of the wall. Most skirtings are made from softwood, but hardwood designs are available.

FITTING COVING STEP BY STEP

You will need
- Coving adhesive
- Mitre box/paper template for cutting angles
- Sandpaper and sanding block
- Tape measure
- Tenon saw

1 Remove any wallpaper or flaking paint from the top of the wall and make sure the plaster is clean and dry. Sand lightly to provide a key.

2 Measure the room, counting the corners, so you know how many angles you need to cut – both internal, such as in a recess, and external, where a chimney breast projects outwards.

3 Cut the lengths to the correct angle using a tenon saw and either a mitre box or a paper template. Smooth the edges by sanding lightly.

4 Apply adhesive generously to the reverse side and edges of the coving (A), and press into place (B). Use a clean cloth to wipe away any excess adhesive before it sets.

Step 3

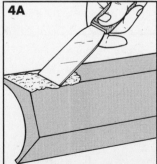

4A

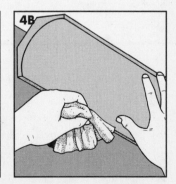

4B

BASIC PICTURE FRAMING

There's no need to restrict the number of pictures you hang or let pictures and photos gather dust until you can afford professional framing. With a few simple tools and materials and basic DIY skills, you can produce excellent frames for minimum outlay. Use the following techniques for prints and inexpensive original paintings.

Anything that is particularly precious or antique should, however, be taken to a professional framer.

WHICH FRAME?

Wooden mouldings suit most pictures. They vary from ornate gilded designs for oil paintings, to waxed, limed or stained frames for water colours, and narrow, plain mouldings for prints. For your first attempt at framing, choose a basic moulding with a rebate (recess), to keep the picture and mount firmly in place.

Aluminium mouldings must be cut with a hacksaw, which can't be used with a mitre box. If you want aluminium frames, it may be better to buy a ready-cut kit.

Clip or 'no-frame' frames sandwich the picture between a hardboard backing and glass front, keeping it in place with clips. This is an economical way of hanging posters and children's paintings but won't protect pictures from dust or damp.

Box or shadow frames are like miniature glass-fronted cupboards. They're ideal for collections and collages that won't lie flat.

TIP To make sure the frame is strong enough to support the picture, the width of the moulding should measure at least ½0th of the picture's longest side.

MAKING A FRAME AND MOUNT

You will need
Tools

- Bevelled mount cutter or sharp craft knife (if using a mount)
- Compasses (if cutting a circular mount)
- Fine-toothed tenon saw
- Corner or frame clamps
- Mitre box, to cut perfect corners. Fix it to a work bench or screw it to a block of wood and then clamp it to a table. (Cover the table with a piece of board to protect it.)
- Metal rule
- Nail punch
- Pin hammer
- Set square
- Small hand drill with very fine drill bit made from a cut-off veneer pin
- Woodwork vice – may be needed to hold wood for sawing

Materials

- Cord or picture wire for hanging
- Fine abrasive paper
- Glass: use non-reflective if light is a problem. Order glass cut to size (take the finished frame to the glazier). Glass is not necessary for oil paintings or prints that are block mounted.
- Hardboard for backing: ⅛in/3mm thick
- Masking tape
- Mounting card
- Veneer pins
- Screw eyes or D clips
- Turnclips
- Varnish, stain or paint
- PVA Wood glue

- Wood filler
- Wooden moulding with a rebate (recessed edge). (To find out how much you need, double the length and width of the picture, plus mount if any. Now add eight times the width of the moulding to allow for mitring the corners, plus 8in/20cm cutting allowance. The moulding can be cut in half for transport if necessary, because that will always allow enough for the longest edge.)

WHEN TO USE A MOUNT

Mounts are traditionally used with watercolours, prints and drawings to protect them and display the delicate colours to their best advantage. Techniques include sticking the picture on top of the mount most easily done using spray photo-mount on the back of the pictures, and (dry mounting) 'window' mounting, where the picture is seen through a hole cut in the mount, recommended for drawings and watercolours, that could be damaged if they came into contact with the glass.

Mount card is available from art shops in thicknesses graded from 1 to 12. Size 6 is a good general-purpose card. Choose a colour that enhances the painting to be framed, not one that competes with it, and look at the depth of colour too. A dark picture on a light mount generally appears smaller than a light picture on a dark mount. Dark mounts should be used with care, because they can detract from the impact of the picture.

TIP Combine two window mounts in different colours, one with a slightly smaller window under the other, to give an impression of depth.

A wide mount defines the picture and separates it from a busy background – worth bearing in mind if the walls are patterned. Very wide mounts are often used to emphasise miniatures though a narrower mount usually makes a picture appear larger.

Professional framers use a special formula when cutting mounts, which gives more depth at the base and makes the picture look central when displayed on the wall. The ratio is complicated, but cutting the mount allowing 10 to 20 per cent extra at the base gives similar results. For most purposes, a border of 2in/5cm at the top and sides and 2¼in/5.5cm beneath looks effective.

If the picture is wrinkled, dampen the back carefully with moist cotton wool before mounting. Leave for about ten minutes, then fix gummed paper to the top of the picture and lay the window mount over the front. Secure the other three sides with tape on the reverse and leave to dry. All but the deepest wrinkles should disappear as the paper contracts when it dries.

MAKING A MOUNT STEP BY STEP

1 Cut the mount board roughly to size using a straight metal rule, and a bevelled mount cutter or a sharp craft knife (A, overleaf). Cut the outer corners into perfect right angles, using a set square as a guide (B, overleaf).

2 Cut backing the same size as the mount from thin card.

3 Using a set square, mark the window in the mount lightly in pencil. Use a bevelled mount cutter, or score along this line with a craft knife held against a metal ruler, keeping the blade at about 60° (to create a bevelled edge, which gives an illusion of depth) and pulling it towards you. Repeat until cut through.

4 Lift out the window, pressing with the craft knife to release the corners, and rubbing the sides gently with fine abrasive paper if necessary for a clean edge.

Step 1A

1B

3

5 Stick the back and front of the mount together along the top edge, using double-sided sticky tape.

PICTURE FRAMING STEP BY STEP

1 Trim the picture if necessary to remove any rough edges and pin holes.

2 Work out the external measurements of the frame by using the following formula. Measure the width of the moulding, deducting the width of the rebate (recess). (See diagram opposite.) Double this and add to the length and width measurements of the picture, adding an extra ⅛in/3mm to the length and width to allow for clearance.

3 Make sure the mitre box is firmly fixed and clamp the moulding into place, protecting it from denting with pieces of card. It should lie flat in the mitre box, with the rebate edge underneath and facing away from you.

TIP Practise mitring offcuts of wood until you're certain of cutting a clean edge and making sure the mitres go the right way.

4 Put the saw in the slot in the mitre box, and cut the first mitre at the end of one of the lengths of moulding.

5 Mark in pencil the external length of the longest side (as calculated in step 2) so you know where to cut. Cut the second mitre, angled in the opposite direction.

6 Using this length as a guide, measure and mitre the other long side.

7 Cut and mitre two pieces of moulding for the width.

8 Return the pieces of moulding to the mitre box and clamp into place to make sure they form a perfect right-angled corner.

9 Place a length of moulding in the vice with the longer outer edge uppermost and drill a tiny hole (two in a wide moulding) near the end of the moulding but not too close to the edges or the wood will split. (Experiment with wood offcuts.) Drill the hole at one end only. Repeat at one end of the other three mouldings.

10 Taking a long piece of moulding, put it in the vice and brush the cut edge of the undrilled end with glue (A, right). Place the pin-hole end of the shorter side on it to form two sides of the frame. Hammer in the pins, punch in and wipe away any glue that's squeezed out (B, right).

11 Remove the two pieces carefully and lay flat to dry. Repeat with the other side and then assemble the frame.

12 When dry, rub down with fine glass paper and stain or varnish the frame if required.

13 Cut the backing from hardboard with a hand saw, marking out the cutting lines with a pencil and set square.

14 Check that the glass (if used) and mount are clean and lay the frame face down on the table. Insert the glass into the rebate, followed by the picture, mount and hardboard. You

may need to use glazing sprigs to keep it all in place if it doesn't fill the rebate, or turnclips if it all lies flush with the surface. Seal the back of the picture so that it stays in place with masking tape.

15 Fix screw eyes or D rings to the back of the frame, one-third of the way down. Attach enough cord or picture wire so that it comes just below the top of the picture. Then measure from the frame to the top of the picture wire or cord when it is fully stretched and mark the same point on the wall. Fix a picture hook to this point and hang the picture, making sure it is straight.

REPAIRING PICTURE FRAMES

Old picture frames can be more decorative than those available today and are often picked up at relatively little cost. Metal plates, from DIY and art shops, can be used for repairs and broken glass can be replaced by a glazier, who will cut a new piece to size. Secure your picture with a piece of thin hardboard fixed to the frame with panel pins or tape.

If the mitres are wobbly, remove the pins with pliers, fill the holes and re-fix. If the

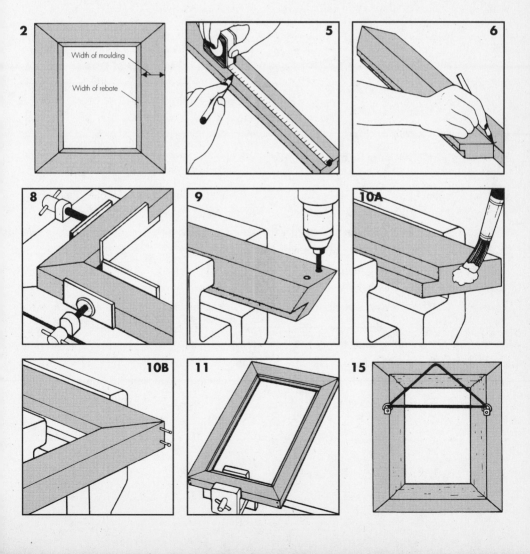

joints are damaged, it may be easier to cut the lengths and re-mitre them to make a smaller, sounder frame.

Check that the screw eyes and cords are in good condition, particularly if repairs make the frame heavier than before. You may need to substitute strong D rings for existing hangings and replace the cord with some picture wire.

RENEWING FRAME SURFACES

• Painted frames can be cleaned with white spirit, sanded and repainted with solvent-based undercoat and paint.

• Polished frames can be revived with methylated spirits that is rubbed in with fine wire wool.

• Gilded frames can be cleaned with acetone. Seal with lacquer for protection.

DESIGN TIPS

• For a lacquered look on a smooth frame, repair chips with multi-purpose filler, and sand lightly when dry. Then apply two coats of enamel paint.

• Mock tortoiseshell has a deep, rich effect. Use artists' water-based acrylic paints that dry quickly and leave a slight sheen. On a smooth, clean base, apply one coat of orange acrylic paint. Allow it to dry, then sand lightly and wipe clean. Dab brown acrylic paint on top of this coat with a cosmetic sponge, allowing some of the first colour to show through. Finish by painting some feathery streaks in black with an artist's paintbrush. Sand lightly when it is dry and then protect with a coat of varnish.

• Lace relief work can disguise chips and cracks. Cover the frame with a ⅛in/3mm layer of ready-mixed filler and press a length of crisp lace into the surface. Pull the lace away carefully when the filler has dried and paint the surface as required.

• Sea-shells make an attractive surround on old mirror frames. Protect the mirror glass with paper and then cover the frame with a ¼in/6mm layer of ceramic tile cement. Press in a variety of shells and leave them for 24 hours or so, until completely dry. Protect the finished image with a layer of clear polyurethane varnish.

• Fabric can rescue damaged frames. Use some strips of light cotton or silk, stiffened on the back with a stiff wallpaper paste. Remember to mitre the corners for a professional effect.

TIPS FOR HANGING PICTURES

Only large, imposing pictures look effective when hung alone in the centre of the wall. They should be positioned at eye level so they can be fully appreciated.

Other pictures are best hung in groups, 'anchored' to furniture or architectural details that provide a reference point. You can use all different shapes and sizes to add variety to the group, but as a rule, the largest should not be bigger than about one-third the size of the total, and the paintings should line up either at the top or the bottom. This arrangement works very well over tables, chests or sofas. You can also line them up along the right- or left-hand side as well as the top or bottom, which gives you extra room to extend the group.

An alternative is constant spacing, where all the paintings are hung the same distance apart: about 4in/10cm often works well. If you start with a central cluster of pictures, you can work upwards and outwards as your picture collection grows.

WINDOW TREATMENTS

Choosing curtains and blinds is one of the most creative aspects of home decorating. There's such a variety of fabrics, headings, tracks and poles to choose from that you're sure to find a style to suit your taste and your room. In fact, if there is a problem, it's that there's such a bewildering choice. Before you start shopping for material, jot down the effect you'd like to achieve and any considerations you should take into account. Ask yourself:

• Are there any practical features that will influence the style that you choose? For example, is there a radiator or window seat beneath the window? Does the window pivot? Is it a dormer, or French doors?

• What shape is the window, and do you want to alter it? A pelmet can help reduce the height of tall windows; long curtains can give importance to a small one. A square bay can be treated in several ways: as a single unit or with separate blinds or curtains.

• How many windows are there in the room? Identical windows can be given the same treatment, while windows that are very different in size and shape can be treated individually. If they're slightly different, or oddly proportioned, it's often best to copy the treatment chosen for the largest window, or to curtain the entire wall, if the windows are next to each other.

• How much clearance is there between the top of the window and the ceiling? This will affect the type of track and heading. Curtain poles need space above and below to look effective. If space is very limited, you may need a ceiling-hung track.

• Is privacy important? If the room is overlooked, you may need to screen the window with sheers or blinds during the day, as well as having curtains that close at night.

• Do you need extra insulation? Full-length lined and interlined curtains, when closed, can help keep precious heat inside the room.

• Will you need to wash the curtains or blinds? Lined curtains should be dry-cleaned even if both inner and outer fabric are made from cotton, because if washed they're liable to shrink at different rates and the seams will pucker. If you want curtains for a kitchen, bathroom or family room, it may be best to choose detachable linings or unlined sheers. Fabric blinds are usually not washed, but roller blinds can often be wiped with a damp cloth.

• Would you prefer an architectural solution? Window coverings don't need to be fabric. Other coverings include shutters, wood-slat blinds and shelves.

• Does the window really need covering? Oriel, round, and stained-glass windows are often best left to speak for themselves. Skylights and high, narrow windows rarely need covering for privacy though you may want to screen out the light. Their proportions may need minimising rather than emphasising so if you want to cover them, it may be best to choose a simple treatment in a colour that blends with the walls.

• Is security important? It's worth fitting simple locks to every window, but you may want to consider special blinds, security grilles or shutters for ground floor or basement windows, or if you live in a high risk area.

WHICH WINDOW?

The way a window opens can affect the window covering you choose, especially if it projects inwards rather than outwards and needs blinds or curtains that pull clear of the pane. Here are the main types to consider.

WINDOW FRAMES

Aluminium is popular for replacement windows, patio doors and double-glazed units. It can be coated as well as plain and is wiped clean easily but the cold metal may increase condensation. To prevent this, a plastic 'thermal break' is often provided in double-glazed windows, to improve insulation.

Plastic window frames are made from unplasticised polyvinyl chloride (uPVC) and reinforced with metal. They provide good insulation but should not be painted.

Galvanised metal windows may be found in some older houses, but are rarely used today because their poor insulation can cause condensation and rot. They need careful maintenance to prevent them from rusting.

Timber provides good insulation, minimising condensation round the frame, but needs to be painted or stained regularly to prevent rot. Timber frames should be treated with preservative, and softwood should be thoroughly seasoned before building, to prevent warping later.

Casement windows are side-opening. They usually have one fixed pane and one or two opening lights.

Sash or double-hung windows are made in two parts that can be raised and lowered independently, worked by sash cords or a metal spiral balance.

Tilting windows include pivoting designs, which turn through almost 180 degrees; projecting windows, which push forward on metal struts; tilting designs which can be tipped ajar for ventilation and pull inwards or pivot to open fully; and louvre (jalousie) windows, made from horizontal glass slats.

Sliding windows are usually patio doors, but small sliding windows are sometimes found in houses near the sea, where they're designed to resist buffeting by the wind.

COMPLEX WINDOW SHAPES

Bay windows extend the floor area of the room, letting in light on three sides. They can be square or angled, made from three separate windows, or a curved unit. You can cover a square bay with four curtains (two in the centre and one at each side); with three separate blinds; with a blind at the centre and show curtains on each side; or a single pair of curtains, provided you use track or poles that bend. You can also 'cut off' the bay by screening it with a pair of full-length curtains.

TIP Before you buy a curtain track, check the tightest angle recommended by the manufacturer for bending it. Some tracks for DIY use won't bend enough to fit a square bay.

Bow windows are curved windows set in a straight wall, and don't extend the room in the same way as a bay. You can fit curtains or blinds to cut off the bow, or hang them from curved track to emphasise the window's shape.

Dormer windows project from the roof. There's usually only one window (though some dormers have windows in the side like a miniature bay), plus a broad shelf underneath. Though charming to look at, dormers may not let much light in, so shutters, simple blinds, or narrow curtains that pull right back from the pane are often a good choice.

French windows and garden doors need curtains that pull clear on either side so that the doors can open easily. Tie-backs or hold-backs that secure the curtains when the doors are open help keep soiling to a minimum.

Picture windows and patio doors may take over most of the wall. In this case, it may be worth covering the entire wall, rather than the window alone, for the best effect.

CURTAIN TRACKS AND POLES

Curtain poles are designed for show; curtain track is often best hidden by a heading or pelmet. But just to confuse matters, there are now a number of curtain tracks that are attractive in their own right and can even be mistaken for poles. Here's a basic guide.

CURTAIN POLES

Poles are usually best for relatively short, straight runs, though it's possible to buy poles that bend round to follow a bay. They are sold complete with fittings such as rings from which to hang the curtains, although it's usually possible to buy some extra rings separately if needed.

Poles are usually made from wood – either stained or sprayed or left natural before painting – or have a metal finish.

Most are fixed to the wall, though ceiling fixing is sometimes possible.

CURTAIN POLE DIAMETERS

Heavyweight
$1\frac{1}{8}$–$1\frac{1}{2}$in/28–38mm

Medium weight
1–$1\frac{1}{8}$in/22–25mm

Lightweight:
$\frac{1}{2}$–$\frac{3}{4}$in/12–20mm

TIP If space is limited, look for 'short reach' brackets, which fix the pole close to the wall.

At the end of the pole is a finial (end piece), which keeps the last curtain ring in place. This can be removed if the pole is a very tight fit because the window is close to a corner.

The diameter of the pole is important. Long, lined curtains need substantial poles to bear the weight. Slim poles (under 1in/25mm thick) are best kept for short or sheer curtains. Long poles (over 8ft/2.4m) need a central support to prevent them sagging, and this can sometimes be used to join two lengths together. Larger poles may come ready corded, so the curtains don't need to be pulled by hand. It's possible to buy a draw rod, attached to the leading ring and concealed by the folds in the fabric, to pull uncorded curtains.

TIP Polish curtain poles from time to time with silicone polish so that the rings run up and down smoothly.

In addition to conventional poles, there are also sprung rods that will fit inside a window recess. These include café rods for café curtains, and lightweight tension rods for lace curtains.

CURTAIN TRACKS

Curtain track can be fixed to walls or ceilings. The track is made from plastic, aluminium or steel and can be used with accessories such as cording sets (to open and close the curtains without handling them), a valance rail for fabric pelmets, or a net curtain track.

It's important to buy track that's strong enough for the curtains, as long, lined curtains and fabrics like velvet need double the support required by light cotton curtains. Many brands of track are suitable for DIY use but the heavier metal curtain tracks may need to be installed by a professional, especially if the window is a difficult shape.

You may need special type of track to fit a square bay window or to sweep each side of a bow window. Some types used by professional fitters will bend around 90 degrees.

TIP   If you like the look of curtain poles but need the flexibility of track, consider a track that combines the features of both.

TIP   To prevent the gliders sticking, spray curtain track with silicone-based polish or a lubricant such as WD-40.

FITTING CURTAIN TRACK

Make sure the track is the right length before you start. Curtain track is either cut or telescoped to fit; poles are cut to size.

Wall fixing

There's usually a concrete lintel above a window, so you will need to use a hammer drill and a masonry drill bit. (While it is possible to drill into a steel lintel, it is easier to hang curtains from the ceiling in this case.) Measure at least 2in/5cm above the window before you start to drill, and make sure the holes are at least 1½in/38mm deep so that you penetrate the wall beneath the plaster.

TIP   If the plaster crumbles, try fixing a wooden batten to the lintel and screw the track to that. This will also cut down the number of holes that are drilled into the wall itself.

Ceiling fixing

It is very important to make sure the track is securely fixed into the timber joists above the ceiling plaster.

You can locate them by tapping the ceiling: Hollow areas will sound hollow and joists will sound duller. Then test with a bradawl, pushing through the plaster to find the wooden joists above. Alternatively, use a battery-operated joint and stud detector (see Putting up a shelf, page 165).

If the joists run parallel to the curtain track, you will need to take up the floorboards in the room above and fit strips of wood between the joists. You may find it easier to fit the curtain track on the wall close to the ceiling.

MAKING A PELMET BOARD

This can be made from a standard 4in/10cm shelf or, for full-length curtains, a shelf 6in/15cm deep. Pelmet boards should be cut 2in/5cm wider each side than the curtain track, and fixed to the wall above the track with strong brackets.

CURTAIN TRACK LOADS	
	Maximum load/ length of track
Heavyweight	6½lb per ft/1kg per 10cm
Heavy/ mediumweight	2½lb per ft/375g per 10cm
Mediumweight	1½lb per ft/225g per 10 cm
Lightweight	1¼lb per ft/175g per 10cm

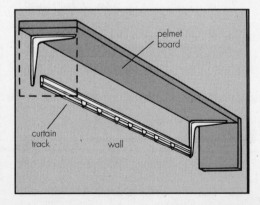

pelmet board

curtain track

wall

SAFETY & SECURITY

HOME SAFETY

Accidents in the home are responsible for about 5,000 deaths a year, and at least three million people need medical attention for injuries sustained at home. Yet many of these injuries could easily be avoided with some common sense, safety measures and greater awareness of potential problems.

Every household is different, so take a good look at your home, room by room, and carry out a safety audit to see where the possible hazards lie.

KITCHEN

NEW

If you are planning a new kitchen, it's easy to get caught up with the overall look and the smart new appliances you would like to include, but don't forget to consider how practical and safe it will be. You'll need to consider the layout, design and positioning of appliances carefully (see Kitchen Planning, page 8).

INHERITING A KITCHEN

If, on the other hand, you have inherited a kitchen, you may also be taking in potential problem areas, and it is important to be aware of badly planned or problematic fitted kitchens, particularly if you have small children.

Ask yourself:
- Is the lighting adequate over the work surfaces?
- Are the plug sockets well positioned or will flexes trail near the sink or cooker?
- Are the edges of work tops or corners of tables sharp? Should you consider using covers for the tables?
- Is the kitchen ventilated adequately? Proper ventilation is vital, especially if you have gas appliances in the kitchen, and to provide a clean, airy environment.
- Are there unhygienic gaps in tiles on work surfaces? Seal with waterproof sealant. Germs can be harboured in crevices.
- Is there safe storage for hazardous cleaning chemicals or medicines?
- Are there glass fronted doors that would be safer with laminated glass?
- How even and ruck free is the flooring?
- Have you inherited electrical appliances with unknown histories? Get them serviced.
- Did the previous owners install the kitchen units themselves? Check how secure they are, especially wall units.
- How strong is the shelving? Don't overload shelves, and put heavy and fragile items in a low but secure position. Make sure the shelves have shelf retainers to prevent them tipping forward if a heavy weight is placed at the front.

KITCHEN HAZARDS

These are used every day and we often neglect to treat them with the respect they deserve.

COOKER

- Don't leave saucepans unattended.
- Try to get into the habit of using the pan that best fits the size of hob ring available. If possible, use the rings at the back of the hob and remember to turn saucepan handles inward (so that they don't hang over the edge of the cooker or get dangerously hot over another hob ring).
- Never fill the pan more than one-third full with oil, or two-thirds full when the food has been added.

- When cleaning, switch the cooker off at the wall panel.
- Don't be tempted to line any part of the cooker with kitchen foil to keep it clean – fat from foods may catch fire.

KETTLE

- If you have a corded kettle, buy a curly cord or check to see if you can wind the flex underneath so that the kettle cannot be sited too near the front of the work surface.
- Switch off and unplug at the wall socket before you fill or pour it. Fill with enough water to cover the element completely.
- If buying new, opt for a cordless kettle and site the power base near the back of the work surface.

KITCHEN KNIVES

- Don't keep sharp knives loose in the utensil drawer. Ideally, use a knife block at the back of the work surface, or a wall rack (but don't overload it).
- Knives should also be washed up separately from the rest of the cutlery to avoid bad cuts from hidden knives in soapy water.

TOASTER

- It's tempting to use a knife to loosen bread caught inside the toaster, but never do this without switching off and unplugging first, otherwise you may get an electric shock. Allow the toaster to cool, and only then remove the bread with a wooden spatula. (If buying a new toaster, look for one with an extra lift facility for easier access).
- Do not disturb the heat elements. Never poke about with a fork or similar metal object as you are likely to break them.
- Follow the maker's instructions for removing loose breadcrumbs. Many models now have removable crumb trays.

IRON

- Fill a steam iron before you plug it in. Make sure the iron base is dry before using it.
- Fit a flex holder to the ironing board. Do not wrap the flex around a hot iron, and never leave an iron face down.
- If you are worried about leaving the iron on after use, buy a model that automatically switches off if left in the ironing position after a few seconds.

MEDICINES

Always lock all medicines and chemicals away in a high cupboard, preferably in the kitchen where there are always more adults around than in a bathroom.

- Try to buy cleaning products and medicines in child-resistant containers.
- Never transfer gardening or cleaning liquids to squash bottles, in case children mistakenly think they are drinks.
- Don't take labels off anything: it may be potentially dangerous.
- If you have medicine left over, don't keep it or throw it in the dustbin. Take it back to a pharmacist so it can be destroyed.

HOUSEHOLD CLEANING AGENTS

This book is full of useful hints on how to cut cleaning costs by using cheap household chemicals but it is important to remember that some of them are potentially dangerous substances that should be treated with respect.

Caustic soda (Sodium hydroxide)

This is a very strong alkali. If using caustic-soda crystals remember they are corrosive and can burn the skin, so follow all the safety instructions on the can to the letter. Wear rubber gloves and avoid inhaling fumes.

Always use in a well-ventilated room and if overcome by fumes, get to an open window as quickly as possible.

For accidental splashes on the skin, rinse the affected area well under some running cold water.

Chlorine bleach (Sodium hypochlorite)

Always store bleach in a safe place. Don't be tempted to add it to any other household chemicals or proprietary cleaners to speed things up, as it may then give off toxic gases which can be extremely dangerous.

If you spill any on your skin, wash the affected area immediately with plenty of cold water. If any is accidentally swallowed, drink plenty of water followed by plenty of milk, then contact your doctor immediately.

Solvents

Include acetone and turpentine.

Keep all grease solvents well away from flames and sparks. Avoid inhaling fumes and vapours, and always work in a well-ventilated room. Avoid prolonged contact with the skin as it may make it feel dry. Keep well out of reach of children.

TIP If you are worried about children and solvent abuse contact the charity Re-Solv for advice (0808 800 2345 weekdays, 9.00am–5.00pm).

Ammonia

This is a poison. Don't allow it to be taken internally, and never open the bottle caps to smell the contents: the result can be most unpleasant. Avoid contact with the eyes, skin and clothing. Wear rubber gloves, always work in a well-ventilated room and store the bottle in a cool, dark place.

If spilt on the skin, flush liberally with cold water. If ammonia is swallowed, make the person drink plenty of cold water, then contact your doctor immediately.

BATHROOM

Many accidents take place in the bathroom. Inevitably, in an area where you are dealing with water and slippery surfaces there are a number of possible dangers.

• Baths should be filled with cold water first, then hot.

• Always use non-slip floor mats and non-slip bath mats. (For awkward shapes, try Slipsafe spray inside baths or shower trays, which bonds to most surfaces).

• Make sure the areas around your bath and sink are properly sealed with bath sealant. This can be a breeding ground for germs in a hot, wet environment, and the sealant will prevent damage to the room below and also prevent wet rot.

• Consider fitting an extra bath grip for elderly members of the family to assist them in getting in or out of the bath.

• There should be no electrical plugs in the bathroom but if you live in an old house which has not been re-wired, watch for this and get in an electrician to advise you. All lights should be on pull cords, not switches.

• Make sure the shaver socket is situated well out of reach of children.

• Radiant heaters, towel rails and mirror lights must be fixed firmly to the wall. They should have permanent wiring (which means sockets) and pull-cord switches. Don't fix them above the bath or near a shower. Heaters must be out of reach of people using the bath and heaters with metal frames must be securely earthed and bonded to other metalwork in the bathroom. Have all work carried out by a qualified electrician.

• All shower heaters should have anti-scald thermal cut-outs. (If buying new, opt for thermostatic models that are designed to stabilise any temperature changes while you're under the shower. Mechanical mixer showers are less expensive but do not offer the same degree of temperature control and safety.)

• If you have a gas water-heater in the bathroom, there should be adequate ventilation at all times.

• Hot-water thermostats should be set at 130°F/54°C.

• Always ensure that the radiators and towel rails are kept at a safe temperature.

• Install bath shower screens or curtains to reduce water escaping from the bath on to the bathroom floor.

• Take care not to leave medicines, cosmetics, household cleaners, razors and razor blades within reach of children.

• Never use loose rugs in bathrooms. All rugs should have safety grips

• Never use a portable electric fire, hairdryer, or other electrical equipment in the bathroom.

LIVING ROOM, STAIRS AND HALLWAY

HEATING

• Never hang things over a convector or storage heater.

• Don't place mirrors over fireplaces: it encourages people to stand too close to them.

• Portable heaters can start a fire if misused. When using, make sure the heater has a permanent safety guard, is used in a well-ventilated area and is clean and well maintained. Always turn them off before going

---

TIME SWITCHES

If you have any heaters on time switches, keep them well clear of curtains and furnishings. Never fit time-switched or delay controls to an electric fire.

---

to bed. Electric heaters should carry the British Electrotechnical Approvals Board (BEAB) approval mark, while portable gas heaters should always carry the British Standard Kitemark.

• Open fires cause 1,400 house fires each year. Use a spark guard over the fire when you are not there to keep an eye on it. Don't forget to have the chimney swept each year.

TV AND STEREO

• Switch off when you are not using them and take the mains plug out of the supply socket.

• Never try to repair them yourself: call in a specialist.

LIGHTING

• Switch off light fittings before removing bulbs.

• To avoid causing a fire, do not use higher wattage bulbs than the makers recommend on shades and fittings.

FLOORING AND STEPS

• Don't polish floors under loose rugs or carpets, or place them in vulnerable areas such as at the base of stairs.

• Ensure stair rods are securely fixed and the stair carpet is not loose.

• Check that banisters and railings are firm.

• Stick down loose tiles and sheet vinyl. Neaten off frayed carpet edges.

• Make sure the lighting is adequate over the stairs.

WHICH SAFETY GLASS?

There are various types, so for guidance, go to an expert: a member of the Glass and Glazing Federation. Use and look for glazing materials that meet BS 6206. As a general guideline:

• Toughened glass is up to five times stronger than ordinary glass so is difficult to break. When it does, it shatters into thousands of pieces.

• Plastic safety film can be stuck on to one side of ordinary glass to hold the pieces together if the glass breaks.

• Laminated glass crazes but the pieces are held together by a strong, transparent interlayer, so minimising any injuries.

WINDOWS

Each year, about 27,000 people in Britain are injured by glass in their homes. If you have young children it may be worth considering safety glazing in fully glazed doors; door side panels, wet areas (eg shower screens), low level glazing and glass in furniture.

Glass in any window, whether it is double glazed or not, can be difficult to break. It is important to have at least one window wide enough to be used as an emergency exit in every room. With double glazing always make sure the key to the window is at hand (put it on a hook on the wall beside the window, out of reach of children).

BEDROOMS

ELECTRIC BLANKETS

Each year British fire brigades are called to some 1,500 fires caused by electric blankets. More than 20 people are killed and 250 injured in these fires. Only use electric blankets which carry the BEAB approval mark and conform to BS 3999, Part 6, or BS EN 60967.

• Not all electric blankets can be left on all

FIRE SAFETY AND FABRICS

If your upholstered furniture and bedding was made before the new fire safety regulations that came into effect in 1988, consider improving their resistance to fire.

If making loose covers for a sofa or armchair, look for match-resistant fabric (ask the advice of your fabric supplier).

Flame retardant sprays can be applied to fabrics, carpets and upholstery. They may not always be as effective as fire resistance treatments that are applied by factory process. Check that the spray is suitable for the fabric on your furniture and follow the manufacturer's instructions carefully. Be

warned: spray treatments that are not water resistant will simply wash out if liquids, eg tea, are spilled on the treated fabric.

If having your furniture re-upholstered, replacement covers and any material supplied in the course of a re-upholstering service must now meet the fire-resistance requirements. But you could also have the filling replaced with a fire resistant one or, at least, use a fire resistant interliner that is fitted between the new cover and the existing filling material to help protect the old fillings in the event of a fire breaking out.

night: check the instructions.
- Over-blankets are designed to be tucked in at the sides and bottom of the bed, without any of the heated area being folded under.
- Follow the manufacturer's instructions, check the blanket regularly for wear, and have it serviced every two to three years.

HAIRDRYERS

- Do not wrap the flex around the handle when you have finished with it.
- Disconnect when not in use.

SMOKING

- Never smoke in bed due to risk of fire.

CHILDREN

What may seem like a perfectly safe home can suddenly become an assault course of potential hazards once there is a child in the house. If you have young children then you've probably spotted most of the danger zones already, but there may be some which still lurk undetected. Pinpointing the hazards is more difficult when your home is only occasionally invaded by small children.

In the last two decades, accidents have emerged as the major health problem for children after the age of one. Home accidents are the biggest cause of death in under fours.

Babies
Babies less than nine months old have limited mobility, and accidents frequently result from the perilous positions they are put in by others. Over half the accidents in this age group are from falls such as rolling off furniture, or out of cots.

Toddlers
Toddlers (nine months to four years) often fall off and collide with furniture. They are also learning to climb stairs and are more likely to set off unaided. The increasingly mobile, active child can come into contact with medicines and household chemicals, small or hot objects, glass doors and other household hazards. A higher proportion of burning, poisoning and foreign body-type accidents occur to this age group.

CHILD-PROOFING YOUR HOME

Realistically, no home can be totally child-proof but here are some of the ways you can make a child's environment a little safer. Don't worry if you are not able to implement all the measures outlined below, but concentrate on those that are most applicable to your children depending on their age and inclinations.

STAIRS

- Fit stair gates: there's little to beat the challenge of climbing the stairs. Barriers or gates should be fitted at both the top and bottom of the staircase. Look for one that conforms to British Standard 4125 as this ensures that the spacing between the bars and the gap between the lower edge and the floor is much too small for a youngster to wriggle his/her head through.

TIP Buy a gate that can be opened easily with one hand.

- Install two-way light switches at the top and bottom of the stairway so you can light your way from either direction.
- Board up horizontal balcony rails so they cannot be used as a ladder.
- Never allow a child to play on or near stairs.
- Fix loose carpets and check that the carpet

tacks are not poking up through worn patches.

- Keep halls well lit and fit a dimmer switch on the landing light, to keep the light on low through the night in case children want to go to the toilet.

WINDOWS

Small children love climbing up to peer out of windows but once up there it is all too easy for them to topple out.

- Vertical window bars may save a toddler's life but do make sure they can be removed quickly in the event of a fire. Less conspicuous are window limiters which only allow the window to be opened a little way – enough to allow fresh air in but not sufficient for a toddler to get out.
- Keep sash windows locked at the bottom.
- Don't put anything that a child can climb on to near a window.
- Check that patio doors, shower screens, glass tables and a conservatory are all made from safety glass. If they are they will be marked with the BS 6206 or Kitemark. If not, replace them with laminated or toughened glass, or at least cover them with safety film conforming to BS 6206.

IN THE KITCHEN

Young children are at risk of serious injury from hot liquids and cooking fat. Every year around 30,000 children go to hospital with scalds.

FIRST-AID TIP If a child is scalded, run cold water over the scald right away. Don't stop to remove clothing. Then get medical help for anything but the smallest accident.

- Always keep hot drinks well out of children's reach. Don't hold a baby when you are drinking. If you're passing a hot drink to someone else, make sure a child isn't underneath.

- Keep the kettle at the back of the work surface out of the reach of toddlers, and keep the lead as short as practical. Alternatively, buy a coiled flex for your kettle, keep it at the back of the work surface or use a kettle guard (which screws to the wall at the back of the work surface).
- Knives and utensils must always be locked away or stored well out of reach.
- Simple child-proof locks should be fitted to kitchen cupboards and medicine cabinets.
- Try to cook on the back rings of the hob, and always remember to point saucepan handles inwards or towards the rear. Use a cooker guard to prevent toddlers accidentally pulling pans off the hob on to themselves.
- An oven built in above floor level ensures that at least one hot area is out of reach of children. If not, buy, an oven door guard which will at least diffuse some of the heat.
- Doors on washing machines, dishwashers and tumble driers should be kept closed always. Don't forget that the doors can get very hot during use (if they are not double insulated).

TIP To prevent children fiddling with the controls on a washing machine or tumble drier get a control visor to cover them.

- Never store soft drinks and alcohol in the same, low-level cupboard.
- Choose bottles with child-resistant lids where possible.
- Keep aerosol cans well out of reach.
- Make sure bookcases and wall units are well-secured and cannot be pulled over or used as climbing frames.

IN THE LIVING ROOM

- Guards should be fitted to all fires and radiators: BS 6539 on guards for open fires;

BS1945 on guards for electric, gas and paraffin heaters. Check that there's at least 8in/20cm between the heat and the guard, otherwise the latter will become dangerously hot.

• Always extinguish cigarettes properly and empty ashtrays. Always keep cigarettes, lighters and matches out of reach.

• Consider fitting door slam protectors to stop little fingers being crushed.

• Rugs can be fitted with adhesive underlay. (From specialist carpet retailers or contact The British Carpet Manufacturers' Association on 01562 747351 for stockists.)

• House-plants should always be checked for poison and possible allergic reactions.

• Consider fixing ornaments and movable objects in position with sticky pads or other fixings.

• Play pens are advisable for toddlers on those occasions when you simply can't be in two places at once. Buy one made to BS 4863.

• Store any alcohol out of reach.

IN THE BATHROOM

• Try to ensure that the floor covering is water resistant without being slippery, and that any rugs have a non-slip backing. In the bath itself, a non-slip rubber bath mat will help prevent the child sliding under the water. Children can drown in only a few inches of water so never leave them alone in the bath – even for one moment.

• Ensure that children cannot reach the lock on the bathroom or toilet door, in case they lock themselves in. Move locks if necessary.

• Baths should always be filled with cold water before hot. Mix the water well and test the temperature with your elbow before you put a baby in.

• If bathing a baby in a baby bath, check that the stand for the bath is solid and fits the bath well. If the bath is part of a changing

unit, make sure that the mat or cover lifts off or slides away completely, and cannot drop down on to the baby while in the bath. Once a child can stand unaided, stop using the baby bath on a stand. Either use an adult bath or put the baby bath inside the adult bath.

• For toddlers who delight in flushing toys, shoes, etc, down the toilet, buy a lid lock.

IN THE BEDROOM

• If the child has just graduated to his/her first grown-up bed, consider using a bed guard to stop them falling out. (This is a tubular frame with a soft, mesh infill. It is held in place with swivel arms which slide beneath the mattress and attach to the opposite side of the bed.)

• Non-toxic nursery paint should be used for children's rooms and furniture. Check that it conforms to BS 5665. (Available from specialist paint and hardware stores.)

• Encourage children to be tidy and put toys away after use, to avoid tripping and falling over objects on the floor.

• Check that the wardrobe doors can be opened from the inside in case your child gets stuck.

• Don't leave medicines (including the contraceptive pill), cosmetics, nail scissors, etc within a small child's reach.

• Don't put under-fives in the top deck of a bunk bed.

• Changing units: make sure the unit is stable when the drawers and cupboard are both open and closed. Make sure you can reach everything you need without leaving your baby alone on the unit.

• Nappy buckets: keep nappy sanitising powder out of reach. Your baby could swallow it and burn his/her mouth and throat. Keep nappy buckets out of the way of the baby. A child could drown in a full bucket or he/she could use the bucket as a step for climbing and reaching hazards like kettles.

• Cribs: make sure the stand for the crib is firm and that swinging cribs can be locked into a resting position.

• Moses baskets: make sure the fabric lining is stitched firmly into place and that there are no loose folds which could smother a baby.

• Cots and cot beds: always put the side up when the baby is in the cot. Drop the mattress base to the lowest position as soon as your baby can sit up. Don't put the cot near curtains or anything that might help the baby climb out.

• As soon as the baby starts trying to climb out of the cot, either switch to a bed or leave the drop side down. Keep the bedroom door closed or put a gate across it so that he/she cannot get out of the room at night.

TIP Move beds and other furniture away from windows to stop children climbing on them and falling out.

ELECTRICAL APPLIANCES

• Use covers on unused electrical sockets. Put furniture in front of electric sockets.

• Use a residual current device for areas in which your children live and play. It will automatically cut off the power in a fraction of a second, before your child receives a serious shock. It plugs into the socket, and you then plug the appliance into it.

HELP WITH SAFETY EQUIPMENT

If you can't afford to buy items such as stair gate, car seats or fire guards, speak to your health visitor, GP or the Social Services about loan schemes in your area.

• Make the TV and stereo strictly out of bounds. You can buy self-adhesive video shields to stop little fingers altering the programming.

• Look out for trailing flexes and clip them out of harm's way.

• Never leave a lamp without a bulb.

CHILDREN'S PLAY EQUIPMENT

• Check that outdoor play equipment is sturdy and well maintained.

• Paddling pools must always be emptied and ponds always covered when children are around. If you have a garden pond fence it or better still, drain it.

• Climbing frames or swings should be placed on a grassy surface or ground covered with bark chippings.

• Sand pits should always be covered when not in use to stop dogs or cats fouling them.

WATER, FIRE, GAS AND ELECTRICS

Most of us worry, at one time or another, whether we've unplugged the iron or switched off the gas cooker when we go out. But few people are aware of the full potential for accidents caused by the domestic services that we take so much for granted. Explosions caused by gas leaks don't just happen from leaving the cooker on accidentally: they are far more likely to be caused by appliances and central-heating systems that don't get regular servicing. Of course, the biggest fear is fire, but most people die without ever seeing any flames as they are overcome by smoke or toxic fumes first.

Make sure that all the family know the location of stoptaps, fuse-boxes, mains power switch, gas mains and what possible exit routes to use in case of fire.

GAS

• Have all gas appliances professionally installed and serviced regularly. Make sure there is adequate ventilation at all times.

• Switch off instant gas water-heaters before getting into the bath.

• Don't look for a gas leak with a naked flame and don't smoke near one. Open windows and phone the emergency gas service. (Look under Gas in the phone book, or better still, keep a list of emergency numbers handy (see Preparing for Emergencies, page 206).

• Always fill a paraffin heater outdoors, and never while it's still burning.

• Gas installers who are registered by CORGI (Council for Registered Gas Installers) must always be used for jobs involving gas appliances, by law.

• For further advice on gas safety and carbon monoxide poisoning, see Gas and Electricity, page 214.

ELECTRICITY

House wiring

Faults in wiring cause 2,200 fires and about ten deaths per year in Britain. You should have your household wiring checked every five years. This may sound excessive, but the cost is a small price to pay for electrical safety.

If your wiring circuits are more than 25 years old, or if your sockets are of the round, two-pin type you almost certainly need to renew them. Before checking or repairing wiring sockets or switches, turn off the power at the mains switch.

Get expert help for all repairs and wiring. If you think there may be a fault, immediately contact a contractor who is approved by the National Inspection Council for Electrical Installation Contracting. There is a list of approved contractors available at all Electricity

RESIDUAL CURRENT DEVICES

Residual current devices can be fitted by a professional at the mains supply where they offer protection throughout the home, or in a plug or socket suitable for portable equipment such as a lawn-mower, drill, or appliances which need an extension lead.

The RCD can detect damage to the cable and other faults through change in the current flow. It automatically disconnects the power, reducing the risk of an accident and warning you that there is a fault.

RCDs must be fitted to any electrical supply expected to serve appliances outdoors.

Board showrooms. Always keep a torch handy in case it is needed during a power cut. Check regularly that the battery is working.

Plugs and flexes

Faulty flexes cause 1,000 fires and several deaths per year.

• Always buy shatter-proof plugs that meet BS 1363 or BS 1363/A, which are stronger than most. Make sure the clamp in the plug properly grips the outer plastic cover of the flex and not just the leads.

• Wire colour codes:
   Live = Brown
   Neutral = Blue
   Earth = Yellow/Green.

• Don't overload plug sockets. Use adaptors as little as possible. Ideally, use a separate socket for every appliance. If you often use two appliances from one point, fit a double socket.

• Make sure you are using the correct fuse for the appliance.

FIRE

No one should underrate the danger of fire. In this country every year there are about 50,000 accidental fires in the home which kill about 800 people and injure over 14,000 others.

Smoke alarms

Over 60 per cent of households now have a smoke alarm. Your chances of surviving a fire are two to three times greater if you have one fitted. Battery-operated models are not expensive. You can also buy mains-powered alarms if you have a large house and need several alarms. You should preferably have one on each floor of the house.

Smoke alarm maintenance

Once you have fitted a smoke alarm, it is easy to forget about it. But it is important to

SMOKE ALARM CRITERIA

Smoke alarms should:
- Comply with BS 5446 and preferably carry the British Standard Kitemark.
- Be placed within 8yd/7m of rooms where fires are likely to start and within 3yd/3m of bedroom doors.
- Be placed at least 12in/30cm from any wall, or from a ceiling light fitting.
- If wall mounted, be between 6in–12in/15–30cm below the ceiling.
- Be fixed in positions that allow maintenance, testing and cleaning.
- Be sited away from areas where steam, or fumes could give false alarms.
- Be away from hot or cold areas.
Mains-operated smoke alarms must comply with IEE wiring regulations, so use a qualified electrician for installation.

SMOKE ALARMS FOR THE HARD OF HEARING

Smoke alarms are available for those with hearing impairment. For details contact The Royal National Institute for Deaf People (020 7296 8000).

maintain it properly: it could save your life.
- Make a note in your diary to replace the battery at least once a year.
- Test the battery once a week.
- Vacuum dust from inside the alarm.
- Test sensor annually by waving a smoking candle under it.

Fire-fighting equipment

For most homes, a fire blanket in the kitchen (to BS 6575) and a multi-purpose dry powder, foam or water-type extinguisher in the hall (conforming to BS5423 or 6165 and the British Standard Kitemark) would be adequate. But it depends on the fire risks in your home and what you can afford. A multi-purpose dry powder or foam extinguisher in the garage, shed or car would complete the package.

If in doubt about which type to have, contact your local fire brigade for advice or contact The Fire Protection Association for useful leaflets (020 8207 2345).

DIY SAFETY

One of the biggest causes of home accidents is the enthusiastic DIYer who overlooks the essential precautions when using power tools, hazardous chemicals or even climbing a ladder.
- Never cut corners, always use the right tool for the job and keep tools in good order.
- When drilling walls, avoid areas adjacent to power sockets and the area at right angles and

vertically above them. Power cables are usually routed in these locations.

- Always take care of hands when working, and wear gloves whenever possible
- Always wear protective clothing – face masks, safety goggles, ear defenders or knee pads – when undertaking jobs which may be dangerous or harmful.
- Prepare yourself and your working area properly before you begin.
- Fuels, glue, cleaners, paints and lubricants all contain chemicals that can be harmful. Always follow the makers' safety guidelines. Ensure that you have adequate ventilation.
- Use residual circuit devices when operating power tools.
- Put blade covers on knives and chisels when not using them.
- Keep children away from all DIY work.

LADDER SAFETY

Falling off ladders and chairs is one of the most frequent DIY accidents.

- Always check that the ladders are suitable for the job.
- Use a special ladder tray that fits on to the ladder instead of carrying paint or tools.
- Never over-extend an extension ladder or exceed the recommended angle of a ladder.
- Use stabilising legs when using a ladder extension.
- Always wear a tool belt (to carry a number of tools) rather than carrying a handful.

THE GARDEN

The most obvious danger is the use of electrical equipment, such as mowers and hedge trimmers, but what about the hazards of barbecues and, of course, plants themselves?

- Never use any electrical appliances outside when it's raining.
- When using mains-powered electrical appliances outside the home, wear rubber-soled shoes. Never mow the lawn or trim a hedge barefoot.
- Keep an electrical cable behind you, and continually check that it is still behind you.
- All electrical equipment should be unplugged during cleaning or adjustment and should be put away after use.

OUTDOOR WIRING

- Use a single flex without joins and never work with wet or worn flex.
- Do not run power tools from a lamp socket. Have a proper earthed socket fitted by a qualified electrician.
- If you use a socket to supply electricity to equipment outdoors, such as lawn-mowers or hedge-cutters, protect it with a residual current circuit breaker.
- Sockets installed outdoors must also be under cover, unless special weatherproof units in a waterproof box are used.

PLANTS

- Think carefully before siting hazardous plants where they will be accessible and attractive to children or animals. If in doubt about certain plants, take a clipping along to your local garden centre. (Be sure to wear protective gloves.)
- Rose bushes (and any other plants with thorns) should be well pruned.
- Dispose of broken or cracked plant pots.
- Always put away garden chemicals, ie. fertilisers, weed killers and insecticides.
- Be extremely careful of poisonous plants. The best-known are laburnum seeds, yew berries and foxgloves, but there other common plants with dangerous seeds or berries such as privet, laurel and rhododendron. Teach your child never to eat garden seeds or berries.

• If your child has eaten parts of, or been poisoned by, an unknown plant, seek medical advice immediately. Don't make the affected person sick, and take a sample of the plant with you.

OUTDOOR GLAZING

Consider installing safety glazing (toughened glass, laminated glass or plastic sheet glazing) in the conservatory, patio doors, at low levels, and in any balustrades. Contact the Glass and Glazing Federation (020 7403 7177) for further advice and local member stockists.

BARBECUES

• Site in a clear location away from fire hazards and children.
• Never sprinkle barbecue coals with flammable fluids. Read the instructions and follow the procedure for how to start or re-light a barbecue safely. The quality of charcoal varies from brand to brand. The better the quality the easier the barbecue will be to light and stay lit. (The British standard for barbecues is BS 5258.)

Barbecue problems

If your barbecue won't light, or the fire is flagging:
• Never use petrol, paraffin, methylated spirits or other flammable fuel to light or revive it.
• Do use special lighting fluid, pastes and fire lighters. Be sure they have totally burned away before you start cooking or they may taint the food with an unpleasant flavour.
• Add more charcoal, not fluid, to sides of barbecue.
• Try a different brand of charcoal.
• Try 'light the bag' instant-burn charcoal. (Place the bag in the barbecue bowl and light it.)

• Buy a grill starter (a mini chimney that uses burning newspaper and the pull of air up the chimney to light the coals. Then pour the hot coals into the barbecue bowl.)
• If the fire goes out, use tongs to place the coals in a steel bucket. Then start again with fresh charcoal.

FIRST AID

Many minor accidents can be effectively treated at home. Anyone can learn the basics of first aid and invest in a practical kit to cater for minor injuries, such as:
• sterile dressings of different sizes
• triangular and crepe bandages
• cotton wool
• individually wrapped assorted plasters
• sterile gauze pads
• safety pins
• thermometer
• mild painkillers
• protective gloves.

St John Ambulance and the British Red Cross both offer first-aid courses. They also have a variety of leaflets on safety and first aid. For details look in the telephone directory for your county headquarters.

TETANUS

Tetanus is extremely common in gardens, so ensure that all the family have had tetanus inoculations in case any garden accident should occur.

FURTHER SAFETY INFORMATION

For further information on safety in the home in general, contact The Royal Society for the Prevention of Accidents (0121 248 2244).

HOME SECURITY

Every year, thousands of people suffer a burglary or break-in. The thought of a thief breaking into your home, picking through your personal belongings, and making off with the most valuable and resaleable items is both unnerving and frightening. Yet, without turning your home into a fortress, you can employ a few simple precautions to make it less attractive – both to opportunist amateurs and to professional thieves who look around for suitable homes to burgle.

Your greatest weapon against a burglar is time. The more barriers you can place in front of him (such as fences, locked doors, windows, alarms) the less attractive your home will appear to be. The chances are he'll give up on your place and move on to try his luck at the next house.

CRIME FACTS

- The average burglary takes place in daylight.
- On average, each of us will be burgled twice in our time as home owners.
- Once burgled, you may have a repeat visit a few weeks later when the thief has calculated that you have received an insurance payment and have replaced your TV and video, etc.
- 80 per cent of thefts are opportunist.
- Most burglaries take place between 2pm and 4pm on a weekday afternoon.
- Thieves are usually aged between 15 and 18 and live locally.
- On average, it takes two minutes for a burglar to go through your home.

The area in which you live

Burglary isn't restricted to poor urban areas, although the chances of being burgled are greater in some areas of the country than others. There are, of course, centres of high risk but burglary is a national problem. According to Home Office statistics, you are least likely to be burgled in Dyfed and Powys in Wales, and most likely in the metropolitan area of London.

Be prepared for house contents insurance to be affected by the level of crime in your area. You may not know whether you live in a high-risk area but your insurers certainly will! Before buying expensive locks, etc, check with your insurer to see if he has any particular recommendations.

Planning home security

When considering home security measures, consider your lifestyle, what restrictions you are willing to impose on yourself and the practical aspects of any security devices.

BASIC SECURITY PRECAUTIONS

Often people could do more to protect their homes and possessions but are put off by the cost. But many homes lack even basic security precautions that cost little or nothing at all. Here are some initial steps:

- Don't leave doors and windows open.
- Use the locks already installed.
- Don't make it easy for the burglar: lock up tools and ladders.
- Don't 'advertise' the valuables you have.
- Don't advertise your absence.
- Ask neighbours to be vigilant (and do the same for their property in return).

- Ask your local crime-prevention officer to visit your home and recommend ways to improve household security.

ENCOURAGING BURGLARS

Take a good look at your house from the outside, and consider whether any of these questions apply:

- Do you live in a quiet area?
- Is the house secluded or hidden from the road?
- Do you live in a poorly lit and neglected area?
- Could a burglar work unseen behind high walls and fences?
- Is there easy access to the rear, eg a footpath or a canal towpath?
- Do you have an open porch where a thief could hide?
- Does the house have side access which would allow a burglar to work unnoticed? Has the side passage been left unlocked?
- Are the locks on your external doors adequate?
- Is there a way through the garage to the house?
- Do you have valuables on display?
- Do you have a shed or garage containing tools, ladders, ropes, etc, that the thief could use to break in?
- If you have a garage (or coal bunker) with access to your house, are the locks adequate?

All these features could encourage a burglar to

HOW BURGLARS BREAK IN

Front door   25%
Rear/side door   23%
Rear/side window   43%
Front window   3%
Upper window   3%

---

target your home, and remedying them will make your house less vulnerable to theft.

THE LIVED-IN LOOK

It is easy for a thief to tell who's in and who isn't. The house may be in darkness, post left in the letter box or milk bottles left out on the doorstep. Over 80 per cent of burglaries occur when a house is empty, so try to keep your house looking occupied when you are out, and even when you're away on holiday.

- If going away, don't leave your car full of luggage overnight. Load it just before you leave. Lock everything in the boot or under the cover of the hatchback if you're trying to save time in the morning.
- Cancel the milk and papers.

TIP Ring your local Royal Mail Customer Care Unit to find out if the Keepsafe scheme operates in your area. Under the scheme the Royal Mail will hold all your mail until you return home – the price varies according to how long you will be away for.

- Curtains closed during the day make it look as if no one is home. It is better to leave them open and get security lighting (see below). If you have a large number of valuables, it may be worth considering an electric curtain-track system. You can programme it to open and close your curtains at pre-set times.
- Tell the local police station you'll be away.
- Mow the lawn before you go away.
- Buy a couple of automatic time switches for inside lights. These can be used to turn on a light, TV or radio and help give the impression that you are in. They work at pre-set or random times.

- Don't announce that you're going away to a shop full of people. Only tell people who need to know.
- Don't leave valuable items like TVs, videos or stereos visible through windows.
- Don't have your home address showing on your luggage for the outward journey. Put this only on the inside of your cases.
- If going out for an evening, leave a light on in a room, not the hall (many people leave the hall light on when they are out); and perhaps leave a radio playing.
- Ask a neighbour to keep an eye on the house, collect post and free newspapers left in the letter box, sweep up leaves, and even mow the lawn if you're going to be away longer than a fortnight. If they have two cars, perhaps one could be parked in your driveway. You can repay the favour by doing the same for them when they go away. Warn the key-holding neighbour not to put your surname, address or even house number on your keys in case they fall into the wrong hands.
- A message recorded by a strange voice on your answerphone announcing that a guest is staying in the house while you are away will fool everyone except close friends. Never leave a message saying you have gone away.
- Just before setting off on holiday, it's worth spending a quiet couple of minutes on the doorstep to check you've done everything, and have taken all you need with you.

HOME SITTERS

Leaving home for the pleasures of a holiday is often marred by the worry of burglary. Although you may be able to enlist neighbours to a degree, if you have pets or a conservatory full of precious plants, it may be worth considering a professional home sitter. Obviously you don't want just anyone living in your home, so be sure to choose a professional company that:

- Has been in business a reasonable length of time.
- Is registered and licensed by the Department of Employment.
- Vets its home sitters/caretakers carefully and takes references.
- Is insured against any problems that might occur such as the home sitter having an accident, simply not being up to the task, or damage to the home.
- Provides full back-up for the home sitter so that if he/she falls ill, or has to leave the assignment, the company is still bound to honour the contract.

The larger companies include Homesitters which employs all its people (charges include all PAYE and National Insurance contributions); Universal Aunts and Animal Aunts which are agencies which link self-employed sitters to homeowners.

TIP For peace of mind and to ensure everything runs smoothly, meet the prospective home sitter/caretaker before the day you hand over the keys. To ensure that things go well, prepare a list of anything that you think might be useful to the sitter.

DOOR SECURITY

Doors are the obvious point of entry for a thief. In 30 per cent of burglaries, life is made even easier by the owner leaving a door or window open.

DOOR LOCKS

Look on the front face of the lock for a BS Kitemark, which ensures that the lock is of a reasonable quality.

If in doubt about the suitability of your existing locks, check with your local crime prevention officer or a locksmith who is a member of the Master Locksmiths Association. Also find out from your insurance company whether the locks are adequate to meet their requirements.

KEY TIPS

- Never leave a spare key in a convenient hiding place. Burglars instinctively know where to look.
- Change locks when you move into a new house, as you don't know how many sets of keys may be around.

When it comes to locks, most of us don't know our twin cylinders from our automatic deadlocks. Luckily, most lock manufacturers now put helpful advice on the packaging of their products to indicate which door it would be suitable for (front/back, internal/external).

TIP New guidelines from the Association of British Insurers recommend which locks householders need to fit to secure their homes adequately.

There are basically two kinds of door locks:
Mortice locks (usually seen on back doors) are sunk into the door so are more difficult to force out.
Cylinder rim locks (usually used on front doors) are screwed to the surface which makes them easier to fit.

When you are buying a lock for an entry/exit door, look for a deadlock, which means the bolts locks into the extended position and can be opened only with a key. This means a thief can't smash a nearby panel, and open the door from the inside, nor can he enter by a window and leave by that door.

FRONT DOOR

- The front door should be a minimum of 1¾in/44mm thick. Check this, especially if you live in a flat with a communal main door.
- It needs a high-security automatic deadlocking night latch with lockable internal knob or handle (to prevent entry by breaking glass and releasing the latch) and a five or seven-lever mortice deadlock (to BS 3621). (A two-lever mortice lock isn't strong enough so you should only ever fit these to inside doors.)
- Fit a spyhole and a door chain.
- The letter box should be at least 15in/40cm away from the locks, so that there is no chance of an intruder opening the door by reaching up through the letter box.
- Fit hinge bolts to reinforce the hinge side of the door.
- Check that the door frame is fixed firmly to the brickwork and is strong enough to hold the lock in place.

BACK DOOR

Over 60 per cent of burglaries occur through the back door so it needs particular attention.
- Fit a high-security two-bolt mortice lock, or ideally a five or seven lever-lock (to BS 3621).

IDENTIFYING MORTICE LOCKS

To find out if you only have a two-lever lock (which is really too lightweight for the back door and only suitable for internal doors) look at the face plate in the edge of the door. This may be marked with the number of levers.

If not, look at the key. If it looks cheap or has very few notches in the bit of the key then it's probably only a two or three-lever lock.

- Fit mortice bolts top and bottom.

TIP Don't forget that it's no use having a top-grade lock if the door itself is of poor quality and can easily be forced. You can strengthen a door by using a door-reinforcement kit which includes two solid plates which bolt on to each side of the door round the lock area (these are readily available from normal ironmongers and locksmiths).

PATIO DOORS

Don't rely solely on factory-fitted locks for patio doors.

These should be fitted with multi-point locks and an anti-lift device to stop a thief from lifting the door off. If the hinges are visible from the outside, the doors should have hinge bolts as well.

GLASS-PANELLED DOORS

These should be fitted with laminated glass, which looks like ordinary glass, but is very hard to break. It may cost more than double the price of ordinary glass, but you should only have to put it in once.

Laminated glass is made of two or more layers of ordinary glass, bonded together with a strong, clear plastic interlayer. When attacked, the glass itself may break but the broken pieces will adhere to the interlayer and remain as a barrier. It's a good idea if there are many youngsters or vandals in the area, and it won't cause serious injury if you fall against it.

Laminated glass is available from members of the Glass and Glazing Federation. For further details contact the Laminated Glass Information Centre (020 7499 1720).

Also fit a cylinder rim lock with a lockable inside handle. If a thief breaks the glass to reach in, the door cannot be opened.

WHO'S AT THE DOOR?

Most callers are genuine, but we've all heard tales of burglars getting into people's homes by pretending to be the gas man or from the council. So it's sensible to be cautious. If you live alone, be especially careful to check the identity of unknown callers.

- Ask to see the identity card of meter readers or service men.
- For blind or partially sighted people, electricity, gas and water services can arrange for their staff to use an identifying code word.
- If callers claim to be from local services, ask them to wait, shut the door and ring the office to check who they are.
- Call a neighbour or ask the visitor to come back when someone else is in.
- Don't keep a door chain on all the time. Only put it on when someone calls, otherwise it may be difficult for others to get in if an emergency happens.
- Don't leave your handbag or wallet unattended in any room where a caller may need to enter. Stay with the caller all the time and keep all other doors closed.

WINDOW SECURITY

The most common way for a burglar to break into your home is through an easily accessible back window.

If you're not sure about whether a window is large enough for a thief to climb through, the rough rule is if you can get your head through an opening, he can also squeeze inside.

TIP Do make sure there are no ladders left lying around and shut all windows – even small cloakroom ones – when you go out.

SECURITY TIPS

• Fit window locks. Over 60 per cent of homes still do not have window locks. You can buy them for casement, skylight or sash types. Pay particular attention to ground-floor windows and those above flat roofs, near drainpipes or fire escapes.

• Glue the slats of louvre windows in place with epoxy resin, or fit them with special louvre locks.

• Consider replacing vulnerable downstairs windows with laminated glass.

• Install security grills on vulnerable windows, especially at the rear of the house. Many DIY stores and ironmongers sell decorative grills that can be attached to the wall quite easily with security screws.

• Shutters can be attached to the exterior wall, although they can be fitted on the interior if you do not want to change the appearance of your property. Both types are operated from the inside. They are usually aluminium or foam-filled aluminium which also provides insulation. Contact the British Blind and Shutter Association (01827 52337) for a list of local suppliers.

• Even small windows, like casement windows, skylights or bathroom fanlights might need locks.

• Check the window frames are in good repair. There's no point having a good lock if the burglar can simply push in a rotten frame.

• Always have internal beading on double glazing: otherwise thieves can simply slit around the rubber seal and remove the whole window with a suction pad.

• If you live in a bungalow, for secure ventilation use window limiters/child safety locks. These limit the window opening to no more than 15 degrees.

NEIGHBOURHOOD WATCH

Setting up a Neighbourhood/Home/ Community or Tower Watch group can help reduce the level of crime and the fear of crime in a neighbourhood. They are not intended to encourage people to set up as a vigilante group, but just to be on the lookout for suspicious behaviour and to enhance the security of the members' own properties.

If you are interested in setting up a scheme in your area, find out first whether others share your enthusiasm before approaching the police.

SECURITY FOR FLATS

• As the front door of an individual flat is often not as strong as the main, outside door, it's worth upgrading a thin door with a more solid one. And it needs as many locks and bolts as the main communal door.

• If a fire escape runs up the side or back of the flats, make sure nearby doors and windows are secure.

• Talk to other residents, or the landlord, about installing a door telephone entry system. Bear in mind, however, these still aren't foolproof and you must use them sensibly. Don't ever let anyone in who says they want to go to another flat or even hold open the door open for a stranger whose arrival coincides with yours.

SECURITY LIGHTING

The more visible the burglar is when he is trying to break into your house, the less he will like it. It will also make him less sure about whether the house is occupied if you have security lighting coming on and off while the house is actually empty.

PLUG-IN TIMER CONTROLLERS

These switch lights, radio, TV, etc, on and off while you are away so that the house appears to be occupied. They are simple to install, not difficult to set and several of them can be used around the home and moved around wherever you need them. The most basic time switches simply plug into a socket outlet (like an adaptor) and then whatever you want the time switch to bring on – such as a lamp or TV – is plugged into it, to give the impression that you are home.

Electromechanical time switches are set by moving little markers or tappets around a dial. They operate, usually to the nearest 15 minutes, at the same time every day (or every week, with a seven-day timer) unless you move the tappets. Some switches will turn on at random within specified active periods. Electronic, programmable time switches can be set more accurately to the nearest minute. There may also be an option for setting different times each day.

SECURITY WALL SWITCHES

You can fit a security light switch in place of a normal light switch to control a central room light, wall lights or an exterior porch light. It will normally be set so that it only brings on the light when it gets dark, but methods vary. There is a wide range of varying levels of sophistication.
• Simple photocells which turn lights on at dusk and off again at dawn.
• Switches that allow setting of the exact times at which lights will switch on and off.
• Switches that come on randomly.
• Switches that re-create the householder's own habits over a 24-hour period.

SAFETY WARNING

Unless you are competent at DIY, mains lighting should always be installed by a qualified electrician. There are strict safety standards for electrical installation to mains supply and you need a separate garden circuit with waterproof external plug sockets.

For a list of electricians in your area ring the National Inspection Council for Electrical Installation Contracting (020 7582 7746), or the Electrical Contractors' Association (020 7313 4800).

TIP You can't use time switches with fluorescent lights, without fitting an adaptor to the lights first.

OUTDOOR SECURITY LIGHTS

If you live in a large property, it may be worth considering illuminating large areas such as a drive or lawn with mains-wired floodlighting. This will spread an even, practical light, which is ideal both for deterring burglars from shady corners, and for alfresco entertaining in the summer.

Alternatively, spotlighting may be more effective. Key areas to spotlight are over the front door, garage, shed, passages and any other obvious entry points.

Rather than having lights that stay on all night and require you to turn them on and off, consider installing some passive infra-red lighting. This only works when someone approaches your home: a passive infra-red detector senses the person's body heat and automatically operates a light (turning it off again after a few minutes). You can buy both integral lights, or separate lights and passive infra-red sensors.

TIPS FOR LIGHTING

• Don't forget that outdoor lighting should have separate wiring from your household system with external plug sockets, and should incorporate a Residual Current Device (RCD) and fuse. For installation, always use a qualified electrician.

• Mount light fittings high so no one can tamper with them and adjust the beam slightly off ground if you have cats or dogs, so they can't activate them accidentally.

• When positioning floodlighting or security lighting bear in mind that your neighbours may not want the night sky illuminated into the small hours. Be considerate.

SAFES

If you live in an area where burglary is common, a safe may be useful for small valuables and cash. Look for one that conforms to BS 7558. It's also worth checking with your insurer whether this will reduce your premium, and how much cover they will give for items in a safe.

Think carefully before buying secondhand (unless you are confident that the safe has been reconditioned to BS 7582). If you move into a house with an old safe, do not use it. Old safes may look quite secure, but the technology used will almost certainly be outdated, making them easy to break into.

The most common types of safe used in the home are wall safes (about £50) which can be set in brickwork or fixed to the wall, and floor safes which are sited under the floorboards. You can buy small, free-standing safes but a thief may think you have something worth taking and decide to remove the whole safe, so it is wiser to fix them to the floor or wall.

It is important to ensure the safe is securely bolted to the floor or wall, and in a position where a thief would have difficulty prising it out. Have the safe professionally installed for maximum security. For a reputable company and details of reliable installation experts in your area, it's best to contact the Master Locksmiths Association (01327 262255).

TIP To store cash, use a small portable unit, such as Safe-Can, which looks like an ordinary tin of food, or Safe Plug, a false double electrical wall socket. Both are available from DIY stores.

BURGLAR ALARMS

If after you've taken as many practical, physical and common-sense measures as you can you still feel insecure, then it may be worth considering fitting a burglar alarm. This isn't a substitute for having good locks, but may be worth it if you live in an inner city or a secluded spot and have a lot of valuables. You will have to use it conscientiously, even if out for only a few minutes – the major danger time for burglaries.

Don't be rushed into a decision by the offer of a discount, or frightening stories of crime levels. You will need to discuss your security risks with a local crime-prevention office. Do not deal with doorstep salesmen of burglar alarms. You'll also need to think about who you would appoint as your key holders for occasions when you are away. You will have to give them – and your family – full instructions on using the system.

If installing a burglar alarm you should always inform the police and environmental health department.

Some insurance companies offer discounted premiums if you have an 'approved' burglar-alarm system. But think carefully before trying to get a reduction on this basis as it often involves you in regular maintenance checks by an approved company and, in the event of a burglary, if the alarm wasn't on you may have difficulty claiming.

An 'approved' installer usually means one registered with the British Security Industry Association (the trade association) or the National Approval Council for Security Systems (NACOSS, the industry inspectorate).

Don't expect any insurance discounts for DIY-installed alarms.

COST

The cost of a professionally installed burglar alarm system will vary according to its level of sophistication. Installation charges, too, will reflect the type of house, its size, the number of entry points, etc. In addition to the initial outlay for the installation, you will have to pay an annual maintenance fee.

A DIY-installed system from your local DIY or hardware store is cheaper than a professionally installed system. Costs vary depending on the complexity of the system. (For more, see DIY Burglar Alarms on page 201.)

To ensure you are charged the right price for the job, it is essential to obtain a minimum of three quotes from reputable installers before making your choice. Quotations are usually free and don't place you under any obligation. Remember, the cheapest installation is not necessarily the best option.

PROFESSIONAL ALARMS

• Check that the system meets BS 4737.
• Be suspicious of firms that offer you a ready-made package. For a burglar alarm to be really effective it needs to be tailored to your home and your particular needs. A professional installer should send someone to look at your home to determine what kind of lifestyle you lead so he can draw up the most appropriate form of protection before quoting. For instance, pets may cause a problem if allowed to run free in the area of movement detectors; or if you are elderly you may have visits from grandchildren who are attracted to personal-attack buttons placed at low level.

• Don't forget to ask how much servicing and maintenance will cost and who pays if the system breaks down, or there is a false alarm.
• You should also check that all equipment has a 12-month guarantee.
• Establish which part of the system you own. Signalling devices are invariably rented from the company. If the control equipment is rented you will lose this if you change companies.

WHAT SYSTEM?

A burglar alarm consists of three main parts:
1 The detection device.
2 The control equipment. You should be able to set just part of the system, such as door, window and living-room detectors at night when you are asleep.
3 The signalling device/s.
Think of an alarm system as a stand-in for you: the detection devices are your eyes and ears, the control unit is your brain and the signalling device is your voice.

1 DETECTION DEVICES

These fall into two categories: fixed-point detectors and movement detectors.

Fixed point detectors
Usually fitted to doors and windows and can be:
• Switches that operate when a door or window is opened.
• Vibration sensors, which can be fitted on walls, windows or doors to detect physical vibration.

• Pressure sensors: hidden pressure pads that trigger the alarm when stepped on.

Movement detectors

Normally fixed to the corner of a wall near the ceiling and can be:

• Acoustic, to sense airborne vibrations such as the sound of breaking glass.

• Passive infra-red, which react to a change in temperature as an intruder moves within a defined area.

• Air-activated, which sense changes in air pressure caused when doors or windows are opened or broken.

2 THE CONTROL PANEL

This is the nerve centre of the alarm system and is usually situated in a cupboard or under the stairs. Once activated by any of the detection devices it sets off the bell/siren, or the central monitoring station.

3 SIGNALLING DEVICES

Bell only

This sort of system makes a noise when set off. These are designed to draw immediate attention to the break-in but rely on neighbours or passers by to alert the police.

Bell-only systems are sometimes fitted with flashing lights fitted on the underside of the bell box. This gives a visual warning that the alarm has activated, which is useful for identification within a row of alarmed houses. The light will continue to flash even after the bell/sounder has cut out.

TIP It's worth having a bell that sounds inside the house as well as out. This is important as you may not be able to hear the outside bell: if you are in bed asleep, for example. It also stops a burglar from hearing what is going on outside, making him more vulnerable.

TIP Remember that a highly visible alarm-bell box will provide a deterrent, and if your house is vulnerable to attack from the rear, it may be worth fitting a dummy bell box at the back. Buy spares at DIY stores.

Monitored system

When a monitored alarm is set off, it sends a coded message down the phone to a central monitoring station, which in turn calls the police or a nominated relative or friend. This system comprises a bell-only system with the addition of a digital communicator to link the alarm to the monitoring station. All the major alarm companies run their own continuously manned monitoring stations.

The police will accept calls signalled over the phone line from these types of system, provided the alarm company is approved (usually if it is a member of NACOSS). A list is available from crime-prevention officers.

Personal-attack button

You press a personal-attack button (usually situated by the bed with a second one by the front door) if you sense an intruder. These are deliberately operated by a push button and reset via a key. This device is used to activate the alarm at any time, whether the control unit is switched on or off.

FALSE ALARMS

False alarms make up over 96 per cent of all alarm calls responded to by the police in England and Wales, wasting millions of pounds in lost police hours per year. If police are called out to false alarms at your property four times in a twelve-month period, you may receive a warning letter from the local police. If the false calls reach seven in a year, the police may stop responding completely.

It's not just the police who are

inconvenienced by false alarms: it could cost you, the householder, dearly too. If your system has been installed by an approved engineer, the British Standard requires him to reset the system once it has been set off, accidentally or not, to prevent burglars cancelling the alarm. Your insurance cover and premium may also be affected if police cover is withdrawn. Find out what caused the false alarms and put it right. There's nothing guaranteed to annoy the neighbours more than an alarm bell continuously and needlessly going off.

DIY BURGLAR ALARMS

If you are a competent DIYer with experience in electrics, you will be able to fit your own system. Wire-free systems are the easiest to fit and should only take three or four hours, but you can also get DIY-wired alarms which are cheaper, but can take a day's work to install.

In a wire-free system there are no wires between the detection devices and the control panel. Each device contains a small transmitting device which signals to a receiver in the control unit.

Apart from simplicity of installation, the advantages of having a wire-free system are that you can also use the system to protect garages and a garden shed, and take it with you if you move house.

Their main disadvantage is that the police won't accept calls signals from them. Therefore they are restricted to local, audible signalling or signals to nearby friends or neighbours.

POINTS TO REMEMBER

• Interfering signals from local police and taxis, etc, can prevent radio systems from working properly, and unfortunately some systems don't show this is happening.

• Effective range of radio systems can be dramatically reduced by internal walls and floors, especially if reinforced with steel.

• DTI approval: it is illegal to sell or advertise non-approved products. Certain radio frequencies have been allocated to these systems so that they don't interfere with the police, emergency services or cordless phones, etc. Talk to other alarm users and a couple of installers about the possibility of radio frequency interference if you happen to live near public services.

• Look for BS 6707 on Intruder Alarm Systems for Consumer Installation.

• Ensure that the control unit is accessible, but out of reach of young children and pets.

• Make sure you can close windows and doors so they don't rattle or vibrate when there is heavy traffic or wind. Physical vibration may set off the burglar alarm.

• If your system has an alarm clearly audible outside your home you should notify the local police station that you've installed an alarm within 48 hours of installation, and give them the names and addresses of at least two key holders. Show the key holders how to operate and silence the alarm. The bell or siren should be set to cut out after 20 minutes.

• Be warned: control panels and bell/siren boxes contain rechargeable batteries to keep the alarm working in the event of a power cut. These must be serviced regularly, so keep a note in your diary as a reminder.

Local authorities' environmental health officers have power to switch off alarms causing a noise nuisance. You may also be liable to a fine if you do not notify the police or keyholders.

Rather than annoy your neighbours through noise, co-operate in looking after each others' property and taking notice if the alarm sounds, or suspicious activity takes place.

NEW HOUSES

If you're buying a brand-new house, look for the builder's Secured by Design symbol. This is awarded to flats and houses that meet police standards for home security, which include substantial door locks, secure boundaries and limited access to the rear.

Secured by Design is a police initiative involving builders and architects to improve home security. It has the support of the Association of British Insurers, the Home Office and the Department of Environment.

HOT PROPERTY

The most attractive items for burglars to steal are portable, high-value goods that can't be identified easily. If you mark your valuables, it will be harder for them to be sold and easier for the police to return them, if they're found.

• For absorbent surfaces, such as documents or fabrics, use a non-absorbent ultraviolet

BURGLARS' TOP TEN MOST VALUED ITEMS

Don't assume you have nothing worth stealing. This is what thieves like most:

1 Video recorders
2 Home computers
3 Cash
4 Stereo equipment
5 Chequebook, credit cards and documents (such as passports)
6 TVs
7 Jewellery
8 Gold and silver ware
9 Cameras
10 Antiques

pen, available from a good stationer's.

• For hard surfaces, such as plastic or metal, use a hard-surface ultraviolet marker. Write in an inconspicuous place, as it's visible and can discolour some finishes.

• Etch your postcode, followed by the house number or the first two letters of the house name on to cameras and stereo equipment. Also make a record of serial numbers. Then if they are stolen and later found, the police can identify them and return them to you.

• Ask your local crime-prevention officer for postcoded property warning stickers to display in the front and back windows of your house.

• Keep a list of valuable items with the make, model number and serial number.

• Hide holdalls and suitcases, as thieves find them handy for taking valuables away.

• Keep a note of your credit cards, cashpoint card, pension/allowance book, bank and building society account numbers and the companies' emergency telephone numbers so you can advise them of the loss immediately.

• It's a good idea to have colour photographs taken of jewellery, antiques, silver, etc that can't be properly marked. Without an accurate description of stolen items there is little hope of them being recovered (see Recovering Stolen Goods, page 204).

• Valuables should be stored in the bank when you go on holiday, and items of lesser value hidden away.

HOUSE CONTENTS INSURANCE

There are over 100 insurers offering household insurance. All cover theft or attempted theft. Decide whether you want indemnity or new for old cover.

Indemnity reduces the amount paid out, to allow for wear and tear, and depreciation.

New for old cover pays out the cost of replacing an old item with a new one, so is more expensive.

Contact at least one independent intermediary to find a variety of quotes.

When you take out cover you will need to estimate the total, new replacement value of all your belongings (with the exception of linen and clothing. Nearly all policies make a deduction for wear and tear on these.)

Most insurers will now insist on you having certain minimum levels of security before they will give you cover. If you improve the security of your home above their minimum requirements, some insurers will give you a discount off your contents policy. For example, if you:

• belong to a Neighbourhood Watch Scheme;

• have locks approved to BS 3621 fitted to all front and back doors;

• have an alarm system fitted and serviced by a member of the National Approval Council for Security Systems (NACOSS).

Insurance tips

• Think carefully before installing an alarm. If you don't have it regularly serviced by a NACOSS-approved company and it wasn't switched on at the time of the burglary, you may invalidate your policy and be unable to make a claim.

• Fitting your own DIY kit alarm won't reduce an insurance premium.

• Check your policy for exclusion clauses. If you fit devices but don't use them, it may affect your cover.

• It's wise to check your policy for holiday cover. Leaving the house empty for over 30 days may restrict it.

• Policies often ask you to specify valuable items worth over £500.

• Check the policy covers garden items.

The Association of British Insurers issues a leaflet, *Beat The Burglar*. For a free copy, send an SAE to 51 Gresham Street, London EC1V 7HQ.

STRANGERS IN THE NIGHT

If you wake in the night and hear intruders, don't rush downstairs and confront them. Dial 999 immediately, if you can. Even if you can't give details, the police will respond. If you can't get to a phone, stay put until the thief has left and it's safe to move.

For the elderly or disabled who may not be able to reach a telephone during a break-in, a community alarm can be fitted. The alarms work as a normal telephone with the additional feature that they can automatically dial a control centre (run by local housing authorities, social services departments or commercial monitoring companies). It is triggered by pressing a button on the telephone or on a pendant around the neck. This service is sometimes provided free or for a a minimal charge per week. Contact your local housing authority, social services or Help the Aged for further details.

TIP Help the Aged (020 7253 0253) also produce a useful home security advice leaflet called: *Security In Your Home*.

STOPPING GARDEN THIEVES

Did you know that there is a one in twenty chance that something will be stolen from your garden in the next two years, whether it is powered tools, plants or ornaments? Garden tools, especially ladders and spades, are often used to assist the burglar breaking into the house.

GARDEN SECURITY TIPS

• Put away all tools and equipment and ensure that all outside sheds and store cupboards are securely locked when not in use.

• Bring the tools inside if you do not have a garden shed or outbuilding.

• Install automatic security lighting outdoors (see Security Lighting, page 197).

• Use good-quality locks to secure your gates.

• If you have a burglar alarm, why not extend it to cover outbuildings and sheds?

• Photograph valuable garden plants or ornaments for identification if stolen.

• Postcode garden tools and equipment.

• Check that your household insurance policy covers theft from the garden and outbuildings.

• Use prickly plants to provide extra natural protection around your property. Suitable thorny defenders include Blue Spruce (dense blue, spiky needles), Creeping Juniper (thorny stem and foliage), Holly, Chinese Jujube (very spiny, pendulous branches), Firethorn (thorny stem), and Juniper (prickly foliage).

RECOVERING STOLEN GOODS

If your home has been burgled, the chances of ever seeing your most valuable belongings again are, realistically, rare. If items are security marked the chances increase considerably, and if you have photographs and detailed descriptions of items, even better.

If the items are antiques, try contacting:

• The *Antiques Trade Gazette* (020 7930 7195), a weekly newspaper with a section on stolen goods, circulated to the antiques trade

internationally will place an advertisement for a fee.

• *Trace* magazine (01983 826 000) publishes details of stolen works of art and antiques. Around 60 per cent of its advertisements are placed by private individuals.

• The *Art Loss Register* (020 7235 3393). Any item worth over £500 in value can be registered for £20 plus VAT, or for free if the item is already insured by one of their members. The information is kept on a permanent database of stolen art and antiques and checked against auction catalogues. There is a small fee if the goods are recovered.

MALICIOUS PHONE CALLS AND HARASSMENT

A harassing or malicious phone caller can make you feel unpleasantly vulnerable in your own home. To combat such calls, phone users should follow the procedure below.

• Call free on 0800 66 6700 for recorded advice on what to do if you get one of these calls. Such advice includes, for example: don't give your name or phone number, say nothing, walk away from the phone and gently hang up without saying anything after a few minutes. For personal advice, ring BT's Malicious Calls Bureau free on 0800 66 1441.

• The operator can intercept all your calls (usually for about two weeks) at no charge.

• Your telephone number can easily be changed and you can go ex-directory.

• BT can organise Malicious Call Identification free of charge but only as part of a police investigation.

EMERGENCIES

PREPARING FOR EMERGENCIES

Knowing how to act in a household emergency is as much about understanding how your house works as staying cool in a crisis.

In an emergency you probably won't have time to read the advice in this chapter, so read it *now* and try to memorise the main points. Emergencies can happen at any time to anyone, so as well as learning what to do yourself, teach your older children.

ESSENTIAL PHONE NUMBERS

First, it's a good idea to keep a list of essential numbers by the phone. Ideally, these should include:

• Family doctor
• Nearest hospital with an accident and emergency unit
• Plumber
• Locksmith
• Glazier
• Electrician
• Electricity company's emergency number
• Local gas emergency number
• Local builder
• Local police station
• Vet (if applicable)
• Your and your partner's work numbers
• School and college numbers
• Relatives or friends that the children can ring in an emergency

TIP If choosing a tradesman for the first time, try to follow a personal recommendation from a neighbour, or at least choose a firm that is a member of a trade association that insists its members follow a code of practice, and that has a grievance procedure for customers to use should you need to complain, such as:

• Federation of Master Builders
• Institute of Plumbing
• National Association of Plumbing, Heating and Mechanical Services Contractors
• Electrical Contractors' Association
• National Inspection Council for Electrical Installation Contracting
• Council for Registered Gas Installers
• Glass and Glazing Federation

While making a list of emergency numbers, group other family details together that might come in handy, such as blood groups, medical card numbers, national insurance numbers and insurance policy numbers. Also list bank, building society and credit card numbers – and where to ring if they are lost or stolen.

FIRE

Take some time now to think carefully about how you and your family would escape from your house in a fire.

• Is there an alternative route down, as well as the stairs, in case they are blocked by fire?
• Is there a window in every room that could be used to climb out of?
• If you have double glazing, is the key kept by the window for easy unlocking?
• If you have secondary glazing, check whether is there at least one window in each room that doesn't have it, that you could use to escape?

Finally, hold regular, family fire practice and make sure the whole family knows what to do if there really is a fire.

FIVE-POINT FIRE DRILL

1 Get everyone out.
2 Call the Fire Brigade by dialling 999.
3 Only attempt to tackle a fire in its earliest stages. Remember that fire extinguishers are only for 'first aid' fire fighting.
4 Wait for the Fire Brigade.
5 Don't go back to the house, until a fire officer tells you it's safe to do so.

FIRE AT NIGHT

If you were to wake up at night and notice the smell of smoke, here's what to do:
1 Wake everyone up (calmly, without causing any panic).

TIP Fit a smoke alarm (to BS 5446) on every floor of the house. It can increase your chances of getting out in a fire by two or three times, giving you precious extra minutes. (See Smoke Alarms, page 188.)

2 Try to establish where the heart of the fire is and close the door to that room if you can. Don't open any door that feels warm to the touch. (Use the back of your hand to touch it).
3 Use the stairs, if safe to do so, and get everyone out of the house. Call the Fire Brigade from a phone box or neighbour's house. Clearly state the address of the fire.

TIP Never store combustible materials, such as paint cans or solvents, under the stairs. They could give fuel to a fire and block your escape route.

4 If the stairs are blocked, use an upstairs window as an escape route – if you can do so safely. Otherwise go to a front bedroom, close the door, block any openings such as vents or skylights, and seal up the gap along the bottom of the door with rolled up clothes or bedding.
5 Go to the window and try to attract the attention of someone outside. Shout and wave something brightly coloured (or pale, that will be seen in the dark).
6 Don't try to get out unless you are forced to. If the room starts to fill with smoke, try not to become panicked. Tie a handkerchief or scarf around your mouth and lean out of the window to breathe. If this isn't possible, crouch down near the floor (the heat and smoke will be less there).
7 Only as a last resort, jump. Drop bedding or cushions to the ground to break your fall, and lower yourself feet first from the window sill to reduce the drop.

FIRE-FIGHTING EQUIPMENT

Kitchen: Fire blanket. Make sure it conforms to BS 6575 and is at least 3 x 3ft/90 x 90 cm in size.
Hall: Multi-purpose dry powder, foam or water type extinguisher (conforming to BS 5423 or 6165 and the British Standard Kitemark).

These would be adequate for most homes, but it depends on the fire risks in your home and what you can afford. A multi-purpose dry powder or foam extinguisher in the garage, shed or car would also be a good idea.

WHAT KIND OF FIRE?

Different kinds of fires require different measures: that is, extinguisher, water, etc.

CHIP PAN/FRYING PAN FIRE

1 Leave the pan where it is.

2 Turn off the heat if it is safe to do so.

3 Protecting your hands, place a damp cloth, a close fitting lid or a fire blanket over the pan to smother the flames.

4 Leave the pan to cool for at least 30 minutes. (The fire can start again if the cover is removed too soon.)

Ideally, use a thermostatically-controlled deep-fat fryer rather than an ordinary hob-top chip pan.

TIP   Never use water or any type of extinguisher to fight an oil fire.

FURNITURE FIRES

Use a multi-purpose foam or a water fire extinguisher.

Fires in upholstered furniture can spread very quickly and produce poisonous fumes. Do not tackle the fire if it is burning fiercely or if there is already thick smoke. Just get out of your home immediately, shut the door properly, and make an emergency call to the fire brigade.

ELECTRICAL FITTING AND APPLIANCE FIRES

1 If possible, turn off the power. (You can do this by pulling out the plug or switch off the appliance at the mains.)

2 Use a dry powder or carbon dioxide extinguisher.

Don't use a water-based extinguisher unless the appliance is disconnected from the mains – but never use one on TV sets, even when they are unplugged.

FIRE PREVENTION

For further advice on fire protection in the home and how to choose and use a fire extinguisher contact your local fire safety officer. Alternatively, for general safety advice you can contact the Fire Protection Association (020 8207 2345).

TIP   Unplug TVs and computers and cover them with a damp blanket or a fire blanket to smother the fire. Don't use water.

MAINS GAS APPLIANCES FIRES

1 Turn off the gas supply and wait until the gas flow stops.

2 Call the fire brigade immediately and tell them that mains gas is involved.

3 If the gas supply cannot be turned off, *do not* attempt to extinguish the burning gas jet, as this allows gas to escape and accumulate to explosive levels.

Tackling a gas leak

See Gas Leaks page 214.

CLOTHES ON FIRE

1 Lay the victim down so the flames cannot reach the face.

2 Douse the flames with water or any other non-flammable liquid such as milk. Or alternatively smother the flames with a blanket or rug.

3 If water isn't readily available, wrap the victim in a fire blanket or rug.

4 Once the flames are out, check that there is no smouldering material.

5 Get medical help immediately.

SEVERE WEATHER

Excessive water or wind, or both at once, can cause major headaches and distress for the householder.

FLOODING

After fire, a flood is the most destructive element that can hit your home. If you live near a river, reservoir, the sea or a water main, get in touch with your local authority who will advise you on the kind of flood precautions you should take.

READY SUPPLIES

It may be worthwhile having a supply of tinned and dried food and bottled water in case you are cut off for any length of time. It may also be useful to buy a camping light, camping cooker and candles, as the first thing you'll have to do in a flood is turn off the mains electricity.

If you have room in a garage or shed, keep a stock of plastic bags filled with sand or soil to block off outside doors and airbricks.

BE PREPARED

Even if a downpour looks as though it is going to turn into a flood, you should have a reasonable amount of time to prepare the house and your family.

- Block off outside doors and airbricks to try to keep water out of the house; place plastic carrier bags filled with soil against the outside faces of doors and airbricks.
- Turn off mains electricity, gas and water.
- Move your family, pets and what possessions you can (furniture, rugs, etc) to upper floors, or move out if in a bungalow.
- Take off downstairs internal doors, if possible. Severe flooding may damage them.

FLOOD SURVIVAL TIPS

- Get everyone to wrap up well, as the house may be cold, with no heating.
- Take an emergency supplies box with candles, a camping stove if you have one, tinned food and bottled water, etc.
- Flood water is almost certainly contaminated so don't use it for anything. Any cooking utensils which have been in the flood should be disinfected. Don't drink tap water until you hear from the local authority that it's all right to do so.

- Wait upstairs for the relief services to tell you what to do next.

CLEANING UP AFTER A FLOOD

Let the emergency services pump as much water out of the house as possible before trying to return. Once back inside, check the damage very carefully.

- If water has got into the electrics, it could be dangerous and you should get the local electricity company to test it as soon as possible. All appliances should also be examined and tested at the same time.
- Call in the local gas suppliers to check the system and any appliances.
- Check with the water company on the state of the water supplies.
- You should be able to hire a pump to clear any remaining water from cellars, and then use a three in one vacuum cleaner to remove any final pools of water.
- Check the loft for any damage. It may need temporary repairs to stop the roof letting in even more water. An uncovered water cistern

in the loft may be contaminated and so you'll need to drain it and clean it out. Throw out soaked loft insulation material.

• Remove furniture and lift floor coverings so you can hose walls and floors down. Scrub all affected surfaces thoroughly with strong disinfectant, as the flood water may have been contaminated with sewage.

• If you didn't get a chance to do this before the flood, take doors off their hinges and stack them flat so they can dry out without warping.

• Lift some floorboards so the underfloor area can dry out or be pumped out if necessary.

• Check that there is no water trapped underneath ground floors, in cellars or cavity walls. If water has got inside them, holes may have to be drilled from the outside to allow it to escape. Also check for trapped mud.

• Outside, make sure airbricks are free of debris. Unblock drains, clean out gully gratings and rod the drains to clear them.

• Keep windows and doors open as often as possible (security permitting) to give good ventilation, even when the heating is on. Good ventilation is crucial. Your greatest enemy is rotting timber.

• At night, you could use a dehumidifier (which removes moisture from the air and collects it in a container which you then empty). When you think the structural and joinery timbers are dry, call in a surveyor to check the moisture content.

• If the wallpaper is ruined, strip it off to help speed up drying out. Leave cupboard doors open and keep furniture away from walls.

• If walls are very damp, it may be necessary to have some of the inside plaster removed to aid drying out.

It can take weeks for the walls and floors, etc, of a house to dry out. A qualified surveyor will be able to tell you when the walls and structural timbers are dry and whether there

---

FLOOD INFORMATION

For further help on floods and storms, *How to Avoid Damage and Injuries during Wind Storms* and *Dealing with Flood Damage* are both available for a small amount from the Building Research Establishment (01923 664444).

---

has been any physical damage caused. It's a good idea to get the underfloor timbers inspected after about six months and again in a year's time, to check for rot.

Once the cleaning and drying are completed, get a qualified electrician to test the electrics for earth continuity and insulation resistance. Then ask him for an inspection certificate. Be on the lookout for any signs of trouble in the electrics such as sizzling, cracking or buzzing. If either occur turn off the supply immediately. Have your electrics inspected every month for the first six after the initial test and at least twice again in the following six months.

MINOR FLOODS

If you suddenly find your home flooding with water:

1 Turn off the electricity at the mains.

2 Find out what is causing the flood (such as an overflowing bath, a leaking washing machine) and if possible, turn it off.

3 If this doesn't stop the flow of water, turn off the water at the mains stoptap.

TIP To turn a mains water stoptap off, turn it clockwise as far as it will go, like a tap. Check where your stoptap is *now*. It is probably under the kitchen sink. In older houses, it could be in the cellar, or possibly outside the house under a small metal flap. Twice a year, check the stoptap hasn't seized up and that you can turn it easily. If it is jammed, don't force it – turn off the one outside. If you don't know where that is ask your local water supplier.

4 Turn off the boiler, immersion heater, washing machine or anything that heats water.

5 If the flood is still in full flow, if possible, turn off the stoptap on the supply pipe from your cold-water cistern. If you cannot reach this easily, open cold taps and flush cisterns to empty the tank as quickly as possible. If water is coming from the hot-water system, turn off the stoptap adjacent to the hot-water cylinder (on its supply pipe).

DRYING OUT

• Once you have stopped the flood, assess the damage.

• If the ceiling plaster seems to be bulging downwards, under the weight of water from above, make a small hole with a skewer, screwdriver or knitting needle in the centre of the bulge, and put a bucket underneath to catch the water. This is important, otherwise the weight of water may bring the entire ceiling down.

• Wait to turn the power back on until any area with electrics in it has completely dried out. Check with a qualified electrician. You may be able to isolate the power and lighting circuits concerned by switching them off at your consumer unit (fuse box), so you have power to the rest of the house.

• Stand mattresses and foam cushions on their edge as seepage is slower on a vertical surface. Take up wet carpeting and loose-laid flooring. Carpets should be professionally cleaned. Don't replace furniture and heavy appliances until the floor has dried out

completely, which may take several weeks. (See Flooding, page 209, for further advice.)

• Contact your insurance company (see Home Insurance, page 220).

STORMS

In an average year in Britain, the wind damages over 250,000 buildings.

You can find out about any approaching strong winds or storms through the Meteorological Office, which operates a severe-weather warning service.

GENERAL PRECAUTIONS

Keep your property in good repair and pay particular attention to the state of:

• Roofs (particularly ridges, eaves, etc)
• Chimney stacks
• Masonry boundary walls
• Aerials and satellite dishes
• Trees (particularly those close to buildings and taller than the building)

IF SEVERE WEATHER IS WARNED

1 Move under cover anything that might blow about, getting damaged or causing damage, such as garden furniture, dustbins, bikes, children's toys. Take pets indoors.

2 Close and fasten doors and windows. (Don't forget the greenhouse, shed or garage.)

3 Park vehicles in a garage, if possible. If not, move your car away from the house, where it might be hit by falling debris.

4 Close and secure trap doors with bolts.

5 Stay indoors as much as possible. (Don't go out to repair damage while the storm is in progress.)

6 Open internal doors only as needed and close them behind you.

7 Move away from windows. Sleep downstairs

if you have any large trees sited near the house. (It will also be less noisy and safer if you are not directly beneath the roof.)

TIP Keep buckets handy to deal with any leaks in the roof and, possibly, heavy-duty polythene sheeting, tacks and a hammer to cover broken windows. Check also that you have candles, matches and a torch to hand, in case of a power cut.

The aftermath

After the storm, check the chimney stack and roof slopes as the wind may have lifted flashings, dislodged tiles and ripped down your roof-top aerial. If you have a flat roof, check it for torn felt. Check for unstable trees, walls and fences.

Notify your insurance company of any damage for which you might want to make a claim.

PIPES & DRAINS

FROZEN AND BURST PIPES

Freezing in winter and corrosion in the heating system often cause burst or frozen pipes. Don't panic. Disreputable plumbers thrive on this sort of problem but a burst pipe need not be a major disaster if you know how and where to turn off the water.

TIP Check your stoptap regularly by turning it off. This will help to stop it from scaling up.

BURST PIPES

1 Turn off the water to the affected pipe quickly. For a burst on the mains-pressure pipes (such as in the kitchen, or an outside tap), turn off at the rising main. For bursts on low-pressure pipes fed from the tank in the loft (such as taps in a bathroom or guest room), turn off gate valves if they are fitted or turn off the rising main stoptap. Then open the hot and cold taps to empty all water from the affected pipes.

If the burst is on the heating pipework, switch off the boiler and turn off the stoptap on the supply to the feed and expansion tank

(if there is one) to stop it refilling. Then attach a length of hose to the lowest draincock on the system (such as from the washing machine) and take the other end through to a drain outside. A draincock is fitted to parts of your plumbing system which cannot be drained via a tap, for example, the boiler. So you will need to open the draincock valve to empty the system.

TIP Make sure you know where all the control valves and drain cocks are in your plumbing system.

THINK AHEAD!

The most useful thing you can do to prevent internal flooding is to make sure that the cold-water pipes in your loft (and the top and side of the cold-water tank) are well insulated to prevent them freezing in winter. If you go away for a few days, leave the heating on low and prop the loft hatch open. If going for a longer period, drain down the plumbing system. This doesn't take long and may save a great deal of aggravation on your return!

WATER AND ELECTRICITY

The greatest danger from a burst pipe is to the electrical system. If water gets into power and lighting circuits it can make the plumbing system live. If unsure about dampness, switch off the electricity and work by torchlight. Then call in a qualified electrician to test the system.

2 Now you have stemmed the flow of water, call in the plumber.

FROZEN PIPES

1 Turn off your water at the mains, as above.
2 If the freeze is on a heating pipe, turn off the boiler as above.
3 Inspect the frozen pipes and try to find out whether they have burst. (You may see ice glistening in the pipe, or feel a split.) If it doesn't seem to have burst, very gently try to thaw it. Working back from the frozen tap, unwind any lagging and use a hairdryer, a warm air gun, a hot-water bottle or even hot cloths to thaw it.

TIP Never use a naked flame. Too much direct heat may cause the water in that section to boil and steam. Be patient.

4 If the pipe has split, bind rags tightly around the leak, or plug it with something. Place a bucket underneath to catch the water as the pipe thaws, and call a qualified plumber.

TIP If replacing a pipe, flexible plastic pipes allow some expansion and although water will still freeze it won't necessarily burst the pipe.

5 If possible, turn off the stoptap on the outlet to the cold water tank. If it is a hot-water tap that has burst, turn off the stoptap controlling the supply of water to the hot-water cistern.

TIP If escaping water cannot be controlled switch off the electrics at the mains, open all the cold taps and flush the cisterns in order to drain the system quickly. (Save some in the bath, jugs and bowls to use until the plumber comes.) Then wait until the area has dried out completely before switching the electricity back on. If you can, isolate that circuit and switch on the power to the rest of the house.

BLOCKED TOILET

Most households have toilets with a wash-down pan: when flushed, two streams of water come from each side of the rim. The water should leave the pan smoothly, not eddying like a whirlpool.
• If the cistern is working properly but the bowl fails to clear, something is obstructing either the flush inlet or the toilet-pan outlet.
• If the flush water rises almost to the pan rim then ebbs away very slowly, there is most likely a blockage in the pan outlet, or possibly in the drain it discharges into.

UNBLOCKING A TOILET

You will need
• Plunger which has a long handle. (You may be able to use a mop or broom tied round with rags. Alternatively, stand carefully on a stool and then tip in a whole bucket of water in one go.)
• Flexible drain auger (plumber's snake)
• Bucket
• Rubber gloves
• Mirror

1 Remove all visible waste. You may be able to clear it with a bent wire that you push round the bend. Wait until the water level has dropped down again and then flush the toilet from a higher level using a whole bucket of water.

2 If this doesn't clear the blockage, take the plunger and push it sharply on to the bottom of the pan to cover the outlet completely. Then pump the handle up and down two or three times.

3 If this doesn't clear what is obstructing the pan, use a flexible drain auger (a plumber's snake) to probe the outlet and trap. If that still doesn't solve it, you may need to call in a plumber or drain specialist who has special equipment that will clear out the underground drain.

4 If when you flush the toilet cistern, water is entering the pan poorly or unevenly, use a mirror to check the flushing rim. Then try and probe the rim with your fingers to feel for flakes of rust or debris that is escaping from the cistern that may be obstructing the normal flush of water. If there is any clean it out thoroughly to prevent it happening again.

GAS & ELECTRICITY

GAS

Never carry out any DIY repairs to gas pipes, fittings or appliances. Gas installation and repair should only be carried out by a CORGI-registered gas installer (Council for Registered Gas Installers).

Make sure everyone in the family knows how to turn off the gas supply at the mains. If you don't know where your gas tap is, ask your meter reader next time he calls. (It is usually a small lever on the gas pipe near your meter.)

THE GAS MAINS

OFF: Turn the lever until the notched line on the spindle points across the pipe. If your tap seems stiff, don't attempt to loosen it yourself: call your local gas service centre who will come and loosen it for you safely, free of charge.

ON: Before turning the gas on again, make sure that all appliances and pilot lights are turned off. The gas tap is on when the notched line on the spindle points along the pipe. After turning the supply on, re-light all pilot lights.

GAS LEAKS

If you smell gas:
- Turn off the mains gas tap (next to the gas meter).
- Put out all naked lights, don't smoke and don't operate any electrical equipment (including light switches and doorbells).
- Open doors and windows to increase ventilation and get rid of the gas.
- Ring the local gas board's 24-hour, 365-day-a-year emergency service: it's still all right to use the phone. Look under Gas in the phone book.

After the gas leak has been dealt with and the gas supply is back on, don't forget to re-light all pilot lights.

CARBON MONOXIDE POISONING

If any of your fuel-burning appliances (including gas central-heating boilers, water-heaters, open fires and wood-burning stoves) use a flue, they must be kept clear. If the chimney or

DOMESTIC GAS AND CARBON MONOXIDE DETECTORS

Gas

Your sense of smell should tell you if there is a gas leak (which could lead to an explosion). But if you are worried about gas or have poor olfactory senses, consider having a gas detector installed (professionally, by wiring it directly to the mains).

There are different types for natural and bottled gas, and each must be installed correctly: high on a wall to detect the lighter-than-air methane in natural gas, and low down for the heavier-than-air propane and butane in bottled gas.

Carbon Monoxide

A carbon-monoxide detector will tell you if you have a leaky flue (which could lead to you getting poisoned).

You shouldn't rely on a gas or carbon monoxide detector to tell you if there is a leak. Carbon monoxide does not have a smell, so you will not be able to detect it unaided.

Follow the advice above if you are at all concerned about leaks. There is no substitute for making sure that all your gas appliances are properly maintained and serviced regularly.

If you are thinking about buying a gas or carbon-monoxide detector, contact the Gas Consumers Council (020 7931 0977) for advice on what is available or ask for assistance at your local gas showroom.

flue does get blocked, the waste gases could spill into the room, polluting the air you breathe with carbon monoxide. This could be fatal. Always ensure there is plenty of ventilation.

If you notice any of the following signs on your gas appliances, stop using the appliance and contact your local gas office immediately.

- Is the outer case discoloured?
- Is the decoration around the appliance stained or discoloured?
- Does the appliance burn with a yellow or orange flame?
- Is there a strange smell when the appliance is on?
- Is the flue damaged or broken?

ELECTRICITY

Unless you are highly competent at DIY, never tinker with electrical wiring or carry out repairs, except for very minor matters such as mending fuses and fitting plugs.

GET TO KNOW YOUR CONSUMER UNIT

This is the heart of your electrical installation, and every circuit in the house must pass through it. Go and take a look at it now, as these guidelines will then be easier to follow

- Every unit has a large, main switch that turns off the power to your house. These are called RCCBs (residual current circuit breakers).

TIP On some units, the main switch will trip automatically if a serious fault occurs, as well as being operable manually.

- With some consumer units you can't remove the outer cover without first turning off the main switch. If yours is not like this, stick a label on the cover to remind you to switch off before exposing any of the elements inside the unit.
- With the main switch off and the cover removed, you can see how the unit is arranged.

TIP The cover must be replaced before the unit is switched on again – and remember that even when the unit is switched off, the cable connecting the meter to the main switch is still live, so take care.

• Look at the cables that feed the various circuits in the house (ideally they should all enter the consumer unit from the same direction) and should be labelled to tell you which area of electrics they cover.

• Each fuse covers a particular wiring circuit in the house. Check which has failed (lights, socket outlets, etc). If a faulty lamp or appliance is responsible, switch off the mains before replacing the fuse or closing a circuit breaker.

REPLACING A FUSE WIRE

To replace the fuse or fuse wire, first switch off the main switch on the consumer unit (or it may be on a separate switch box nearby).

Re-wirable fuses

1 On a blown re-wirable fuse you should be able to see the broken wire and scorch marks on the fuse carrier. If the fuse is one on which you cannot see the whole length of the fuse wire, pull gently on each end of the wire with the tip of a screwdriver to see if it is intact.

2 Loosen the two terminals holding the fuse and extract the broken pieces.

3 Wrap one end of a new length of wire (of the correct rating) clockwise round the terminal and tighten the screw on it. Then run the wire through the fuse carrier across to the other terminal, leaving it slightly slack, and attach it in the same way and cut off any surplus.

4 Replace the fuse carrier.

5 Refit the fuse-box cover and switch on the mains.

Cartridge fuses

1 Unscrew the fuse carrier.

2 Fit a new fuse of the correct rating.

3 Put together the carrier and screw tight.

4 Replace the fuse carrier and put back the fuse box cover.

5 Switch on the main switch.

MINIATURE CIRCUIT BREAKERS

Instead of the usual fuse holders, you may have MCBs. These are amp-rated, like fuses, but instead of removing an MCB to isolate the circuit you merely operate a switch or button to switch it to off. When a fault occurs the circuit breaker switches to the off position automatically, so the faulty circuit is obvious.

1 Turn the main switch off.

2 Correct the cause of the fault.

3 Close the switch on the MCB to reset it. (There is no fuse to replace.)

4 Switch on the mains.

RESIDUAL CURRENT DEVICES

If all the power to your house has gone off, it may be the residual current device (RCD) that has tripped. The RCD will operate quickly if there is an earth fault.

1 Correct the fault: unplug the faulty appliance or replace the light bulb.

2 Try to close the RCD.

3 If it opens again, switch off the mains,

WHICH FUSE TO FIT?

Always fit a fuse of the correct rating for the job.

5 amp: Lighting circuits

15 amp or 20 amp: Immersion heater

30 amp: Socket outlets and average sized cooker

45 amp: Large cooker

SAFETY AND FUSES

• If a fuse continues to blow or the breaker keeps opening, don't fit a larger fuse. If in doubt, consult a competent electrician.

• If the RCD re-opens, ring an electrician or your local electricity company. Don't try to repair the problem yourself. For further advice on electricity in the home, visit your local electricity showroom for a range of practical leaflets.

remove all the circuit fuses or breakers and replace or reset them one at a time until you find the faulty circuit.

4 Leave the faulty fuse or breaker out and ring an electrician, or ask your local electricity company for help.

TIP Put a note on the consumer unit saying what you've done so that nobody else will try to replace that fuse.

5 Replace the cover before switching the electricity on again.

WHEN WILL A FUSE BLOW?

• When too many appliances are operated on a circuit the excessive demand for current will blow the fuse in that circuit.

• When current re-routes to earth because of a faulty appliance, the flow of current increases the circuit and blows the fuse. This is called short circuiting. You will have to deal with the original fault before replacing the fuse.

MAINS POWER CUT

1 Organise light: make sure that you know where to find torches or candles and matches.

2 Ring your local electricity company to report the problem and find out when you can expect a return of power.

3 Take care if using candles, putting them well out of reach of children. When the power comes back on again, make sure all candles are put out and that any appliances that you turned on before the power cut are not left on, such as a cooker, an iron or an electric blanket.

TIP Leave the fridge and freezer switched on. Check that the fridge drip tray is in position and keep the fridge door closed. Don't open your freezer; its contents will remain frozen for about eight hours. The more food inside, the longer the contents will keep without thawing. Food that has started to thaw shouldn't be re-frozen. To save uncooked but thawed meats and vegetables, make them into pies or casseroles, etc, and then re-freeze them.

4 When the power comes back on reset electric clocks, for example, on central heating, cooker and video.

BURGLARS & INTRUDERS

BURGLARY

If you find you have been burgled, call the police immediately.

While waiting for them to arrive, don't move or touch anything except to minimise any damage. Check whether valuables have been stolen so you can give their details to the police when they arrive.

If you arrive home and think a burglar is still inside your house (due to an open door or window) don't go inside. Go to a neighbour's house or phone box and ring the police, then keep a discreet watch so you can give the police a description of anyone leaving.

Coming home to a burglar

If you arrive home to find an intruder in the house with you:
- Ask calmly what he wants.
- Don't get angry or attempt to prevent him from leaving: he may get violent.
- Try to remember what he looks like in as much detail as possible.
- Call the police as soon as he has gone.

If you suspect a prowler

If you hear a noise as though someone is in the house, or someone is trying to break in:
- Switch the lights on and make plenty of noise. Most burglars will flee immediately.

IMPROVING HOME SECURITY

For comprehensive advice on how to keep burglars out of your home with sensible security measures, see Home Security, page 191.

- Stay upstairs or out of the way, call the police if you have a bedroom/extension phone, and find something you can use as a weapon to defend yourself if you are attacked – but don't go in search of him.
- As soon as you hear the intruder leave, try to see what he looks like and what he is wearing, which way he goes and whether he has a car or van. Then ring the police.

TIP If you get a good look at an intruder, try to memorise details to help the police: age, sex, height, build, skin colour, hairstyle and colour, facial characteristics, clothing. For vehicles, note the type, model, colour and the registration number.

MENDING A BROKEN WINDOW

A broken window is both a safety and a security risk and should be dealt with as soon as possible. It's not a difficult job to tackle yourself as long as you have or can borrow the right tools.

If the window is hard to reach, it's safer to remove the frame and work on it at ground level. Make sure you protect your hands with strong gloves and wear safety goggles.

There are two methods for fixing glass into a wood frame. With wood beading, you simply lever off the beading, replace the glass in mastic (sealant) and re-fix the beading. The method using putty is explained below, and applies equally to wooden and metal-framed windows.

You will need
Materials
- Glazing nails, ⅝in/15mm long, or glazing clips
- Glass: ask your glass merchant to advise you

on the correct glass for your purpose as this will depend on the type and size of the frame and whether it is in a vulnerable position or area of high risk.

- Primer
- Putty

Tools

- Chisel
- Pincers
- Protective gloves
- Putty knife
- Safety spectacles
- Small hammer
- Steel measuring tape

1 Carefully remove all the loose glass and dispose of it safely (wrapped in newspaper).

TIP If the window is only cracked, stick tape over it in a criss-cross pattern to contain fragments and then tap out the pieces from the outside with a hammer.

2 Hack out the old putty and any remaining bits of glass from the rebate (the groove where the glass sits) with a chisel.

TIP With metal frames, the glass will have been held in by small clips. Take these out carefully with pincers as you uncover them, mark the hole positions on the frame and save them for later.

3 Brush out dust and loose bits of putty from the rebate and apply a coat of wood or metal primer to the rebate.

4 Measure up for the new glass. Check that the rebate is square by measuring all four sides, and use the smaller measurement in each case. Subtract ⅛in/3mm from each measurement to allow for clearance. Then order the pane and appropriate putty from your glass merchant. If in doubt, cut a paper pattern and take this to your glass merchant.

5 Put a layer of putty in a thinnish bead all around the rebate (A), rest the bottom edge of

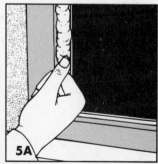

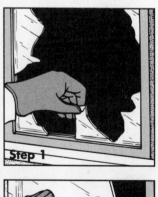

the pane in the rebate and push it gently and firmly into place, pressing round the edge rather than in the centre of the pane to compress the putty evenly (B).

6 To hold the glass in, tap glazing nails in the rebate, at about ½–⅝in/12–15cm intervals in a wooden frame, or use glazing clips in a metal one. Trim away excess putty from the inside of the frame with the putty knife.

7 Finish off with a layer of putty around the outside of the frame. Wet the blade of the putty knife to prevent it from sticking, and shape off at an angle. Finish off by trimming away the bedding putty where necessary and cleaning off the putty marks with methylated spirits.

8 Allow the putty to dry for two weeks before painting.

HOME INSURANCE

MAKING A CLAIM

If, unfortunately, you have to make a claim on your home insurance, here is how to make the process as smooth and fast as possible.

• Read your policy carefully. Does it cover the cause of the damage or loss? Should you claim under 'buildings' or 'contents'? Some policies cover both.

• Ring your insurer and ask for a claim form, quoting your policy number. Don't forget to quote the number on any correspondence as well, and keep copies.

• If temporary emergency repairs are needed, arrange these immediately and let your insurer know. The cost may form part of your overall claim, so keep all the bills and any damaged items as the insurers will probably want to see them. Take photos if necessary.

• Some insurers offer a 24-hour emergency help line which can give details of local tradespeople.

• While waiting to receive a claim form, get repair estimates from at least two specialist contractors, list all items lost or damaged, and find the original receipts if you can. If you can't, estimate their current value and check the price of replacements. Remember that some policies offer replacement as if the items had been new, while others take wear and tear into account.

• Complete the claim form and return it quickly, with any estimates, receipts and valuations you can find to support your case.

• The insurers will either pay your claim, or arrange for their claims inspector to call on you, or send a loss adjuster to assess the loss or damage.

INDEX